Seeing

Spartanburg

See-ing

Spartanburg

ing

a history in images

by

Philip N. Racine

HUB CITY writers project

1999

ISBN 1-891885-10-3, soft cover
ISBN 1-891885-11-1, hard cover
Third printing, March 2007

Hub City editor, Lisa Isenhower
Cover and book design by Mark Olencki
Editorial assistance, Betsy Teter and John Lane
Digital technician, Christina Smith
Darkroom technician, Karen Huff
Family support, Diana and Weston
Printed and bound by McNaughton & Gunn, Inc. in Saline, Michigan

Hub City Writers Project
Post Office Box 8421
Spartanburg, South Carolina 29305
(864) 577-9349 • fax (864) 577-0188
www.hubcity.org

For Kit and Dan
who embody the grace
that is the South at its very best

Publication of *Seeing Spartanburg*
has been made possible by
a substantial gift from
the *Herald-Journal*
and its Celebrate 2000 Partners:
Vic Bailey Automotive Superstores,
Spartanburg Regional Medical Center,
Spartanburg Technical College,
and Westgate Mall.

Celebrate 2000™
envision the future

The Hub City Writers Project would like to thank
its other Friends who made contributions in support of this book:

Phifer/Johnson Foundation

Arkwright Foundation
The Arts Partnership of Greater Spartanburg
Jo Ann Bristow
Mr. and Mrs. Winston Hardegree
Agnes Harris
Dorothy and Julian Josey
Mrs. Roger Milliken
Olencki Graphics, Inc.
Price's Store for Men

Bea and Dennis Bruce
Colonial Trust Co.

Dr. and Mrs. Mitchell H. Allen
Mr. and Mrs. Robert Allen
Mack and Kathy Neal Amick
B & B Studio
Mr. and Mrs. W.D. Bain Jr.
First South Bank
Carolina Southern Bank Foundation
Valerie and Bill Barnet
Mr. and Mrs. Thomas Bartram
Dr. and Mrs. Charles Bebko
Shirley Blaes
Mr. and Mrs. Glen B. Boggs II
Dr. and Mrs. James Bradof
Susan Bridges
Pat Brock
Mellnee G. Buchheit
Mrs. W. Marshall Chapman
Mr. and Mrs. Arthur Cleveland
Mr. and Mrs. John Cleveland Cobb
Dr. and Mrs. Robert Cochran
Mr. and Mrs. Paul Cote
Nancy Rainey Crowley
Frances Davis
Mr. and Mrs. James Dunlap
Mr. Duncan and the Rev. Beth Ely
Jean Erwin
Dr. and Mrs. Harold E. Fleming

Gordon and Karen Floyd
Dr. and Mrs. Sidney Fulmer
Mr. and Mrs. Billy Gossett
Margaret and Chip Green
Mr. and Mrs. Tom Grier
Benjamin and Tanya Hamm
Mr. and Mrs. Peyton Harvey
Mr. and Mrs. J. Thomas Hollis
Sallie and Bill James
Mr. and Mrs. Stewart H. Johnson
Wallace Johnson
Mr. and Mrs. Charles W. Jones
Mr. and Mrs Charles D. Kay
Dr. and Mrs. Cecil F. Lanford
Mr. and Mrs. Paul Lehner
Mr. and Mrs. Fred M. Lockman Jr.
George Loudon
Alan and Mary Beth Lyles
Dr. and Mrs. Nathaniel Magruder
Dan and Kit Maultsby
Dr. and Mrs. Dean McKinney
Bob McMichael
Les and Betty McMillan
Mr. and Mrs. E. Lewis Miller
Karen and Bob Mitchell
Nancy Moore
Mr. and Mrs. Douglas B. Nash

Nancy Ogle
Mr. and Mrs. Dwight Patterson
Mr. and Mrs. Edward P. Perrin
Mr. and Mrs. Robert V. Pinson
Sigmund Pickus and Janet Wilson
Gary and Anne Poliakoff
Dr. and Mrs. Jan Postma Jr.
Norman Powers
Mr. and Mrs. Norman Pulliam
Mr. and Mrs. Philip Racine
Eileen Rampey
Mr. and Mrs. William B. Ramsey III
Angela Rogers
Gail D. Rodgers
Spartanburg Development Council
Mr. and Mrs. Jess G. Taylor
Bill and Kristin Taylor
Betsy Wakefield Teter
Elizabeth H. Wakefield
Mr. and Mrs. J. W. Wakefield
Mr. and Mrs. John T. Wakefield
Mr. and Mrs. David Weir
Mary G. Willis
Jeffrey R. Willis
Dennis and Annemarie Wiseman
Cynthia and Stephen Wood
Wm. Grantham Wood

Publication of this book is funded in part by the Arts Partnership of Greater Spartanburg and its donors, the County and City of Spartanburg, and the South Carolina Arts Commission which receives support from the National Endowment for the Arts. All proceeds from the sale of this book go to the Hub City Writers Project.

Contents

— *Introduction*

*A*fter the publication of the initial edition of this book, I was often asked where and how I had obtained its photographs. I take the occasion of its revision to share some of the story of its inception and creation. Twenty years ago, a publisher approached me about writing a photographic history of Spartanburg. Because such a thing did not then exist (there have been several subsequent projects) and because I had been working on a history of Spartanburg for a number of years, the idea of using photographs to tell the story intrigued me, and I accepted.

The *Herald-Journal* published a letter in which I asked for photographs. The response was gratifying. It was a revelation for me to encounter so many people who wanted to participate; many other people hesitated, assuming that such a book would be filled only with well-known buildings and portraits of "important" people. But as soon as they realized that I was primarily interested in depicting daily life, they became enthusiastic and generous in sharing their family photographs.

After collecting some 300 photographs and writing their captions, I then went looking for people to tell me more than I already knew about the pictures. Among the numerous helpful people, Lionel Lawson and Ann Sanders stand out. One in his late eighties and the other in her early nineties, they brought old Spartanburg to life with their keen, long-lived minds that seemed to frolic through the past. I was fortunate to have known them then, and I miss them now.

The proposal by the Hub City Writers Project to revise and reissue the *Spartanburg County: A Pictorial History* gave me an

Spartanburg County

A PICTORIAL HISTORY

Philip N. Racine

opportunity to do it all over again. The new project allowed for many more photographs than the original had; also I discovered more old photographs from the turn of the century than I had expected. Consequently, I could substitute new photographs for some I had previously used, as well as add to the total number for the period from 1880 to 1920 and greatly expand the sections on the Great Depression, World War II, and its amazing aftermath.

I went to Washington and the Library of Congress looking for Depression-era photographs, hoping that some of the famous photographers of that era had passed through Spartanburg and had recorded what they saw. I had to calm myself when I found some taken by Dorothea Lange and Jack Delano, both of whom had worked for the Farm Security Administration and had become icons of documentary photography.

As I sat at the microfilm machine and stared at the Depression-era images, I wondered what those people were thinking when the photographer snapped the shutter. Did they know how they looked? Did they have any idea that in the future someone like me would be scrutinizing their lives, speculating—probably totally incorrectly—about how they felt or how they saw themselves? Did they know that they were poor, that other people laughed at them, that they were despised or pitied, each possibility as heinous as the other? Would they have minded my using them? I guessed not, for they had allowed outsiders to photograph them. And I believed strongly that people needed to know, needed to be reminded of what life was like for most people in Spartanburg during the Great Depression, needed to see the despair and the poverty that were the enemy of the New Deal. All of contemporary intellectual posturing aside, what made Franklin Roosevelt more popular in the South than in any other region of the United States was that he fought to change those conditions.

After the Library of Congress, I went to the National Archives where a group of Camp Wadsworth and Camp Croft photographs awaited me—at Wadsworth, young Americans from New York had been sent to what must have been to them a hell-hole in the stricken South. Showing humor and determination under adverse circumstances, those boys adopted this Southern town and in turn were accepted. Some 23 years later the whole process was repeated at Camp Croft where trainees came from all over.

Yet most of my best discoveries took place in Spartanburg. I went to a corporate building, and Susan Dunlap led me into a paneled room to sit at a large, highly polished table surrounded with hard leather chairs, the kind that mean business. On the table was an old, battered scrapbook that looked as if it would fall apart if I touched it. But that was what I was there for, and so I plunged in. Turning the first page, I just knew that this scrapbook was going to be something special. Old, torn, and battered photographs were attached helter-skelter to the pages of the album; the pictures dated from the late nineteenth century. Over the years various family members had written descriptions of the photographs on scraps of paper, on the photographs, and on the pages of the album.

These were not professional photographs but pictures taken by family members of their elegant home on North Church Street and of important events in their lives—not only of the people, but of the surroundings. I was privileged to gain permission to snoop, to look at the fashions, to see the details of daily life and special occasions, all of which depicted the world of Spartanburg through the first half of the twentieth century in a way I had never seen it before.

As had been true in the first edition, much of the life of these new pictures comes from interviews. The most memorable conversation was with Lewis P. Jones, a warm, sharing, and sensitive person—the finest historian Spartanburg has ever had. John Lane and I went to Lewis' house early one morning with a stack of photographs and lots of questions. We sat around the small kitchen table and went through the stack, Lewis constantly complaining that he could not remember, while I was furiously writing down what he could not remember so that I would not forget it. All of us fed off one another; with John and me occasionally prompting, Lewis told the story. In the end, there were lots of notes. Lewis had enjoyed himself, and John and I had benefited from the willingness of a sensitive student of humanity to share.

Again, John Lane accompanied me out to the Williams Place where the owner, Steve Baker, proudly showed us around. He had a stack of photographs taken by a man from the Library of Congress that he gladly shared with me. Mixing stories from the past with recent anecdotes, he brought to life the buildings and the land itself. The farmstead is once again a living thing, a living museum reconstructed by lots of hard work and pride to approximate the owner's vision of what the place must have been like in the middle of the nineteenth century. I want to do justice to a dedication like that.

Now, it was time to choose. Over and over, I sat and looked at heaps of pictures, trying to decide which ones were the most representative, of what, of whom, and why. That was the task I had set myself, and often I regretted ever agreeing to take it on. Did I know enough of Spartanburg's history to do justice to it? And then I would see a photograph that cut all that analysis short, like the pictures of the trains derailed and wrecked by a Pacolet River gone wild; or the supreme dignity of a turn-of-the-century woman sitting in her living room with a hand-crocheted neckpiece, dignity and grace personified; or the black woman, eyes downcast and staring into nothing while she sits in her rocking chair, a symbol of resignation; or the smile of a man whose elderly, country-sounding voice I had first heard over a local radio station giving hog prices, a man much younger-looking than he had sounded. Those photographs stopped me short; they screamed at me to be included. Yes, they were all real to me; they were Spartanburg, and I listened.

1903 PACOLET FLOOD DAMAGE

Many photographs in this book were taken by professional photographers, persons who made a living recording people and events. Even within professional ranks there are differences between the journeymen and the artists. The professionals distinguished their work from the amateurs by taking the photographs with better equipment, with a knowledge of better techniques, and with the practiced eye of the well trained. Simply, they did what they did better than most.

Yet, amateurs, intending to record a special moment for the future, took most of the book's pictures. The photographers were not artists, just ordinary people trying to aid memory. But for a book like this one, ordinary pictures become something special, for they take us back in time by helping, in conjunction with our imaginations, to recreate what it was like to be alive during a given historical period. Indeed, what ordinary people in the past chose to record—to better remember—shows us what they valued. The inexpensive camera has become a unique resource for historians because the lives of the majority of people are the most difficult to re-create. Those lives were so normal, so mundane, that few people wrote their details, and those details have become obscure. The inexpensive camera, the old "Brownie," has helped fill in the gaps in the historical record.

Historians work with myriad sources—photographic, oral, written—to reconstruct the past. They hope that by checking all of them against one another they will be able to come close to reconstructing the way things were. One does well to remember, however, that it is all flawed. At best, it is a careful approximation. Historians may never be certain about any of their sources, and, in the end, they must rely on their best judgment. This book is, after all, one historian's photographic history of Spartanburg.

In the main, l have left the interpretation of these photographs of Spartanburg's past to the reader. I have tried to provide context; I have included anecdotes, most of which are unverified, for the enjoyment of the reader, with the understanding that they have been shared to give the flavor of the time. Just as novelists and poets generally have "license," in this case, this historian chooses to claim somewhat the same. So the enjoyment of the following becomes a joint enterprise, and I welcome you to it.

In a very important way this book is a joint effort. Linda Taylor Hudgins' work with the photographs that appeared in the original 1980 edition is still evident here, now much enhanced by the brilliant work of Mark Olencki (the layout of the book and many of its finest photographs are his). Lastly, for this edition I have

PHOTOGRAPHER ALFRED WILLIS
& COMPANY

had full access to the Willis collection purchased by the *Herald-Journal* and donated to the Spartanburg County Public Libraries. This is the single finest collection of photographs of Spartanburg, and all of us owe the *Herald-Journal* thanks for its foresight in donating it to the people who can properly care for it. Many other photographs in the book were taken by the talented Harry White, chief photographer for the *Herald-Journal* from 1962-1980 and long-time owner of B & B Studio.

For Wofford College, where I have made a career, l have abiding respect. President Joab Lesesne and Dean Dan Maultsby have continuously supported my efforts, most effectively by fostering a climate of trust and mutual support among faculty, staff, and students. I could not have chosen a better school to which to devote my career. And as for Spartanburg, where else would a poet (John Lane), a freelance writer (Betsy Teter) and a graphic artist (Mark Olencki) create one of the wonders of small press publishing—the Hub City Writers Project? Many thanks also go to this book's editor, the tireless Lisa Isenhower, and the many proofreaders, including Tina and Steve Smith, Bob Isenhower, and Ellen Autenzio.

I am also deeply appreciative of all the people who shared their treasures with me, whether they were in the form of photographs, stories, or anecdotes. The many archivists and lay persons who care deeply about the history of Spartanburg are reassuring to this historian. I hope that the area continues to be worthy of their affection. Any errors found herein are my fault, and I can only ask everyone's good humor and indulgence. Enjoy yourselves!

Philip N. Racine
Wofford College

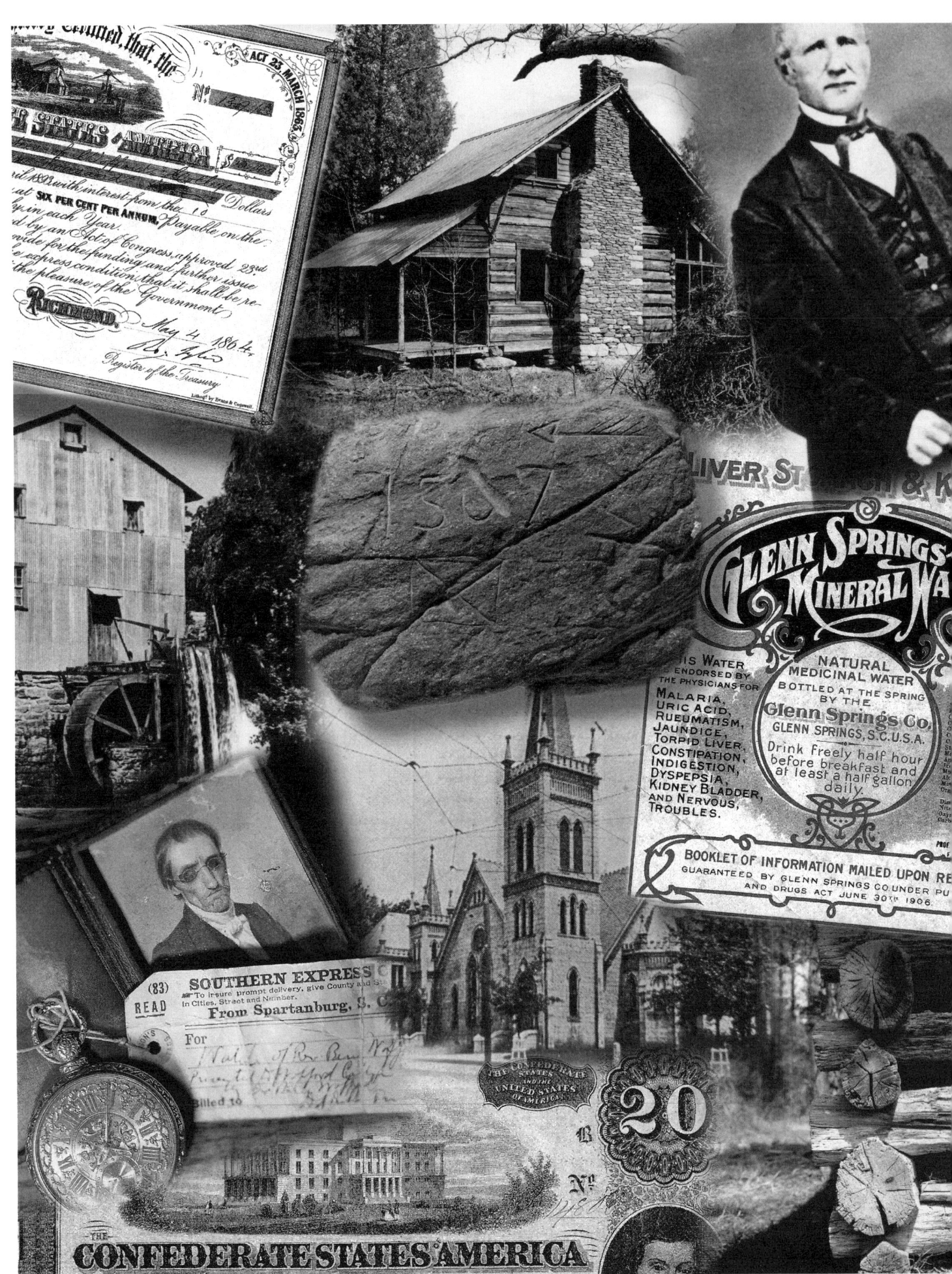

ACT 23, MARCH 1863

No.

SIX PER CENT PER ANNUM, Payable on the

RICHMOND

May 4 1864

Register of the Treasury

OLIVER ST

GLENN SPRINGS
MINERAL WA

IIS WATER
ENDORSED BY
THE PHYSICIANS FOR

MALARIA,
URIC ACID,
RUEUMATISM,
JAUNDICE,
TORPID LIVER,
CONSTIPATION,
INDIGESTION,
DYSPEPSIA,
KIDNEY BLADDER,
AND NERVOUS,
TROUBLES.

NATURAL
MEDICINAL WATER
BOTTLED AT THE SPRING
BY THE
Glenn Springs Co,
GLENN SPRINGS, S.C.U.S.A.

Drink freely half hour
before breakfast and
at least a half gallon
daily.

BOOKLET OF INFORMATION MAILED UPON RE
GUARANTEED BY GLENN SPRINGS CO UNDER PU
AND DRUGS ACT JUNE 30TH 1906.

(83)
READ

SOUTHERN EXPRESS
To insure prompt delivery, give County and St
In Cities, Street and Number.
From Spartanburg, S. C.

For

Billed to

THE CONFEDERATE
STATES
AND THE
UNITED STATES
OF AMERICA

20

R

Nº

THE
CONFEDERATE STATES AMERICA

White men who came to the South Carolina backcountry in the early eighteenth century found few Native Americans living in the Spartanburg area. When the whites did encounter them, the Indians were hostile. Not until much later did whites discover that the Spartanburg area was a favorite Cherokee hunting ground and that the presence of whites constituted a threat to the Cherokee's source of meat and

From Wilderness to City

Origins 1763–1880

clothing. At some time in the past, Native Americans had inhabited the area, for they had burned the underbrush and many of the trees to provide growing areas for their crops. When the whites arrived, they found fields, meadows, hardwoods, and little thick vegetation to hinder the grazing of cattle. The Cherokees were powerful enough to discourage immigration of all but the bravest and hardiest whites into the Spartanburg

A soapstone bowl, circa 7000 B.C., discovered east of Spartanburg.

area. After the Europeans defeated theCherokees in the Cherokee War of 1761, settlers from Pennsylvania and all along the Appalachian Mountains poured into the South Carolina Piedmont.

Most of the settlers came into the area from the north, and communications with the coast were almost nonexistent. The backcountry (Spartanburg County was in an area known as the Ninety-Six District) was wild, and roaming bands of brigands moved through, robbing and molesting the population. All legal authority was located in the lowcountry, and the coastal inhabitants showed little concern for the needs, desperate though they may have been, of the backcountry settlers. Finally, in the late 1760s, the backcountry people took the law into their own hands and formed vigilante bands to rid themselves of the outlaws. The vigilante activity, known as the Regulator Movement, did succeed in getting courts and officers of the law to keep the peace. Not that the area after 1769 was civilized in the minds of the colony's coastal inhabitants, but at least there were people to turn to if the law was being grossly violated.

Projectile points used in prehistoric Spartanburg County.

Although the Regulator Movement of the late 1760s focused the attention of the lowcountry on the affairs of the interior parts of the colony, that interest did not outlast the coming of peace. Even though by 1775 two-thirds of the population of the colony of South Carolina lived in the backcountry, the lack of easy land and water travel between the two regions, and the difference in their needs and interests, acted to separate their existence as if they were two separate colonies. Unless something special happened, people along the coast ignored the nether parts

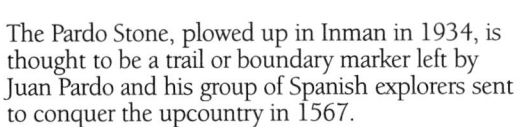

The Pardo Stone, plowed up in Inman in 1934, is thought to be a trail or boundary marker left by Juan Pardo and his group of Spanish explorers sent to conquer the upcountry in 1567.

—*Artifacts courtesy Spartanburg County Regional Museum*

of the colony. Such an occasion was brewing in the 1760s and early seventies when the interests of the lowcountry planters, lawyers, and commercial elements came into conflict with the British authorities. As the colonials and the mother country found themselves increasingly at odds with one another, it became clear to the coastal interests that the support of the backcountry in the forthcoming struggle would be important.

Oak leaves from the white oak tree adjacent to Walnut Grove. The tree dates from 1570.

Backcountry settlers, having no important and immediate relationship either with the lowcountry or with the British government, were not party to the squabbles so dear to coastal Carolinians. Generally, they had little reason to be antagonistic to the British and not much more reason to be favorably disposed to the cause of Charleston. When rumors reached colonial rebels that the backcountry militia had loyalist leanings (that is, loyal to the king), the rebels sent representatives to gain the support of the militia for the rebel cause. The trip of William Henry Drayton and William Tennant on behalf of the rebels to the upcountry in 1775 proved the extent of the loyalist feeling in the Ninety-Six District. Only in the area of Lawson's Fork, around present-day Spartanburg, did Drayton and Tennant find significant support. Colonel John Thomas of Lawson's Fork raised a militia company, called the Spartan Regiment, to counter the royalism of the other militia groups in the area. Tradition has it that the county derived its name from this military band. Why the militia chose it is anybody's guess.

The ensuing struggle between loyalist and rebel militia groups in the district during 1775 amounted to a civil war. The key issue turned out to be which group could best ensure the safety and peace of the inhabitants. As it turned out, the loyalists could not do so, and they were ultimately driven underground and dispersed. But the American Revolution would not ignore the backcountry. In 1779 the British decided to concentrate their efforts on the South, where rebel military leadership had been relatively unsuccessful. Regular British troops were sent into the area to ferret out rebel militia, to establish control over the colony, and to demonstrate the ability of the British army to keep the peace. In a series of battles in the Spartanburg District (Cedar Springs, Wofford's Iron Works near modern Glendale, and Musgrove Mill), the rebel militia mauled the British regulars and loyalist recruits.

The British general for the Southern theater, Lord Cornwallis, developed a strategy for moving from South Carolina through North Carolina to crush George Washington's army in Virginia. He ordered Colonel Patrick Ferguson to cover his western flank. Ferguson was a fine soldier who had succeeded in rallying support for the British in the backcountry but had failed to quell the activities of the rebel militia. Ferguson publicly announced his contempt for the rebels, and they in turn determined to destroy him. As Ferguson moved toward King's Mountain in North Carolina to protect Cornwallis, the rebels pursued him. Contrary to his orders, Ferguson decided to make a stand on the mountain and destroy the militia. In the ensuing battle the rebels killed Ferguson and most of his force, thereby making Cornwallis temporarily give up his plan.

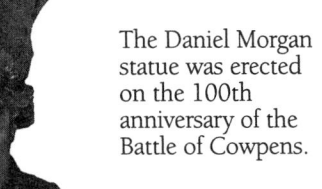

The Daniel Morgan statue was erected on the 100th anniversary of the Battle of Cowpens.

In 1781 Cornwallis tried again and gave orders to the most hated and feared of the British cavalry leaders, Colonel Banastre Tarleton, to destroy the rebel forces in the back-country. This order pitted Tarleton against Colonel Daniel Morgan of the regular American army. On January 16, 1781, realizing that Tarleton was on his heels and that he could not escape, Morgan took his men to Hannah's Cowpens, named for the man who had grazed his cattle there. Because, like other regular army officers, he thought militia unreliable, Morgan placed them on the top of a gentle sloping hill about five miles away from the swollen Broad River, an action which prevented any escape for the rebel troops. As Tarleton later admitted, the disposition of Morgan's troops and the lay of the land were all in the British officer's favor. Due to a mix-up in orders during the battle, part of Morgan's troops retreated when they were supposed to charge. The British troops gleefully pursued, but Morgan's quick recovery in ordering a turnabout left the British troops facing a wall of firing troops, only ten feet away. The British fled the field, and the rebels won a complete victory. Cowpens was the last battle in the backcountry, and it thwarted the plans of Cornwallis, whose movement to Virginia ended at Yorktown. Although American generals had contempt for the militia, it proved its worth in the South Carolina piedmont.

Gravestone of Charles Moore, original resident of Walnut Grove. Moore died "in January 1805 in his 78th year."

Before and after the Revolution, life in the backcountry was harsh. Most people lived in lean-tos or one-room cabins; some lived in a two-room house divided by a hallway or a single fireplace. They eked out an existence by growing corn and a few other vegetables and by keeping hogs. Eighteenth century settlers grazed cattle on the bottom lands, but during the nineteenth century those lands were converted to the growing of crops. The good land seems to have been shared by both the small and large landowners. Farming, which was the occupation of over ninety percent of the population, required working from sunup to sunset. Most slave owners worked in the fields with their slaves, for most people who owned slaves owned only a few. Until the 1840s, the large majority of farmers did not grow enough to be able to sell much. Most people lived on the edge of subsistence. Although there were small settlements of a few families scattered in the county, there was only one village, Spartanburg, founded in 1831.

In 1789 settlers decided to locate a jail and courthouse near a spring on Williamson's plantation. They placed these public buildings facing each other at either end of a large rectangular plot of open land around which lots were laid out. Thus they formed a nucleus which drew business people of various kinds to settle

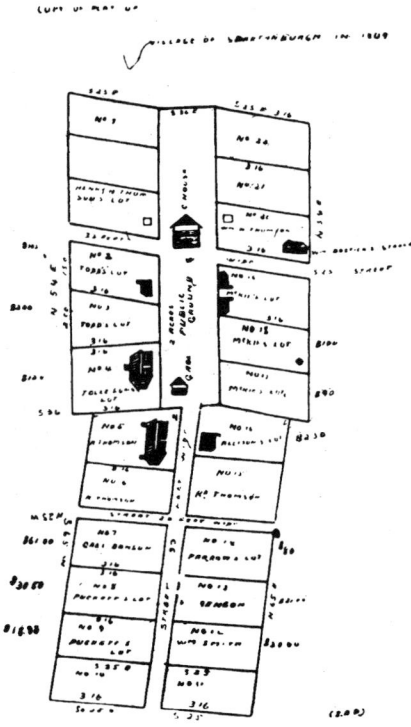

This map of the village of Spartanburg in 1809 shows the location of houses and public buildings. The land surrounding the "public ground"—what we now know as Morgan Square—had not as yet all been purchased. The courthouse stood in the middle of the square at the intersection of Main and Magnolia streets (the old location of the Morgan monument) and the gaol (jail) stood where the Morgan monument now stands. —*Courtesy of Wofford College*

near the public buildings. Today, this area is known as Morgan Square (in 1881 the statue of Daniel Morgan was placed at the west end of the open space where the first courthouse had stood). The spring—the public water supply for man and beast—was located on the north side of the square between Church and Magnolia streets. Although during the early nineteenth century the village brought together lawyers, merchants, and artisans, life in the county remained rural.

There were some families in the eighteenth, and more in the early nineteenth centuries, who had already built substantial homes in the county. The two Moore houses, Walnut Grove and Fredonia, the Price house, and several others, especially the small but elegant Camp Hill, lent an air of elegance and sophistication to the county. The rich and powerful demonstrated such by their fine manor houses and their entertainments. Yet we must not forget that in most instances those homes look far prettier and better kept now than they did when they were new. Not only were the trees surrounding them much smaller, and their condition not nearly as pristine as it is now, but they were working farms. There were pigs and cows around and perhaps a horse or two; slaves and white laborers, working either for wages or for a share, were ever-present. The roads were mud in the rain and dust in the sun; the air smelled of sweat, manure, and other odors of farm life; the wives of owners spent much of their time tending gardens to feed the family; most women made their own clothes; men made their own furniture and tools. Life was constant work. That world is now, in some sense, lost to us, and we can hardly imagine what life was like for the people who lived in those fine houses we see today.

In the two decades before 1860, Spartanburg did not escape

Confederate bond purchased by Wofford College trustees in 1864.
—*Courtesy of Wofford College*

the apprehension that filled the hearts of Southerners at the attack on slavery being waged by other Americans. In 1822 a supposed rebellion had been discovered in Charleston, and subsequent slave insurrections in Haiti had frightened Southern slave owners as to the reliability of their own slave population. In the 1830s two events occurred that sealed the attitudes of white Southerners toward their human property. One was Nullification and the other was Nat Turner's rebellion.

In the late 1820s a tariff had passed the Congress that served to protect infant manufacturing in New England at the expense of Southern cotton growers. The main fear in the South was not so much that imported manufactured goods would now cost much more, as indeed they would, but that if the European countries decided to retaliate, they were bound to lay heavy import duties on Southern cotton. Thus the staple would be less competitive on the world market. By 1832 South Carolina was in the throes of Nullification, which was John C. Calhoun's doctrine that a state had the right to nullify a federal law (in this case the tariff) that the state felt was detrimental to its interests. In the midst of this acrimonious debate, Spartanburg County residents disagreed with Calhoun and took a pro-unionist stand. Leaders of the unionist forces in the county argued that it was not constitutional for a state to nullify a federal law and that remedies short of such drastic action were possible.

The youth of this Confederate soldier represents the pressure and strains placed on the manpower of the South during the Civil War. —*Courtesy of J. H. McMillin*

Although Spartanburg remained unionist during the nullification controversy, it had become secessionist by 1850. This drastic change came about largely because of the controversy over slavery. In 1831 the Nat Turner Rebellion in Virginia, in which marauding slaves killed several white families, frightened unionists into becoming secessionists. Throughout the South, whites, both slave owners and people who did not own any slaves, became frightened of the potential for violence in their midst. In addition, throughout the 1840s and 1850s the activities of the abolitionists in the North seemed intent on provoking that violence. In general, Northerners, although they did not wish to do away with slavery immediately, were becoming amenable to restricting its existence to the Southern states. Southerners, who had once looked upon slavery as a necessary evil, now saw slavery as the cornerstone of all that was good in their society, and they reacted with great emotion to all anti-slavery talk because they saw it as an attack on their superior way of life. During these years residents of Spartanburg County saw things no differently. Even the leaders of unionism in 1832 were, by mid-century, calling for secession from the United States.

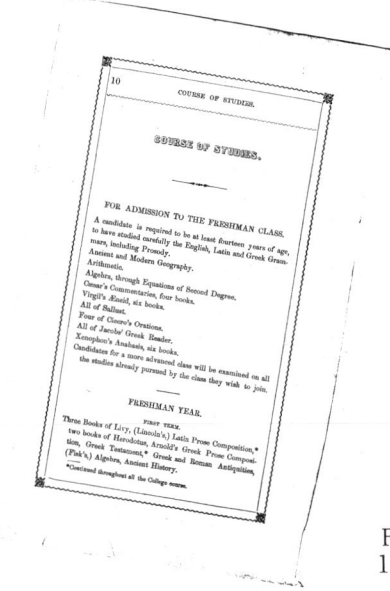

During the 1840s and 1850s, Spartanburg County took on the trappings of civilization. In 1845 the Limestone Springs Female High School was founded; in 1849 the Reverend Newton Pinckney Walker opened a school for deaf children at Cedar Springs; in 1854 the doors of Wofford College, as well as those of Spartanburg Female Academy, opened under the auspices of the Methodist Church; and in 1857 schools for boys and girls opened at Reidville. All of the schools not only established reputations for academic work, but also provided local residents

Front cover and admissions requirements from the 1858 Wofford College Catalog. *—Courtesy of Wofford College*

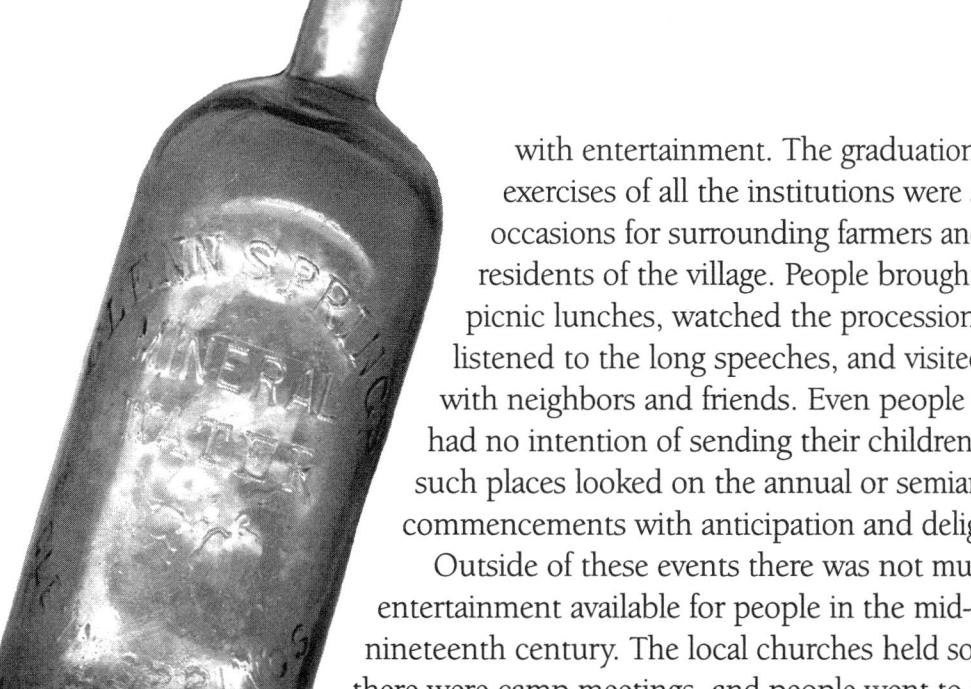

Bottle and label from Glenn Springs Mineral Water, advertised as "unequaled," "delightful," and "a sure cure for rheumatism."
—*Bottle courtesy of Dr. Charles Webb; label courtesy of Spartanburg County Regional Museum*

with entertainment. The graduation exercises of all the institutions were social occasions for surrounding farmers and residents of the village. People brought picnic lunches, watched the processions, listened to the long speeches, and visited with neighbors and friends. Even people who had no intention of sending their children to such places looked on the annual or semiannual commencements with anticipation and delight.

Outside of these events there was not much entertainment available for people in the mid-nineteenth century. The local churches held socials, there were camp meetings, and people went to the village on the first Monday of every month for sales day. People from all over the county and some from the mountains brought their goods to sell, and the horses and wagons would fill the village square. For those residents of the county and other parts of the state who could afford the time and money, Spartanburg County offered a number of springs at which people could board for a time and enjoy "the waters" and the leisure. Most famous was Glenn Springs, which was located southeast of Spartanburg village. In addition to the large hotel run by John C. Zimmerman, Glenn Springs had several other homes that opened up to summer visitors. Glenn Springs was located in the heart of a particularly fertile and successful farming region, and its paths and byways were beautiful to stroll and ride along.

By the end of the decade of the 1850s, Spartanburg County had become a substantial rural community. There were a few farmers who had one hundred or more slaves (John C. Zimmerman owned the most) and grew cotton

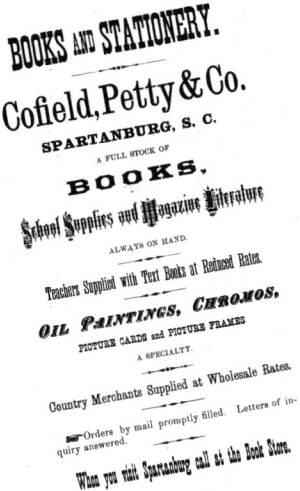
in large quantities, and there were some indus- tries. The textile industry got its start before the Civil War with mills in Bivingsville (modern Glendale), Crawfordsville (modern Fairmont), Fingerville, and two very small operations—Valley Falls and Hills. In addition, the county boasted a substantial iron industry with foundries located primarily in the north central and northeastern parts of the county. Most of these were in present day Cherokee County just southwest of the city of Gaffney. During the Civil War both of these industries produced goods for the Confederacy.

Even though there were no military engagements in Spartanburg, the war was a traumatic time for the people who lived there. With sons and husbands away, many never to come home, the county lived on the verge of severe want throughout the war. The years that followed were marked by the strife between rival political factions caused by the resentment at efforts to bring blacks into the political process, the fraud and corruption which accompanied many of those efforts, and finally the violence of Ku Klux Klan activity in the county. Amidst the trouble that marked the 1870s, the population of the county tripled, and the economy of the village boomed. In spite of the deprivation of the war years, somehow, somewhere, people got money and spent it. People craved the goods the war had made them do without. Stories abound of merchants making trips north after the war to buy goods and selling out in only a few days or weeks after returning. Some fortunes were made in the village in those post-war years.

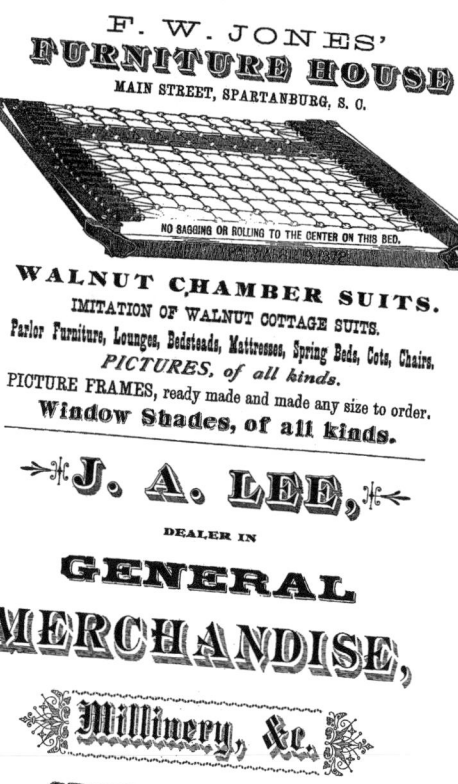
Ads for Spartanburg businesses from 1879.
—*Courtesy of Wofford College*

Landscape & Architecture

ABOVE: Charles Moore began building Walnut Grove in 1765 on land granted him by King George III. Moore emigrated from the north of Ireland to Pennsylvania and then to Spartanburg in the early 1760s. He received several grants, which amounted to about 3,000 acres. His land, located on the Tyger River about ten miles south of the village, has been controlled by his family ever since. The house, restored in the 1960s, was modest yet grand when compared to those of most of his neighbors in the eighteenth century. It should be remembered, however, that this was a working farm and was probably not in as pristine a condition in its heyday as it appears in this photograph.
—*Courtesy B & B Studio*

OPPOSITE PAGE TOP: This covered bridge is typical of late nine-teenth-century bridge construction in Spartanburg. —*Courtesy of the Herald-Journal Willis Collection, Spartanburg County (SC) Public Libraries*

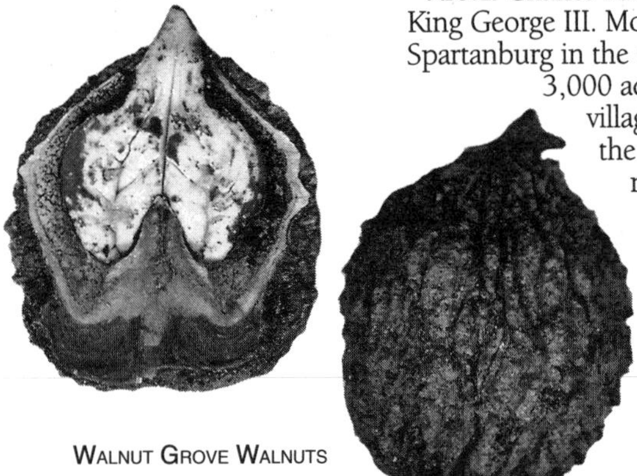

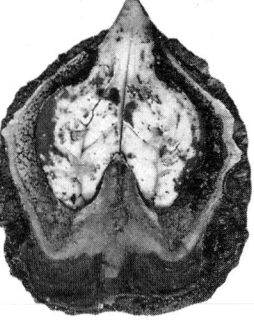

WALNUT GROVE WALNUTS

Thomas Price owned 2,000 acres and 28 slaves, ran a post office, operated a general store, and offered lodgings for stagecoach travelers. He did all this in and around one of the most unusual houses in Spartanburg County. This house, built in 1795, is exceptional because of its steep gambrel roof, its inside-end chimneys, and its totally brick structure. The bricks were all made on the premises and laid in elegant Flemish bond. The house (located just off I-26 at the junction of SC-199, 86, and 200) was carefully restored in the 1970s by the Spartanburg County Commission. —*Courtesy of B & B Studio*

—*Courtesy of B & B Studio*

Jammie Seay fought in the Revolutionary War as a rebel. He owned about 500 acres on Darby Road, where his son, Kinsman, built this house. A modest home for a substantial landowner, the house was far more typical of the structures most people of substance lived in during the eighteenth century than were the more elegant homes represented on these pages. People who owned less acreage lived in even more modest houses of one or two rooms. Jammie Seay died in 1850 at the age of 93 and was buried in the churchyard cemetery of Saint Timothy's Chapel near Arkwright. The top image was taken in the early 1960s. During the 1990s, the property and house were a site for archeological studies and historical preservation and renovation, similar to Walnut Grove Plantation.

—*Photographs courtesy of Terry Ferguson, Mark Olencki*

Smith's Tavern was built about 1795 and was restored in the mid-1970s. The tapestry chimney is one of the few remaining in the county. An itinerant Dutch mason came through the county in the mid-1770s and hired himself out to construct them.
—*Photograph by Robin Smith, courtesy of the Spartanburg County Regional Museum*

Dr. James Bivings left two imposing houses in the county. The first he built in 1830 at the site of Wofford's Iron Works (modern Glendale), where he pioneered in cotton manufacture on a large scale when he erected a large cotton factory in the early 1830s. The area came to be known as Bivingsville, and cotton manufacture continued there without interruption until the mid-twentieth century. Bivings soon lost control of his mill, but he remained undaunted about the prospects of cotton manufacture in the district, and in the mid-1840s he took over a mill at Crawfordsville. He successfully operated this enterprise until he sold it in 1856. In that same year, Bivings completed a beautiful residence in Spartanburg village, setting it on a hill, as he had his house in Bivingsville. This latter home, shown at right, passed into the Evins family and was the residence of John H. Evins, a Congressional representative from Spartanburg in the 1870s and 1880s and an important political figure in the state. Bivings pioneered the concept of the mill village in the upcountry. He set high moral standards for his workers and provided a village for them in order to keep them away from bad influences and under his protection.
—*Photograph by James Buchanan, courtesy of the Spartanburg County Regional Museum*

James Bivings also built this home in the antebellum period at his mill at Wofford's Iron Works (modern Glendale). Later John Bomar made it his home when he purchased a large interest in the mill, and it has since been known as the Bomar house. The photograph was taken in the twentieth century.
—*Courtesy of the Herald-Journal Willis Collection, Spartanburg County (SC) Public Libraries*

Built in 1834 by Dr. John Winsmith, this small but elegant house, known as Camp Hill, is fronted by the original boxwood garden and has an original slave cabin in the back. The house belonged to one of the most colorful politicians in Spartanburg. Dr. Winsmith (who had his name changed by the legislature from Winn Smith) and his brother, Elihu Penquite Smith, were leaders of one of the two most powerful pre-Civil War political factions in the county. Dr. Winsmith challenged the head of the rival faction, James E. Henry, to a duel in 1822, a challenge that Henry treated with contempt. Winsmith, one of the largest slaveholders in the county and a fire-eating leader for secession, did everything in his life with vigor and bravado. After the war he became a leader of the local Republicans. This shift in loyalties made him the target of much hatred, and not surprisingly the Ku Klux Klan visited and threatened him one night in 1871. Sixty-eight years old at the time, he walked out onto his front porch to face his tormentors with pistols blazing in his hands and was shot several times. He was too ornery to die and went on to testify against the Klan before a Congressional committee holding hearings in the area. —*Courtesy of the Spartanburg County Regional Museum*

This rural slave cabin located behind Camp Hill near Glenn Springs is typical of dwellings for slaves. It is one room constructed of mud-chinked logs.
—*Courtesy of the Spartanburg County Regional Museum*

In the last two decades of the antebellum period, one-third of the population of the county was slave. Some of these African Americans lived in the village, usually quartered in buildings with access from the yard but not from the street. Unlike similar quarters in larger cities such as Charleston, they were not surrounded with high brick walls, but short of that, all was done to discourage unsupervised fraternization among slaves. These quarters are somewhat unusual in that they are brick and built like a motel. Normally, slave quarters were either very large rooms accommodating a number of people or they were individual cabins. The quarters in this photograph were located on the southern side of East Main Street in downtown Spartanburg. —*Photograph by James Buchanan, courtesy of the Spartanburg County Regional Museum*

Revolutionary War soldiers discovered that bathing in a certain spring located on the Means Plantation cured the "itch." Since problems like the "itch" were common to frontier living, the spring became quite popular. In 1816 Means sold the spring and surrounding lands to John B. Glenn, who intended to build a house to board summer visitors. In 1845 John Conrad Zimmerman purchased what had become known as Glenn Springs. Under Zimmerman's keen guidance the hotel was built, and the area became one of the most popular vacations spots in South Carolina. Even at this early date the water was bottled and sent to eager customers all over the Southeast. The hotel burned in 1941. This image dates from the 1880s. —*Courtesy of the South Caroliniana Library*

1906 Glenn Springs Mineral Water label.
—*Courtesy Spartanburg County Regional Museum*

Located at one of the major crossroads in the eastern part of the county, Foster's Tavern served as a "public house" from the time it was built in 1807. The tavern was a popular resting-place for travelers going to Glenn Springs from the upper part of the county and is frequently singled out in letters of the antebellum period for its hospitality. In the fashion of the day, columns were added in 1845 and piazzas in 1915. The house stands at the intersections of SC-56 and SC-295. —*Photograph by James Buchanan, courtesy of the Spartanburg County Regional Museum*

Glenn Springs Hotel brochure advertised "unsurpassed" mineral water, "polite and attentive" staff, and rates of $2.00 a day. —*Courtesy Spartanburg County Regional Museum*

John Conrad Zimmerman built this Greek Revival house in 1854 in Glenn Springs. It was a fitting house for a successful farmer and owner of the famed hotel. Zimmerman owned thousands of acres of rich farmland, and his fortune permitted him to help underwrite some of the most successful textile manufacturing ventures in the county. —*Photograph by James Buchanan, courtesy of the Spartanburg County Regional Museum*

The Walker House (later known as the Piedmont House) built much of its early business on the reputation for cool and pleasant summers in the upcountry. This house, built in the 1840s, stood on East Main Street about where the Advantica building is presently located. It burned in 1882.
—*Courtesy of Converse College*

Variously known as Nicholl's Fort, Tanner's Mill, and Anderson's Mill, this structure sits on a foundation that dates from about 1780. The first court in the county met here in 1785. The water mill continued operation into the 1970s. It is located southwest of the city of Spartanburg where SC-64 crosses the North Tyger River. —*Photograph by James Buchanan, courtesy of the Spartanburg County Regional Museum*

As seen here in the interior of Anderson's Mill, the heart of a gristmill is its grinding stones. One of the base stones is seen in the foreground; notice that it has grooves carved into it. The whole grain kernels came from the upper story down a chute into a triangular shaped hopper, which in turn fed the kernels through the center of the top stone. The upper stone was located in the wooden, vertically slatted housing seen here. As the kernels fell through the upper stone, they were caught between the rough surfaces of the revolving stones. The revolution of the stones crushed the kernels into powder, which worked its way into the grooves toward the outer edges of the revolving stones. From there the powder dropped into a small chute and fell into a bag, seen here in front of and to the right of the woman. Over time the constant friction wore the stones too smooth, and periodically, the workers had to lift the stones out of their casings using a block and tackle apparatus and "sharpen" them by roughing up the surface of the stones and deepening the grooves. Unfortunately, Anderson's Mill is the last of the intact gristmills in the county and is deteriorating at such a rate that it may soon be beyond restoration. —*Courtesy of the Spartanburg County Regional Museum*

Beautifully sited on top of a hill, Shiloh Church was built sometime between 1825 and 1830. It is the oldest church building in the county. Tradition has it that Bishop Francis Asbury, the well-known itinerant Methodist preacher, held meetings nearby. Whether the good bishop ever preached here or not, records show that many camp meetings were held on this spot. Located on the Old Blackstock Road, an old Indian trail that linked settlements on the Tyger River with Tryon, North Carolina, the church's location made it a natural gathering place for area Methodists. Religion played an important role in the lives of the frontier people, and their simple and strong faith is reflected in the simplicity that marks the construction of this church. Unadorned, either inside or out, the building has not been altered over the years. The original candleholders still line the walls; the benches and stone foundation attest to a primitive craftsmanship. Since 1915 a service has been held here every year, usually on the third Sunday in May. *—Courtesy of B & B Studio*

Presbyterians organized what is now the oldest congregation in the county in 1765. They built the present structure, known as Nazareth Church, in 1832. *—Photograph by James Buchanan, courtesy of the Spartanburg County Regional Museum*

Two of the first schools in the county. The top image is typical of a one-room construction plan. —*Photographs by James Buchanan, courtesy of the Spartanburg County Regional Museum*

Preachers do not often see quick and practical results from their sermons. However, in 1857, the Reverend R. H. Reid of Nazareth Church preached a sermon on the importance of education, and a few months later, that congregation established a school for males. A village was laid out (the first effort at urban planning in the county) with the male school at one end of the main street and the female school, established in 1859, at the other. The trustees elected Reverend Reid to head the schools, and he served in that capacity for forty years. Throughout the county, the Reidville schools had a well-deserved reputation for scholarship, and colleges were pleased to enroll their graduates. The building in the photograph is the school for girls. —*Photograph by J. M. Taylor, courtesy of the Spartanburg County Regional Museum*

A Webster's spelling book of the type likely used in Spartanburg's first schools. —*Courtesy Spartanburg County Regional Museum*

THE

SOUTHERN HARMONY, AND MUSICAL COMPANION:

CONTAINING A CHOICE COLLECTION OF

TUNES, HYMNS, PSALMS, ODES AND ANTHEMS:

SELECTED FROM THE MOST EMINENT AUTHORS IN THE UNITED STATES.

TOGETHER WITH NEARLY ONE HUNDRED NEW TUNES, WHICH HAVE NEVER BEFORE BEEN PUBLISHED; SUITED TO MOST

OF THE METRES CONTAINED IN

WATTS' HYMNS AND PSALMS, MERCER'S CLUSTER, DOSSEY'S CHOICE, DOVER SELECTION, METHODIST

HYMN BOOK AND BAPTIST HARMONY;

AND WELL ADAPTED TO

CHRISTIAN CHURCHES OF EVERY DENOMINATION, SINGING SCHOOLS AND PRIVATE SOCIETIES.

ALSO, AN EASY

Introduction to the grounds of Music, the rudiments of Music, and plain rules for beginners.

BY WILLIAM WALKER.

Sing unto God ye kingdoms of the earth: O sing praises unto the Lord.—DAVID.
Speaking to yourselves in psalms and hymns, and spiritual songs, singing and making melody in your hearts to the Lord.—PAUL.

SPARTANSBURG, S. C.

Sold by the AUTHOR, at Spartansburg, S. C.; Rev. S. S. BURDETT, Pleasant Hill; MATTHEW LYON, Cheraw;
ROBERTS AND WADDLE, Union; WILLIAM RILEY, Charleston; J R. AND W. CUNNINGHAM,
Columbia; and by MERCHANTS generally in the Southern States.

1835

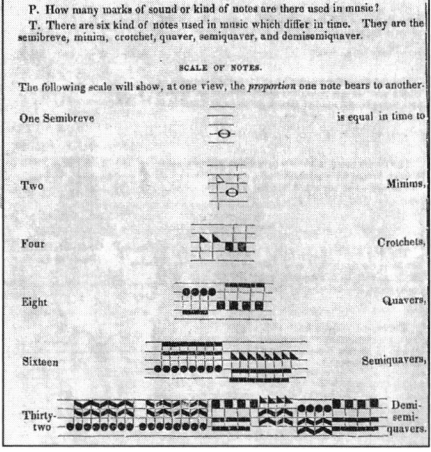

TOP: Title page of William "Singin' Billy" Walker's *Southern Harmony and Musical Companion.* CENTER: Shaped notes examples. BELOW: The hymn tune "Spartanburgh" from Walker's *Southern Harmony.*
—*Courtesy of Spartanburg Historical Society*

Spartanburg's "Singin'" Billy Walker sold over one million copies of his religious songbook, *Southern Harmony and Musical Companion,* which he published in 1835. His work used "shaped notes," musical notations that could be understood by people without formal musical education. *Southern Harmony* preserved hundreds of popular religious songs, including "Promised Land" and "Wondrous Love." —*Courtesy of Wofford College*

Central United Methodist Church is the oldest church in the city of Spartanburg. Built in 1837, the church has undergone multiple renovations, the largest of which took place in 1885. Note the tower on the left, now missing. The church has always occupied this site on North Church Street. —*Courtesy of Wofford College*

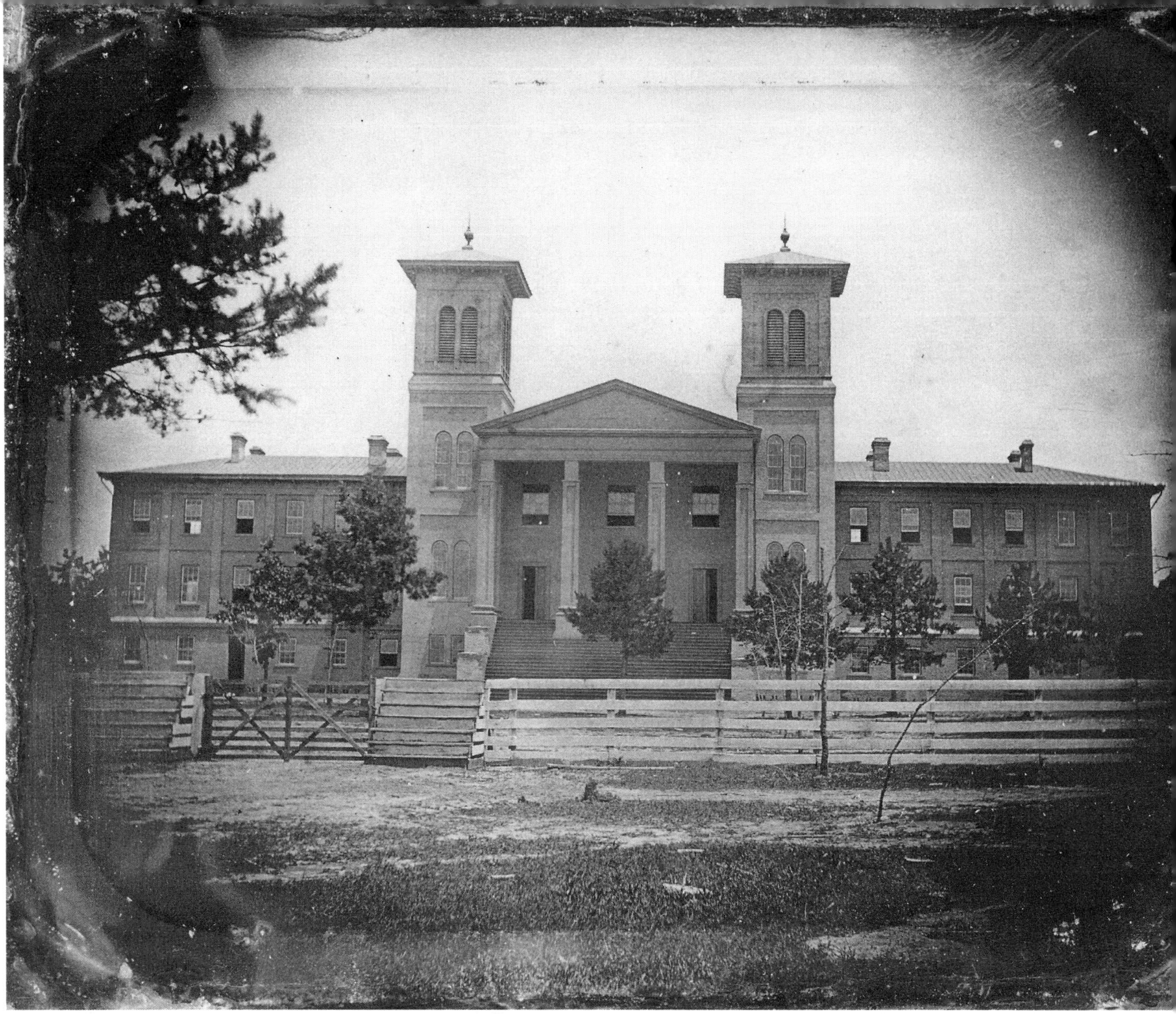

SIX PER CENT.

ACT 23, MARCH 1863.

It is hereby Certified, that the Confederate States of America

are indebted unto

or Assigns in the sum of

Dollars

with interest from the

redeemable on the first day of

day of February 1864 inclusive at SIX PER CENT PER ANNUM, payable on the first days of January and July in each Year.

This Contract is Authorized by an Act of Congress approved 23rd March 1863, entitled "An Act to provide for the funding and further issue of Treasury Notes", and is upon the express condition that it shall be redeemable five years after date at the pleasure of the Government.

RICHMOND, May 4 1864.

Entered

Recorded

Register of the Treasury

Lithog^d by Evans & Cogswell

Wofford's Confederate Investment

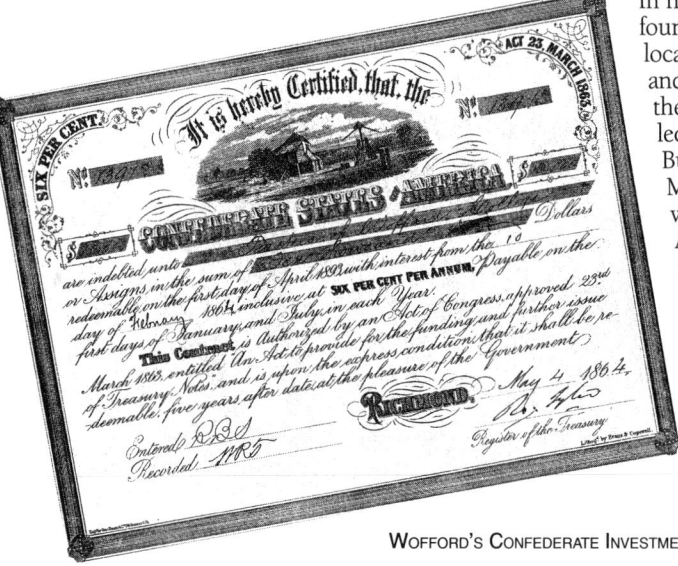

In his will of 1850, the Reverend Benjamin Wofford left $100,000 for the founding of a college "for literary, classical and scientific education, to be located in my native District of Spartanburg, and to be under the control and management of the Methodist Episcopal Church...." For many years the Main Building (circa 1854) was the entire college, housing a chapel, lecture rooms, laboratories, offices, and a museum. At present the Main Building houses classrooms, offices, a chapel, and an auditorium. The Main Building was designed by Edward C. Jones of Charleston and built with slave labor by Clayton and Burgess of Asheville, North Carolina. Although the exterior of the building was impressive, the materials used in its construction were weak. The interior of the very thick walls was constructed of soft brick, and during construction the western tower collapsed and killed one man. Note the double gates in the fence (probably there to keep large animals out) to permit the entry of wagons, and the stairs on either side of the gates to permit free movement of students and faculty. This mid-1850s daguerreotype is one of the oldest photographs of Spartanburg County.

—Courtesy of the University of Georgia Library

An early image of Benjamin Wofford, his gold pocket watch, and the 1900s repair ticket still attached to it.
—*Courtesy of Mark Olencki*

The Reverend Newton Pinckney Walker opened a school for deaf children in 1849 at Cedar Springs. In 1855 the curriculum was expanded to care for the blind, and two years later the state of South Carolina purchased the school and built this fine classical structure. It was always one of the hallmarks of this institution that it kept close ties with the surrounding community. Graduation exercises and other social and academic functions were often open to the public, and the entertainment-starved farmers looked forward to these events. —*Courtesy of Mark Olencki*

A Spartanburg couple, Judge T. O. P. Vernon and Harriet Bomar
Vernon, photographed some time around the Civil War.
—*Courtesy of the Horace L. Bomar family*

Jesse Cleveland, the founder of one of the eminent clans of
Spartanburg, came to the county in 1810 and set up store
keeping directly behind the present Cleveland Hotel. He
was a keen merchandiser who early realized that he could
buy goods more cheaply by making the long trek to
Baltimore or Philadelphia himself rather than by trying
to get goods in Charleston. He would set out with
wagons, slaves, and a parcel of dogs; on his return the
dogs would precede him to the village, thus informing
everyone that Cleveland would soon be there with new
goods to sell. In 1825 he received a land grant of 578
acres, which he increased over the years. He owned
much land in the area of the village, especially from
Main Street north past Wofford College. Jesse Cleveland
was one of the early supporters of education for the
youngsters of the community, inaugurating a tradition of
philanthropy in his family that would
benefit the village greatly in the future.
—*Courtesy of Jesse Franklin Cleveland*

Two of these young men were native Spartans: the future physician Jesse Cleveland in the middle and Barnett Franklin Cleveland on his left. The two Spartans and their unidentified friend were serving in the South Carolina Militia, guarding the coast in Charleston some time in the 1860s, when this picture was taken. Jesse seems either to have given up a Napoleonic pose, outgrown his coat, or become absentminded about his appearance.

—*Courtesy of Jesse Franklin Cleveland*

LOCAL CURRENCY ISSUED DURING THE CIVIL WAR
—*Courtesy of James Crocker*

The Williams Place

The "Williams Place" is a collection of eleven buildings that form a farmstead in the southern part of Spartanburg County around Cane Creek, a tributary of the Tyger River. Of the eleven buildings, only one, believed to have been a slave house, has been destroyed, leaving only the original fieldstone piers. All of the buildings appear to be made of pine logs (cleared off the farm to create fields) that are held together with V notching and half dovetailing.

The farmstead is named for John Williams, who purchased land on both sides of Cane Creek in 1800, and his descendants, who continued to live on it until the 1970s. The National Trust for Historic Preservation considers the Williams Place to be one of the best preserved collections of "open log" construction in the nation. By any measure, it is the finest example of how middle-class farmers of the nineteenth century lived in upper South Carolina. Although the main house has been added onto over the years, its central portion may date as early as 1777 but certainly dates from at least 1800. Most of the other buildings on the Williams Place date from between 1839 and 1850, when the farm was owned and operated by John Williams and his son Robert. In the middle of the nineteenth century, the Robert Williams family owned four slaves and 813 acres of land, 200 acres of which were under cultivation. In addition to the usual food crops, the farm produced one acre of cotton for the family's use. The map shows the location of the various buildings, the state road, and the current dirt paths and farm roads; however, in the nineteenth century another road (marked by the broken lines) ran between the main house and the detached kitchen on past the smoke house and eventually into Blackstock Road, one of the major roads in the district at that time. It was the usual practice to build houses in the country close to the road to facilitate transportation, social interaction, and merchandising.

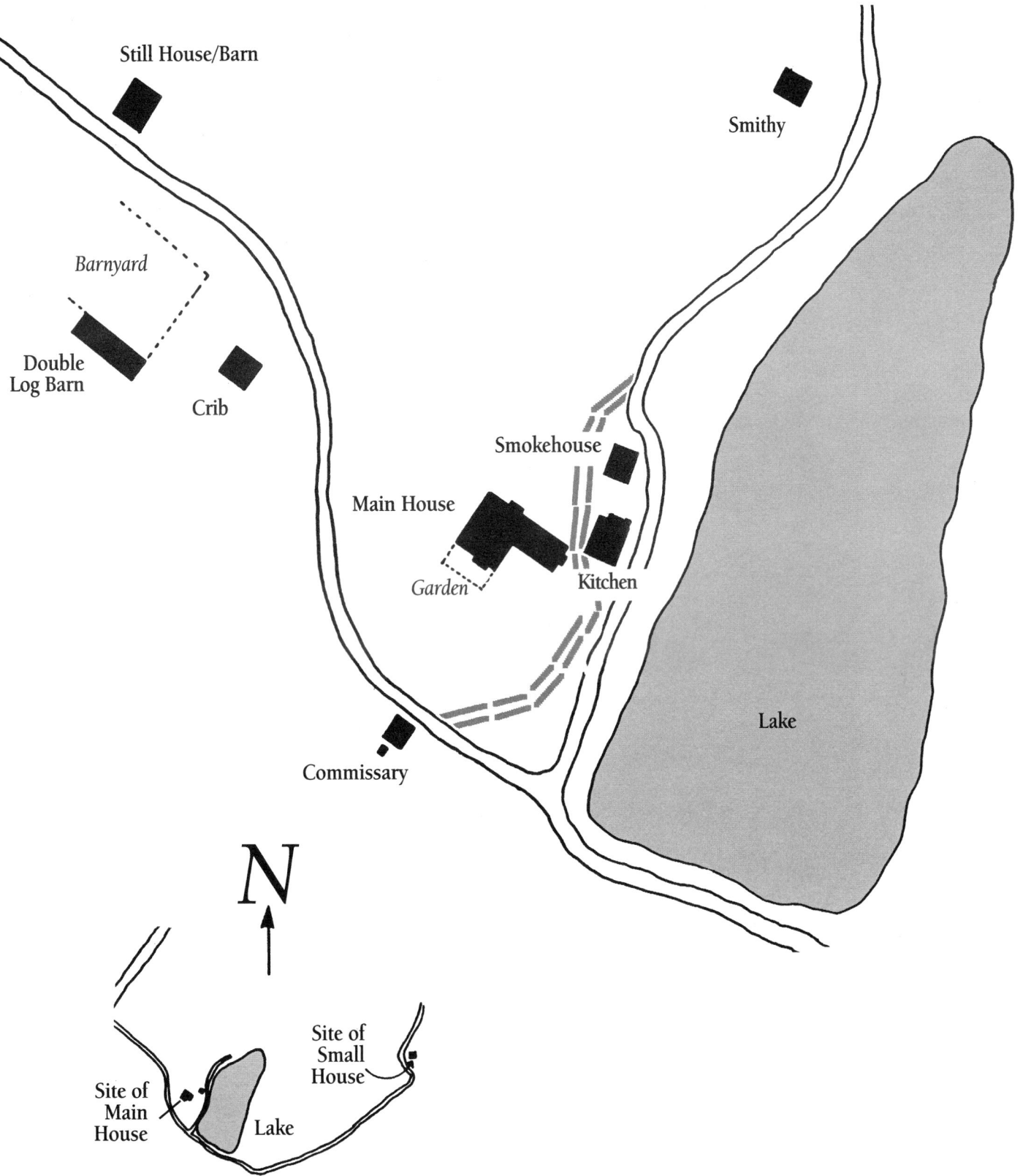

Still House/Barn

Smithy

Barnyard

Double
Log Barn

Crib

Smokehouse

Main House

Garden

Kitchen

Lake

Commissary

N

Site of
Small
House

Site of
Main
House

Lake

—*Williams Place photographs courtesy of the Library of Congress*

MAIN HOUSE

The central portion of the main house is a two-room structure with one door. The front of the house faces the detached kitchen, and in the nineteenth century it would have faced the road that ran between the house and the kitchen. Later additions include the lean-to at the rear of the house which was divided into three rooms, including a preacher's room on the end for itinerant preachers, also known as circuit riders. The L-shaped section of the house, which protrudes toward the front, was added about 1900. The fireplace in the living room has a root cellar just to the front of it. The sleeping quarters upstairs are reached by way of an enclosed staircase, which is narrow and steep.

The Kitchen

The detached kitchen protected the main house from the hazard of fire and from the heat of cooking in the summertime. The structure is made of hewn horizontal logs connected at the corners by V notching. The structure sits on fieldstone pier foundations, one of which is almost five feet high. The chimney is also made of fieldstone up to the shoulders and of brick from the shoulders up through the roof. In the end of the structure opposite the fireplace, there is a notch in the logs for firing a musket. The spaces between the logs of the walls are covered with horizontal planking thus avoiding the necessity of chinking the walls with mud. The fireplace is four feet two inches high and has an eight-inch thick solid lintel taken from a nearby quarry. Also, the planking that forms the doorway is secured to the logs with wooden pegs.

Commissary

The Williams family had a commissary (top image) from which they sold farm goods to neighbors and travelers. The upper story was used for storage while the main story had shelves, which at an earlier time may have held the family's canned goods and later held the goods for sale. The commissary was located close to the road that ran between the main house and the kitchen. Also, a large root cellar was located under the commissary. Note that the buildings necessary to the domestic chores of the women of the family (the main house, the kitchen, the smoke house and the commissary) were located close to each other while other buildings used for animals and general farming were clustered away from the main house. The crib (bottom image) was used for grain and crop storage.

Barn

Notice that the barn is of open-log construction. There was no mud chinking, and animals were left partly exposed to the elements.

Notched logs

Here can be seen the V notching that holds the structure together. There are no vertical supports in the middle of any of the walls, so all of the structure's support rests on the notched ends of the logs. Note how carefully the notches are cut so the fit is tight.

SMALL HOUSE

Sometime after the Williams family built their main house, they constructed this smaller home several hundred yards from the main farmstead. At one time, it may have been the home of a favorite slave named Dave, and at another, the home of one of the Williams family's sons. This small house is more typical of housing for yeoman farmers in Spartanburg County than is the main house. It is a one-room structure with a loft, probably for the children. The structure is constructed of hewn logs, about eleven inches square, held together with half dovetailing. The spaces between the logs are covered inside and out by horizontal boards nailed over the spaces. The structure is typical of Scots-Irish construction in the upcountry with its opposing doors to permit free circulation of air and its two porches on either side of the dwelling. These photographs illustrate the skill of the builders. The logs are very large for such a small structure (11 inches square), and they are notched and dovetailed with extreme precision. The fit is so tight that a sheet of paper cannot be inserted between the various pieces. On the other hand, the lack of any glass in the house and the quality of the workmanship in the window shutter and door illustrate a cavalier attitude at odds with the care taken in the basic construction of the structure. The Williams family was Scots-Irish, and their farm has the characteristics of Scots-Irish farmsteads. Historians and cultural anthropologists have long noted the apparent lack of concern among Scots-Irish immigrants with creature comforts. The narrow stairway, which was never enclosed, leads to the half-story sleeping quarters most likely reserved for the children of the family. The stairs are narrow both because they were for the use of children and to conserve as much space as possible in the one room downstairs.

WADSWORTH GAS ATTACK
AND
The Rio Grande Rattler.

CAMP WADSWORTH, SPARTANBURG, S. C., February 9, 1918

No. 12

DISCIPLINE

TEN CENTS

United States of America
STATE OF SOUTH CAROLINA.
The Converse College Company
OF SPARTANBURG, S. C.

This is to Certify, That L. G. Potter

entitled to one

In 1880 Spartanburg became a city. The threefold increase in the town's population during the 1870s had prompted town officials to make that request of the state legislature. It may have seemed presumptuous of the leaders of a town of 3,200 to change their official status from that of a village to that of a city, but in some ways the next 20 years made them look like seers. In the last two decades of the nineteenth

Boom and Subsistence
Paradox
1880 - 1920

century, Spartanburg acquired many of the trappings of the larger cities it emulated. In the early seventies, kerosene lamps dotted the square, but gas lamps replaced them in 1882. The beginnings of a firefighting unit organized in 1873 achieved the status of a fire department some nine years later when the city bought its first fire engine. The equipment was the city's, but the firefighters were volunteers. Water, first obtained from the spring behind the courthouse and then

Music festivals drew people from all over the East Coast.
—*Courtesy of Converse College*

from a public well in the middle of the square, became available through the Home Water Supply Company in 1888. The company supplied 50 hydrants and four public drinking fountains for man and horse in the last two decades of the nineteenth century. Anything calling itself a city had to have paving and open space to show off the buildings of progress, so the trees lining the square were cut, the old public well was filled in, and bricks were laid to cover the square that had always been dust or mud, depending on the weather.

In 1889 several citizens, under the leadership of Dexter Converse, established Converse College and thereby took a step that had a profound effect on the cultural life of the county. The college not only provided good education for young ladies, but it also sponsored and hosted musical and theatrical productions that became an important part of the county's intellectual life. With the inauguration of the South Atlantic States Music Festival in 1895, the close relationship between town and gown in entertainment and musical education became fixed.

A Converse student received this medal for achievements in math.
—*Courtesy of Converse College*

The beginnings of modernization that took place in the eighties bore fruit in the nineties. The city let contracts for electric street lights and sewage disposal in 1890 and began a program of expensive street renovation. One mile of macadamized street was laid and the sidewalks were cemented. In 1892 that symbol of mass transit, the streetcar, appeared on East Main Street, running from the railroad crossing just west of Liberty to Pine Street. It resembled New York City's 1820s horse-drawn car that had inaugurated mass transit in the United States. There was a Southern touch in Spartanburg, however, for its car was drawn by a mule. An engine replaced Spartanburg's mule within a week, but it promptly blew up. Not all innovation can be trouble-free.

The Spartanburg Railway, Gas and Electric Company replaced the pioneer traction company in the early nineties and eventually constructed a city system running from Union Station on Magnolia to Main Street. From there the tracks went east to Church, where they ran both north and south. From the corner of East Main and Church the tracks went up Main to Pine Street, where they connected with a suburban line which ran along Pine to Country Club Road and on to Glendale, Clifton, and Converse. From the corner of Pine and Main Streets the city line continued east up Main to Rock Cliff Park on Heywood Avenue. Another line turned westward on Main at Morgan Square and went to Saxon. By 1906 this company had some 15 miles of track; popular routes on weekends were those to Rock Cliff Park and to Glendale Park, which bordered the Glendale Mill. Spartanburg, city and county, prospered during these years from 1880 to 1920. Downtown Spartanburg city bustled with stores, people, and traffic. The automobile appeared, and in those first years when cars, horses, trains, and trolleys vied for the right-of-way, pedestrians jeopardized their lives just by being on the streets.

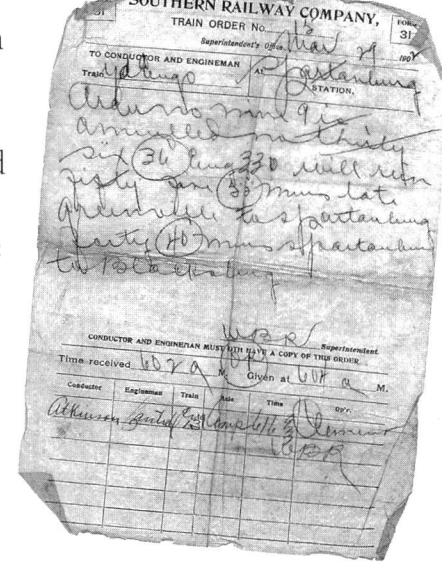

GLENN SPRINGS RAILROAD PASS
—*Courtesy of Spartanburg Regional County Museum*

Early in the 1840s, the Spartanburg business community realized that it was in keen competition for rails, for the cities that got the railroads would prosper. Spartanburg owed much of its prosperity to the railroads. Men with capital would be willing to invest in the area because the railroads would be here to transport goods. By 1900 rail lines crisscrossed the county to all four points of the compass. From the North to Atlanta and from Asheville to Charleston, Spartanburg was "on the way" to almost everywhere. Local capitalists invested in and used the rails. When Dexter Converse built additional mills, he constructed rail lines to connect them with the major railways; when the Charleston and Western Carolina line went broke, a Spartanburg man, John B. Cleveland, bought it. Cleveland abandoned the old emphasis on passengers and concentrated on freight, a wise choice which presaged the future and made him some money. By the late nineteenth century the promoters had been successful and the rails had

ORDERS FOR A SOUTHERN RAILWAY ENGINEER
—*Courtesy of Liz & Dwight Patterson*

come: the Charleston and Western Carolina, the Southern, and the Piedmont and Northern.

The county's income and pride suffered in 1897 when Gaffney, its largest town, and the upper northeastern part of the county split away and joined with parts of York and Union to form Cherokee County. In the long run, the increase in textile activity during the last part of the nineteenth century overshadowed the economic loss of Gaffney. Investors built several mills in the county, and Captain John H. Montgomery, who had first come to the county as a fertilizer salesman, built the first cotton mill in the city of Spartanburg. He named it Spartan Mill. Two years later, in 1890, a subscription was launched in the city to start Beaumont Mills; by 1909 there were nine mills in or near the city of Spartanburg.

There was little concentration of population outside of the immediate villages, and textile mills had to provide living quarters for their employees. As early as the 1850s, John Bivings had erected a small village at Crawfordsville to provide living space for his workers. In the latter part of the nineteenth and the early twentieth centuries, other mill owners also built villages around their plants in order to have their workers close to the mill, to provide them with the necessities of life, and to have some control over the type of worker which they employed. The mill owned the houses and rented them to workers; stores owned by the company provided workers with the basic necessities, including credit. This process created some distance between the mill workers and the inhabitants of the city, a situation that worsened as the two groups came to distrust, resent, and even fear one another.

In spite of the increase in the number of textile mills, the county remained overwhelmingly agricultural. After the Civil War the number of large farms decreased as land was divided among sharecroppers and tenants. With the dismantling of slavery, landowners realized that the cost of large-scale farming was prohibitive, so they took on families to whom they rented land. The most common method of farming was sharecropping, under which arrangement the landowner would rent the land

Textile tools used to retrieve broken threads on looms.
—*Courtesy of Spartanburg Methodist College*

either for a portion of the crop grown on it or for cash. The local merchant (country stores were located throughout the county) granted the tenant credit for fertilizer, seed, and other goods against a lien on the future crop. When the harvest came in, the sharecropper or tenant sold it through the local merchant. Since the merchant took a risk that the crop might be small or might fail completely, he usually charged the tenant from 20 to 75 percent interest on the loan. Cotton prices were not good, and most tenants were in perpetual debt to landowner and merchant.

In general, farming had two primary obstacles before the Civil War. The first was erosion, and the second was partly a consequence of the first —loss of fertility in the soil. Heavy rains and habitual planting without taking precautions to prevent erosion left the rolling hills of the county barren of good topsoil. Farmers in the antebellum South did little to try to restore fertility to the soil, believing that the effort and time required were not worth the gain. Even when crop yields fell, local farmers did surprisingly little to restore the growing power of their soil. By the 1880s, however, the problem seemed to disappear as new fertilizers that re-enriched the soil became available. Because of fertilizers and a rising price, people grew more cotton in Spartanburg after the Civil War than before it. After the turn of the century the boll weevil, which could destroy an entire crop, arrived. Yet, farmers were stubborn, and the weevil was just another problem in a long list of troubles associated with tilling the soil.

Cotton seemed the best and possibly the only cash crop available to them, so the farmers of the county, no matter how small an operation they had, devoted themselves to raising the staple of their ancestors. Fertilizers allowed them to produce much more per acre than ever before. Because of this single-mindedness, they would sometimes profit and oftentimes suffer. When cotton was plentiful and prices went down, farm-

Locally-made corn whiskey filled this bottle.
—*Courtesy of Dr. Charles Webb*

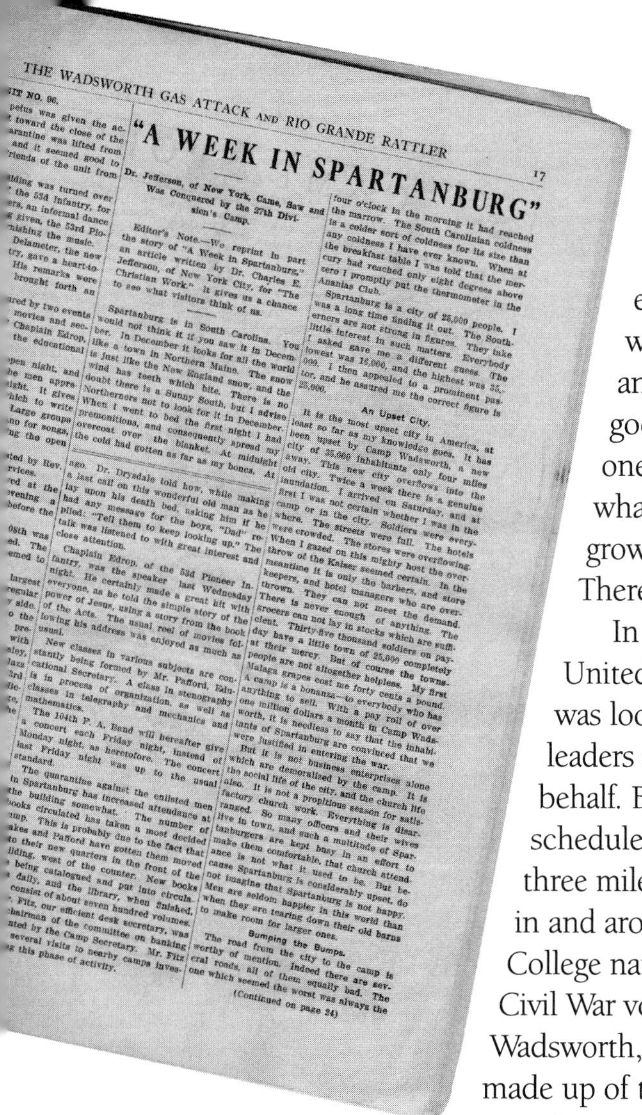

THE WADSWORTH GAS ATTACK AND RIO GRANDE RATTLER 17

"A WEEK IN SPARTANBURG"

Dr. Jefferson, of New York, Came, Saw and Was Conquered by the 27th Division's Camp.

Editor's Note.—We reprint in part the story of "A Week in Spartanburg," an article written by Dr. Charles E. Jefferson, of New York City, for "The Christian Work." It gives us a chance to see what visitors think of us.

Spartanburg is in South Carolina. You would not think it if you saw it in December. In December it looks for all the world like a town in Northern Maine. The snow is just like the New England snow, and the wind has teeth which bite. There is no doubt there is a Sunny South, but I advise Northerners not to look for it in December. When I went to bed the first night I had premonitions, and consequently spread my overcoat over the blanket. At midnight the cold had gotten as far as my bones. At four o'clock in the morning it had reached the marrow. The South Carolinian coldness is a colder sort of coldness for its size than any coldness I have ever known. When at the breakfast table I was told that the mercury had reached only eight degrees above zero I promptly put the thermometer in the Ananias Club.

Spartanburg is a city of 25,000 people. I was a long time finding it out. The Southerners are not strong in figures. They take little interest in such matters. Everybody I asked gave me a different guess. The lowest was 16,000, and the highest was 35,000. I then appealed to a prominent pastor, and he assured me the correct figure is 25,000.

An Upset City.

It is the most upset city in America, at least so far as my knowledge goes. It has been upset by Camp Wadsworth, a new city of 35,000 inhabitants only four miles away. This new city overflows into the old city. Twice a week there is a genuine inundation. I arrived on Saturday, and at first I was not certain whether I was in the camp or in the city. Soldiers were everywhere. The streets were full. The hotels were crowded. The stores were overflowing. When I gazed on this mighty host the overthrow of the Kaiser seemed certain. In the meantime it is only the barbers, and store keepers, and hotel managers who are overthrown. They can not meet the demand. There is never enough of anything. The grocers can not lay in stocks which are sufficient. Thirty-five thousand soldiers on pay day have a little town of 25,000 completely at their mercy. But of course the towns-people are not altogether helpless. My first Malaga grapes cost me forty cents a pound. A camp is a bonanza—to everybody who has anything to sell. With a pay roll of over one million dollars a month in Camp Wadsworth, it is needless to say that the inhabitants of Spartanburg are convinced that we were justified in entering the war.

But it is not business enterprises alone which are demoralized by the camp. It is the social life of the city, and the church life also. It is not a propitious season for satisfactory church work. Everything is disarranged. So many officers and their wives live in town, and such a multitude of Spartanburgers are kept busy in an effort to make them comfortable, that church attendance is not what it used to be. But because Spartanburg is considerably upset, do not imagine that Spartanburg is not happy. Men are seldom happier in this world than when they are tearing down their old barns to make room for larger ones.

Bumping the Bumps.

The road from the city to the camp is worthy of mention. Indeed there are several roads, all of them equally bad. The one which seemed the worst was always the

(Continued on page 24)

ago. Dr. Drysdale told how, while making a last call on this wonderful old man as he lay upon his death bed, asking him if he had any message for the boys, "Dad" replied: "Tell them to keep looking up." The talk was listened to with great interest and close attention.

Chaplain Edrop, of the 53d Pioneer Infantry, was the speaker last Wednesday night. He certainly made a great hit with everyone, as he told the simple story of the power of Jesus, using a story from the book of the Acts. The usual reel of movies following his address was enjoyed as much as usual.

New classes in various subjects are constantly being formed by Mr. Pafford, Educational Secretary. A class in stenography is in process of organization, as well as classes in telegraphy and mechanics and mathematics.

The 104th F. A. Band will hereafter give a concert each Friday night, instead of Monday night, as heretofore. The concert last Friday night was up to the usual standard.

The quarantine against the enlisted men in Spartanburg has increased attendance at the building somewhat. The number of books circulated has taken a most decided jump. This is probably due to the fact that [Bl]akes and Pafford have gotten them moved to their new quarters in the front of the building, west of the counter. New books being catalogued and put into circulation daily, and the library, when finished, consist of about seven hundred volumes.

Fitz, our efficient desk secretary, was chairman of the committee on banking ... by the Camp Secretary. Mr. Fitz several visits to nearby camps investigating this phase of activity.

A soldier describes Spartanburg in the Camp Wadsworth newspaper.
—Courtesy of Spartanburg County (SC) Public Libraries

ers refused to limit their production; there was no organization to help them to do it, and every farmer believed he could get a good price by selling his crop before everyone else did. Even when farmers realized what was going on, they had no choice. To grow less while others grew more was folly. There seemed no way out of the dilemma.

In 1917 America declared war. When the United States government announced that it was looking for training centers, several city leaders successfully lobbied on Spartanburg's behalf. By the middle of 1917 the War College scheduled a camp to be placed a little more than three miles west of the city (the camp was located in and around present-day Westgate Mall). The War College named the facility in honor of a New York Civil War volunteer, Brigadier General James S. Wadsworth, partly because a New York division, made up of that state's national guard, was to be trained in Spartanburg. So the 27th Division, a rather bluestocking crowd of "Yankees" commanded by Major General John F. O'Ryan, was to descend on the rural and small (about 22,000) city of Spartanburg. And descend they did. Even before they arrived, the enormity of the project began to dawn on the city and county. The camp required 915 buildings besides ten storehouses and a hospital unit, all to be built within a few months. The men would sleep in tents. Upwards of 40,000 men who eventually moved through the camp swamped the little town of Spartanburg and taxed it beyond its limits for entertainment and diversion. The almost two years of the camp's existence was a difficult but rewarding time for the county and city.

Between 1885 and 1920 Spartanburg's architecture underwent a change so radical as

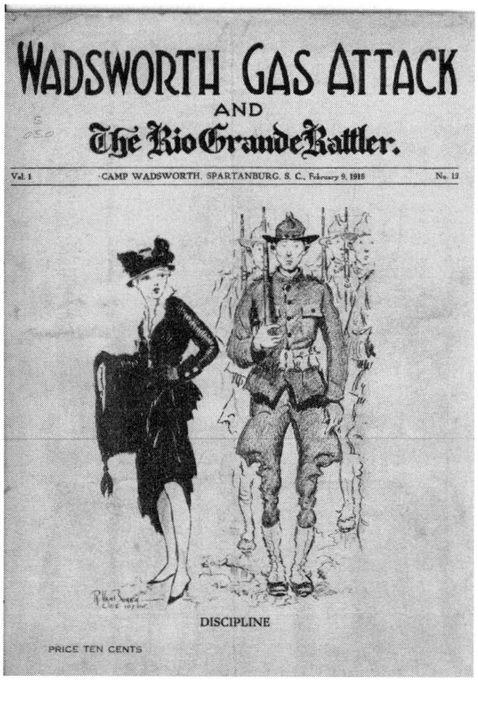

Wadsworth soldiers received this publication weekly.
—Courtesy of the Spartanburg County Regional Museum

to leave it a different city. It was as if the spirit of optimism that infused the leaders of the village drove them into an unthinking destruction of the old so they could build all anew. The old village landmarks went one by one, some by hazard and most by design. The square, which was really a rectangle, had assumed its character from a row of interesting buildings on its north side, beginning with the Opera House and moving eastward to the Palmetto House. By 1910 all were gone, some replaced with buildings of distinction, others with buildings of mammon. It seemed as if structures on the north side of Daniel Morgan were especially ill-fated; many buildings on the south side remain there still. Unfortunately, those structures were considerably less distinguished. The destruction went on laboriously: the Palmetto House, the Courthouse, the Opera House, the First National Bank, and the Spartan Inn. Other interesting earlier buildings that were not on the square, such as the old jail, also disappeared during these years.

The city that grew in its place carried the stamp of the Victorian era. Although somewhat out of favor in our own day, much of the architecture and building of the turn of the century was a credit: the Cleveland Law Range, the new courthouse, and the many Victorian houses on Pine and Church streets. There were also some classical buildings, such as the city hall and the United States Post Office, which added a new dimension and a change from the Victorian. The two finest additions to the new city were exquisite products of the new age: towering skyscrapers; each, in its heyday, harkened to a style that went back to the late nineteenth century. This was lucky for Spartanburg, for they both reflected an artistry in architecture that in many ways was indigenously American. The Andrews Building (originally called the Chapman Building) was constructed in 1912 and the Montgomery Building in 1923. The architectural details and the holistic impression of both of these buildings is impressive, even if it can only be appreciated in photographs, for one building is gone and the other radically changed: the Andrews destroyed in an aborted demolition attempt in 1977 and the Montgomery stripped of its coloring, its marquee, and its street-level character. Yet such change was part of a wider reconstitution of the city that occurred after World War II, when, in an attempt once again to reflect progress as others saw it, Spartanburg destroyed this second generation of buildings to construct yet a third. These last, unfortunately, reflected a new presence in American architecture that denied the local and copied the international, a style that was particularly subject to bad imitation. So the post office, the courthouse, the city hall and the Andrews Building all went the way of their precursors. Although not destroyed, other buildings were critically marred as owners adapted them as inexpensively as possible to air conditioning, a technology that made the South a much more attractive place for people from other parts of the nation to live and work.

THE NEW HOME OF THE CENTRAL NATIONAL BANK

CHAPMAN BUILDING   **MORGAN SQUARE**

1918 ADVERTISEMENT IN THE WADSWORTH *GAS ATTACK*

Landscape & Architecture

This view of Morgan Square was taken from the east end looking northwest in the 1890s. There is still no paving; the fountain fronted by small, bare trees and surrounded by an iron fence marks the center of the Square. The First National Bank is on the west side of Magnolia Street. On the right from Magnolia is the Duncan Building, which housed Greenewald's clothing store (the first two awnings) on the first floor. Under the third awning was a shoe store, then a men's clothing store, a drug store where the sign says "SHOES," a grocery store, and G. L. Cannon's roofing business. —*Courtesy of the Herald-Journal Willis Collection, Spartanburg County (SC) Public Libraries*

EARLY 1900s CITY LETTERHEAD

PREVIOUS PAGE: The big event of the week in the nineteenth century was sales day. The first Monday of every month, wagons carrying provisions and goods from the county and from the North Carolina mountains would gather in Morgan Square. People who had traveled far camped out by the spring behind the courthouse. Not only was this market day for everyone in the area, but it was also an opportunity to exchange gossip, visit with the neighbors, and frequent the local shops and saloons. This earliest picture of Morgan Square shows the Opera House with the tower and clock on the right. Notice the open space under the tower, where ladies could be let off a wagon or buggy to enter the building without getting wet in the rain. Actually a city hall, the building included a hall for theatricals and special events. Next to it stands the Merchant's Hotel, later known as the Spartan Inn, and the building with the columns on the far right is the courthouse. The third courthouse in the county's history, it was built in 1856 entirely of brick, and the columns were coated with white plaster. The monument that gave its name to the square was placed there with great ceremony in the spring of 1881 to mark the one hundredth anniversary of the Battle of Cowpens. Spartanburg was chosen as the place to commemorate the battle because of the inaccessibility of the battleground itself.
—*Courtesy of the Herald-Journal Willis Collection, Spartanburg County (SC) Public Libraries*

1914 PROPERTY TAX RECEIPT

As part of the extensive and expensive program to improve the streets between 1890 and 1910, these workers are laying "vitrified" brick in Morgan Square in 1900. This glasslike surface was considered the most advanced and beautiful paving material in that day, and its appearance led some citizens to refer to Morgan Square as a "courtyard." Whether said in jest or not, almost anything was an improvement over the sea of mud that for years had brought everything to a standstill on wet days. In 1882 the city had macadamized (packed small broken stone on a roadbed) some streets only to find that dirt stuck to them with a vengeance. By 1900 the macadam had been completely covered with a thick layer of dirt. Vitrified brick was considered superior to macadam because mud washed off the former when it rained. —*Courtesy of Wofford College*

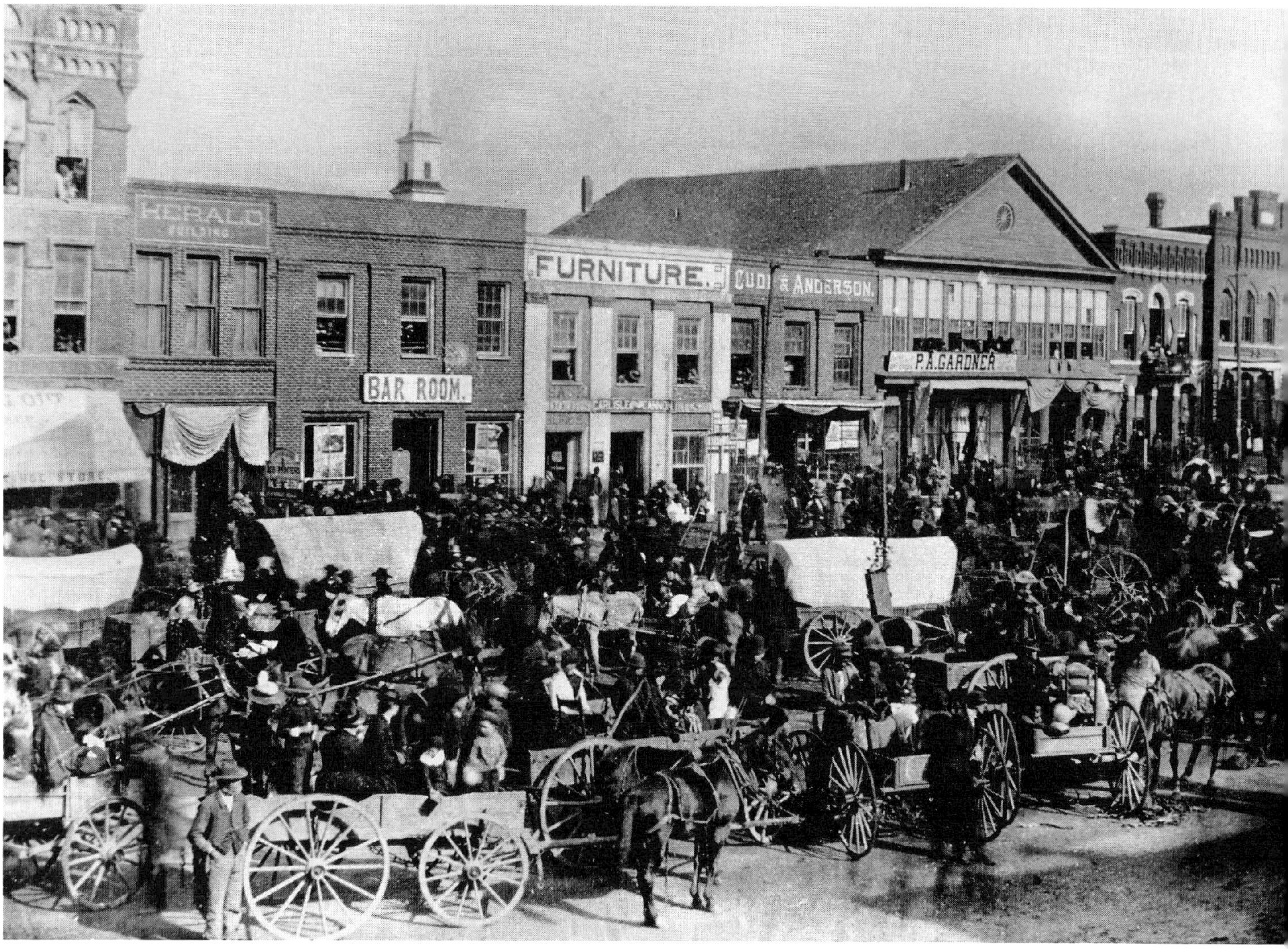
HERALD
FURNITURE.
BAR ROOM.
& ANDERSON.
P.A.GARDNER

It is unknown why these families are gathered in Morgan Square. The photograph is of the south side of the square. Notice the prominent sign showing where a person could get a drink of spirituous liquor.—*Courtesy of the Spartanburg County Regional Museum*

VISIT
The only Basement Cafe in Town. Good things to eat at reasonable prices. Everything clean. You will feel at home here. Regular dinner every day.
THE MAIN STREET CAFE
Located in Basement
NEW REX THEATRE BUILDING
EAST MAIN ST.

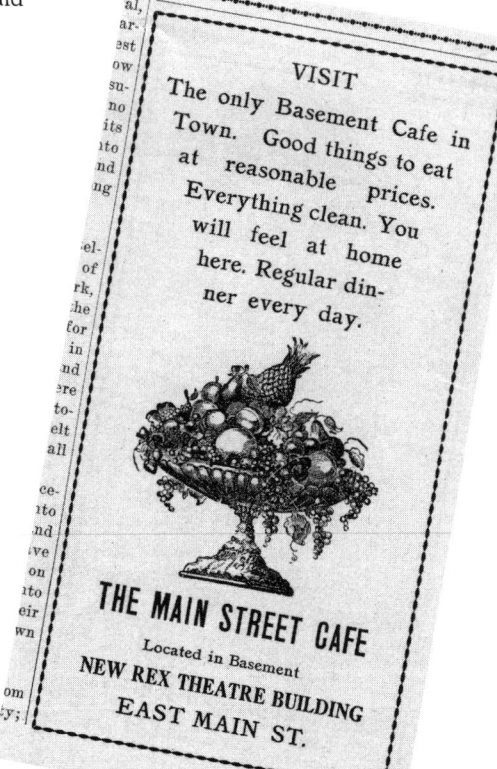

1918 Advertisement Targeted at Camp Wadsworth Soldiers

A long view of Morgan Square looking east taken before 1910. Notice the statue of Daniel Morgan, the tall trees around the fountain, and the streetcar on upper West Main Street. The buildings directly behind the fountain are no longer standing, and Daniel Morgan's statue has been moved to the edge of North Church Street. The street running from the Square to the left of the two buildings beyond the fountain was known as Kennedy Place, for the Kennedy Free Public Library was located on its north side.

—*Courtesy of the Herald-Journal Willis Collection, Spartanburg County (SC) Public Libraries*

In this 1905 picture of Morgan Square, Greenewald's has moved out of the Duncan Building and True's department store has moved in. True's opened for business in 1905, saying it would sell quality merchandise for the lowest prices Spartanburg had ever seen. True's advertised that the store bought for cash and expected to sell for cash. The opening of a new department store was news in itself, but True's had an extra attraction—the first elevator in Spartanburg. Floyd Liles had installed the elevator when he operated a store here, but True's made the most of the novelty by bringing people in "just for the ride." To the left of True's, just across Magnolia Street, is the First National Bank, and farther down the street the Spartan Inn and the Opera House.

—*Postcard view courtesy of the Spartanburg Herald-Journal*

In this Magnolia Street scene, you can see the clock tower of the county courthouse on the left and the Cleveland Law Range on the right. Also note the cannons and cannon balls flanking Daniel Morgan, the vitrified brick covering the square, the street railway tracks, and the street lamps featuring fancy globes. You might also notice the Masonic emblem on the upper story of the Duncan building on the right-hand corner of the square and Magnolia Street.

—Courtesy of the Herald-Journal Willis Collection, Spartanburg County (SC) Public Libraries

TOP: In 1909 a photographer visited Spartanburg to take some panoramic photographs of its two colleges, some of its mills, and its downtown. It is the first panoramic view of Morgan Square known to the author. The photograph stretches from the intersection of Kennedy Place and Morgan Square on the right to Cantrell's Carriage Shop on the extreme left. The space between Cantrell's Carriage Shop and the Spartan Inn had been the site of the Opera House, which was torn down in 1906. —*Courtesy of the Library of Congress*

BOTTOM: By 1915 trolley cars were in their heyday. The trolley in the middle is coming from Magnolia Street, and the other, on the right, is headed for East Main Street. Notice that the elegant globes that earlier had provided light to the square have been replaced by what was a far more efficient but much less elegant lighting system.
—*Photograph by Alfred T. Willis, courtesy of the Herald-Journal Willis Collection, Spartanburg County (SC) Public Libraries*

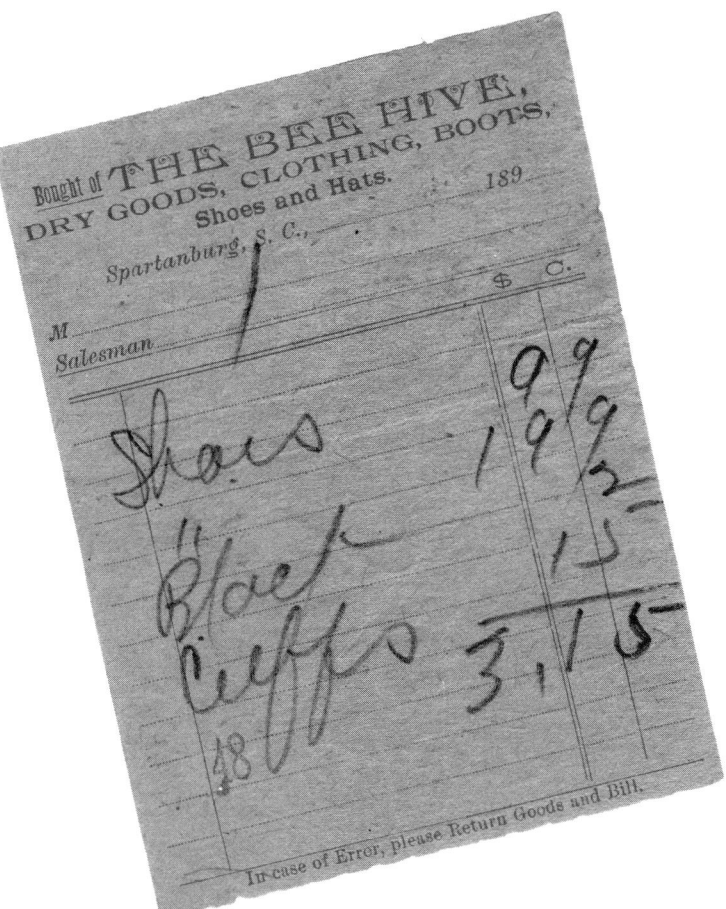

The Bee Hive was a popular downtown department store at the turn of the century.
—*Courtesy of the Spartanburg County Regional Museum*

OPPOSITE PAGE TOP: The iron fountain on Morgan Square in winter; the Chapman (Andrews) Building provides the backdrop. The picture was taken on what was obviously a cold day. From the journals, letters, and newspapers of the latter half of the nineteenth century, it appears that cold weather was more prevalent than it is today. The fountain now stands on the Converse campus. When the city council ordered the fountain removed from the square, Converse asked the city to give it to the college. The council refused and ordered it sold at auction; Converse College was the highest bidder.
—*Courtesy of the Herald-Journal Willis Collection, Spartanburg County (SC) Public Libraries*

LEFT BOTTOM: East Main Street after a heavy snowstorm.
—*Courtesy of George Mullinax*

By 1915 East Main Street had undergone some changes. The Southern Bell Telephone office was located above the Elite Ice Cream Parlor, and F. W. Woolworth Company had moved in next to Kress. Just beyond the Southern Railway crossing, the Grand movie house had opened in 1913. The trees just beyond the last building on the left mark the beginning of the residential portion of Main Street. The building in which Kress is located was the Argyle Hotel. As in the other, older hotels in the city, the Argyle had shops (a barber shop, a pool room, and Kress's) on the street level and its guest rooms on the upper floors.
—*Courtesy of the Spartanburg Herald-Journal*

Magnolia Street looking north from around the intersection of West Wofford
Street. The church on the right is Trinity A.M.E. Church.
—*Courtesy of the Herald-Journal Willis Collection, Spartanburg County (SC) Public Libraries*

Magnolia Street looking south toward Morgan Square (the streetcar tracks
appear to run directly into the statue of Daniel Morgan).
—*Courtesy of the Herald-Journal Willis Collection, Spartanburg County (SC) Public Libraries*

Main Street running from Liberty through Morgan Square was the main business street in the city until the 1960s. Even at 9 a.m. East Main Street looked busy in 1912. In 1912 the two top floors of the building on the extreme left—which still stands—comprised Dr. Benjamin B. Steedly's Private Hospital and the bottom floor was Nicholas Trakas's fruit store. The white railroad crossing barriers behind the automobile on the left were located at the Southern Railway crossing, and the Bee Hive was a department store. The clock on the right belonged to Crosby's Jewelers; just beyond it was Paul and Leroy Dunbar's shop where they repaired, built, and sold wagons. The wagons on the right (with the horses that would not keep still for the photographer) were probably owned by people seeking help in Dunbar's shop. Dunbar Street, which is one block to the right running parallel to Main, was named for the men who worked there.

Around 1900 the city of Spartanburg spent a great deal of money on its streets. By paving some streets and curbing and making sidewalks on others, the city fathers hoped to enhance the progressive reputation of the area. This view of West Main Street looking west was taken from a point just beyond the Opera House. The granite stone for the curbing came from a quarry off to the right at the bottom of the hill just behind where the Steeple Drive-In is located today. The building to the left was a feed store and stable owned by L. E. Castleberry and P. J. White. Next to that was an establishment that bought bottles. The house on the top of the hill to the left belonged to A. J. Gwynn, who was a real estate broker. The Western and Carolina Railroad ran at the base of the hill. The house on the extreme right with the tall columns belonged to Fielding Cantrell, who sold buggies and wagons in a shop next door, about where the photographer is standing. Cantrell's shop stands there to this day next door to the Masonic Lodge across from the Herald-Journal building. The boarding house in the photograph was known as the Carolina House and was owned by Miss M. T. Lipscomb. Into the twentieth century it was not unusual to find businesses and residences—some very nice ones—side by side. It was the automobile and the trolley that made it possible to develop areas strictly for housing and others devoted only to business.

—*Photographs by Bernhardt, courtesy of the Spartanburg County Regional Museum*

This view of Trade Street when it was not much more than an alley was taken about 1912. The photographer was looking toward Dunbar Street from Elm (Saint John). The building on the left with the letters "ON" on the side was the Weddington Hardware Company, and just beyond was Thad C. Dean's feed store. Dean constantly advertised in the newspapers, once claiming "I have a [railroad] car of choice Timothy Hay, the best ever—It will make the 'horse laugh.'" Trade Street was the birthplace of a number of Spartanburg businesses, among them C. L. Cannon Company and the Community Cash stores owned by Broadus Littlejohn. —*Courtesy of Wofford College*

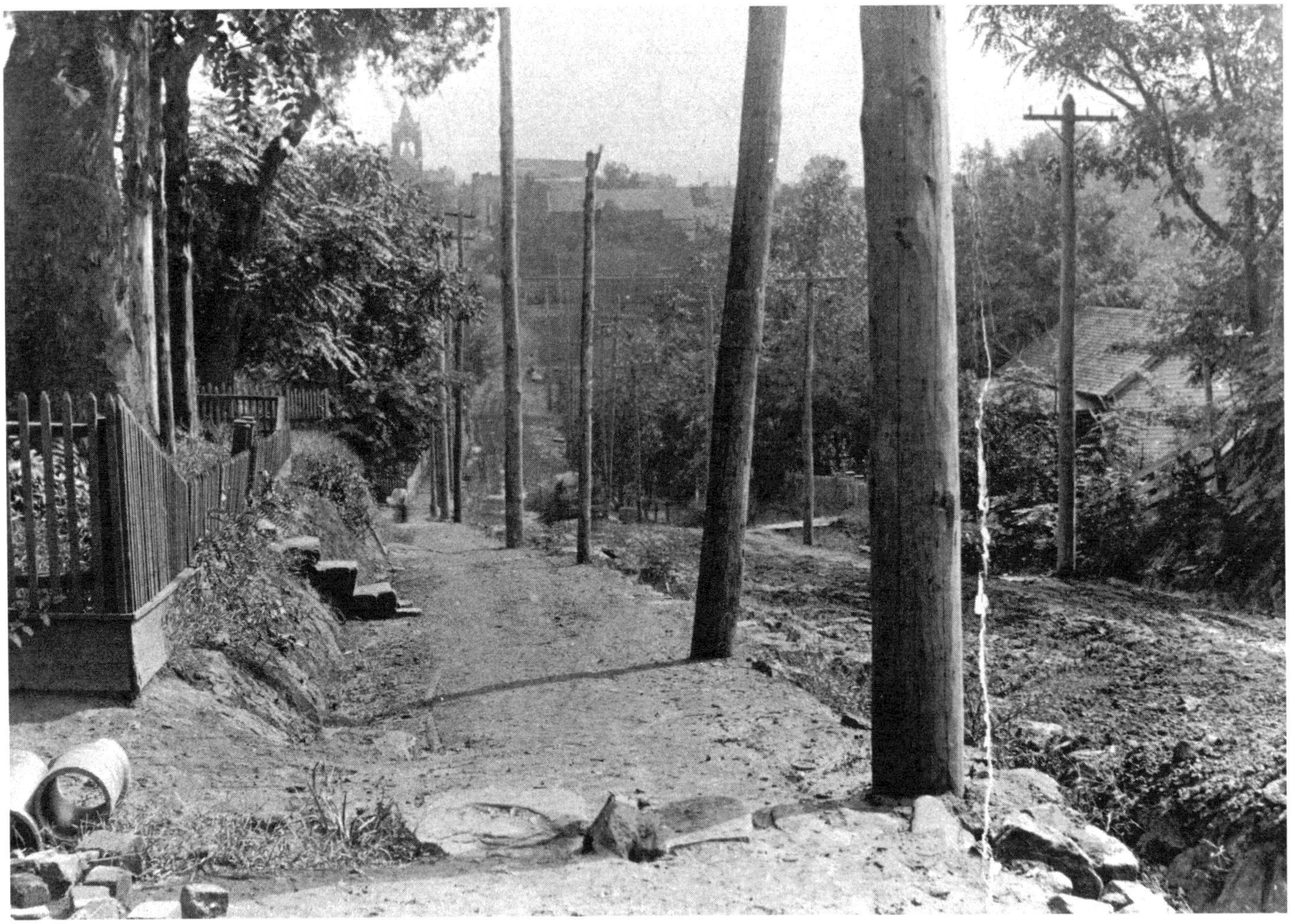

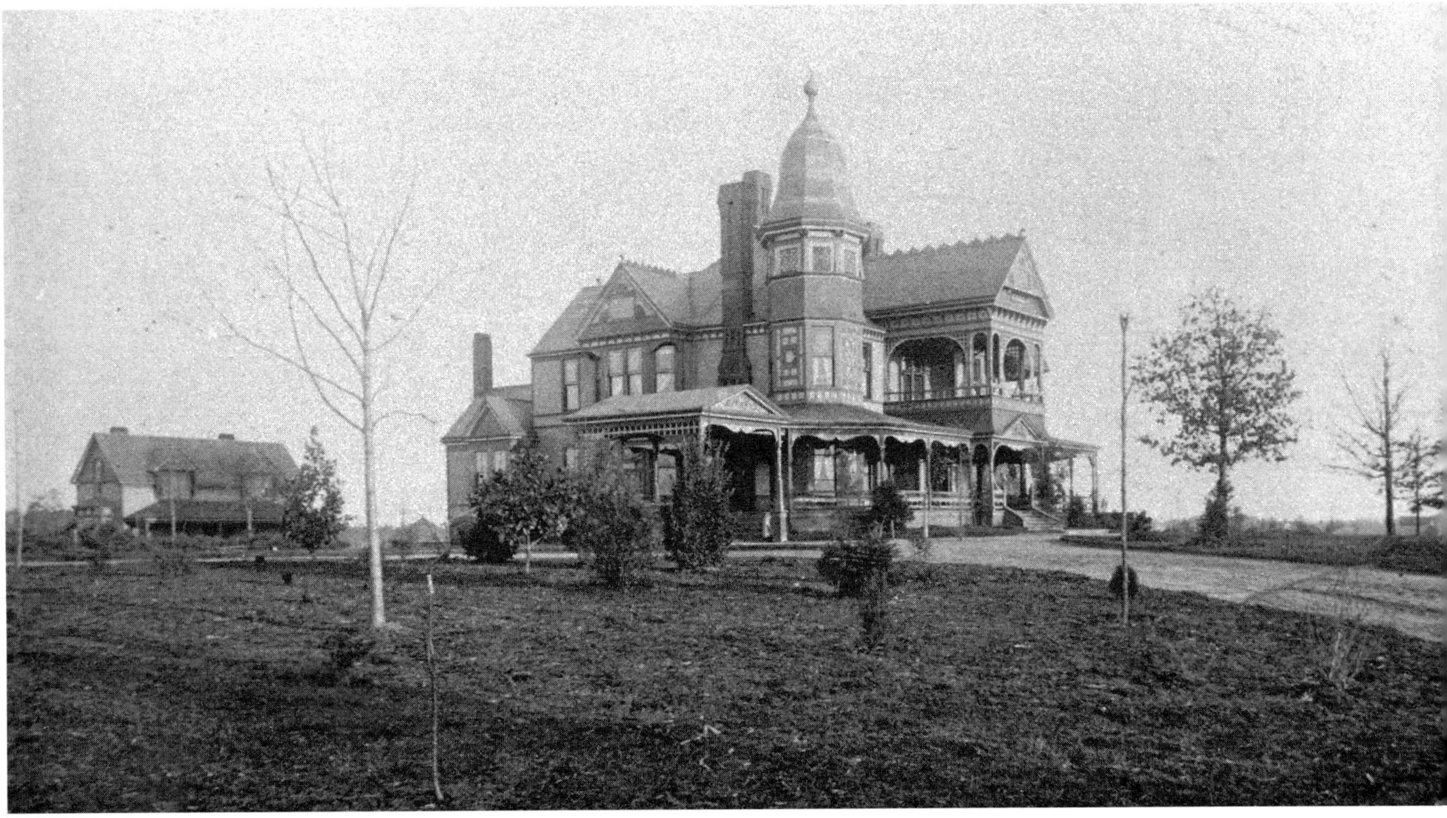

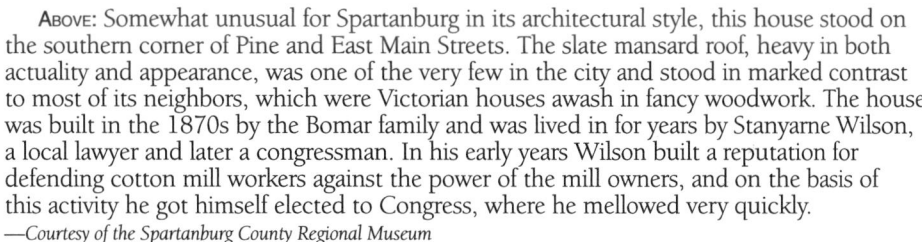

ABOVE: Somewhat unusual for Spartanburg in its architectural style, this house stood on the southern corner of Pine and East Main Streets. The slate mansard roof, heavy in both actuality and appearance, was one of the very few in the city and stood in marked contrast to most of its neighbors, which were Victorian houses awash in fancy woodwork. The house was built in the 1870s by the Bomar family and was lived in for years by Stanyarne Wilson, a local lawyer and later a congressman. In his early years Wilson built a reputation for defending cotton mill workers against the power of the mill owners, and on the basis of this activity he got himself elected to Congress, where he mellowed very quickly.
—*Courtesy of the Spartanburg County Regional Museum*

OPPOSITE PAGE TOP: Taken prior to 1903, this photograph of West Main Street looking east toward town shows the condition of streets at the time. The woman trudging up the hill illustrates what it must have been like to walk to town for shopping before Spartanburg's hills were cut down. The pipes on the left indicate that the street crews were trying to alleviate the washing problem that plagued the town. In the distance stands the tower of the Opera House. —*Photograph by Bernhardt, courtesy of the Spartanburg County Regional Museum*

OPPOSITE PAGE BOTTOM: Dexter Converse built his mansion on North Pine Street in 1889. This home was torn down in the early 1960s to make way for the Spartanburg County Public Library. Note the wide expanse of lawn that surrounds the home. Today, the Converse Heights neighborhood stands here. —*Courtesy of the Spartanburg County Regional Museum*

The home of Dexter Converse, 1898. —*Courtesy of Stanley Converse*

Albert H. Twichell built this house in 1882. Twichell came south in 1859 to help his brother-in-law, Dexter Converse, run the Bivingsville Mill. In 1870 he joined with Converse and others in buying the mill and became the treasurer of the D. E. Converse Company. For many years Twichell served as organist in the First Presbyterian Church, and in 1895 he founded the annual Festival of Music which became one of the special cultural events in the area. His interest in education was as keen as in music; he was one of the original subscribers of Converse College. The Twichell house (known to some older Spartanburg residents as the "Fretwell House") stood on the corner of Pine and Glendalyn streets before it was torn down in the 1970s.

—*Photograph by James Buchanan, courtesy of the Spartanburg County Regional Museum*

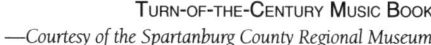

TURN-OF-THE-CENTURY MUSIC BOOK
—*Courtesy of the Spartanburg County Regional Museum*

ABOVE: George Roswell Dean, a Spartanburg physician, built this home on the corner of North Church and St. John Streets directly across from John H. Montgomery's home where the Montgomery Building now stands. On the porch from left to right are Dr. Dean's children: Jesse; Dot, who was a freshman at Converse and has the book bag on her shoulder; Marie, who is sitting on the banister; and Anne, who is holding roses sent her by her fiancee. Next to Anne are Mrs. H. C. Dean and Prof. H. P. Young of Furman University. In the yard from the left are Don, Thad, and Lois, who is sitting on the stump of a locust tree. —*Courtesy of the Johnson family*

A typical turn-of-the-century bedroom in one of Spartanburg's large middle class homes. Note the gas lamp, the iron fireplace, the wallpaper on the ceiling and on the upper border of the walls, and the elaborate picture frames.
—*Courtesy of the Johnson family*

Someone in the Dean family had the foresight and interest to photograph the demolition of the house, which, in the long term, becomes a symbolic act of how people in Spartanburg destroyed much of the architecture that had graced the city during the late nineteenth and early twentieth centuries. In the first photograph Harriet Dean stands with her dog; in the second photograph Harriet Camp Dean, Dr. Dean's wife, and her son Thad are on the porch; and in the third the photographer could see Central Methodist Church over the empty lot that had been the homestead.

—Photographs courtesy of the Johnson family

This typical, small turn-of-the-century house on North Fairview bordering Converse College is no longer standing. Bicycles and tricycles were very popular items around the town in 1915 when this photograph was taken. —*Courtesy of Converse College*

ABOVE: Victorian-style building in the 1880s was not confined to Pine Street. Bishop William W. Duncan of the Methodist church built this house on North Church Street, just north of Central Methodist Church, in 1885. The photograph dates from the turn of the century. —*Courtesy of the Herald-Journal Willis Collection, Spartanburg County (SC) Public Libraries*

LEFT: John Gary Evans, former governor of South Carolina, built this residence in Converse Heights for $9,900 in 1901. It was also the residence of the late Judge Donald Russell.
—*Photograph by James Buchanan, courtesy of the Herald-Journal Willis Collection, Spartanburg County (SC) Public Libraries*

Standing as a symbol of the changes in transportation that transformed Spartanburg from a remote country village into a modern city in the years around 1900, this covered bridge in disrepair speaks of a bygone age dependent on road travel.
—*Courtesy of the Herald-Journal Willis Collection, Spartanburg County (SC) Public Libraries*

The railroad station on the Southern line at Wellford was photographed in the early 1890s. By then Spartanburg County's rural areas were connected to the city by several of these rural stations along the major and feeder rail lines. The man to the left of the post is Dr. Hugh R. Black, who was destined to become Spartanburg's leading physician and founder of the Mary Black Hospital.
—*Courtesy of Rosa Black*

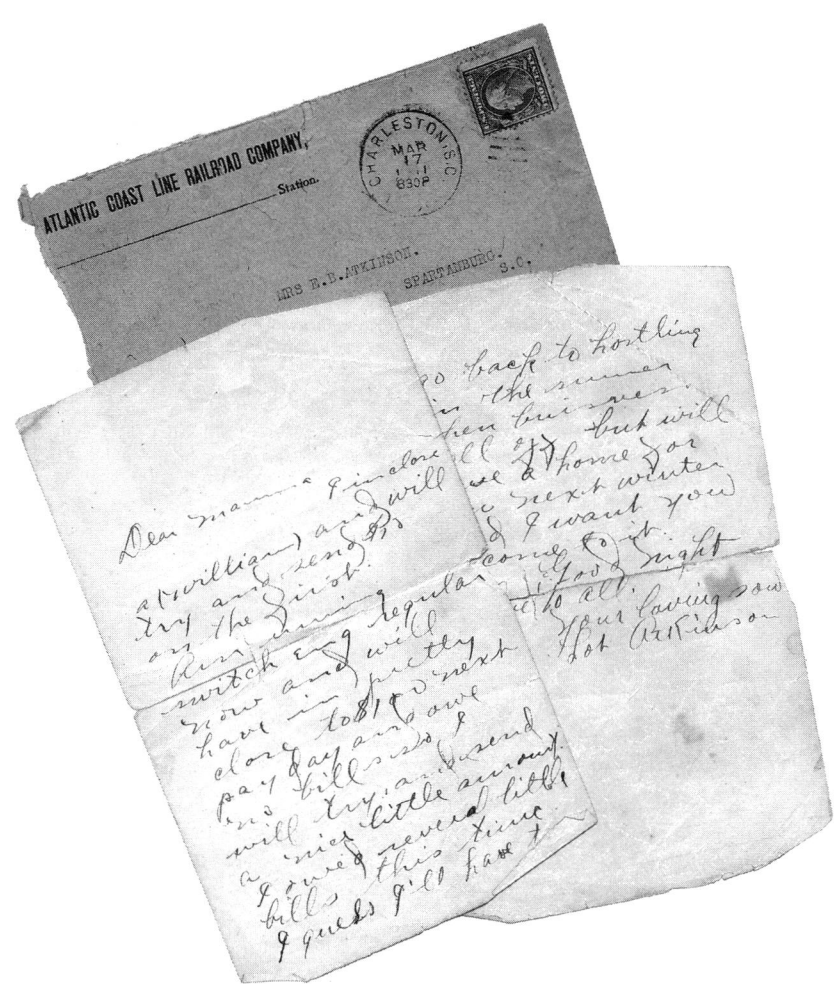

Letter from Lot Atkinson, railroad employee and uncle of Liz Patterson, to his mother Minnie. Atkinson was sending money home from Charleston along with the promise to have a place for her to visit next winter.
—*Courtesy of Liz and Dwight Patterson*

The crowd at the Southern Depot on Magnolia Street attests to the importance of rail travel at the turn of the century. Spartanburg was unusual in that two Southern Railway main lines converged here at Union Station. Passengers could travel in any of the four compass directions from Spartanburg. The trains sat side by side in front of the station, and a mad scramble took place as passengers changed trains or simply tried to board the right train. The presence of the Charleston and Western Carolina trains on the other side of the station only added to the confusion. The feeling was not unlike the sensation shared by passengers at one of our major airports.
—*Courtesy of the Spartanburg County Regional Museum*

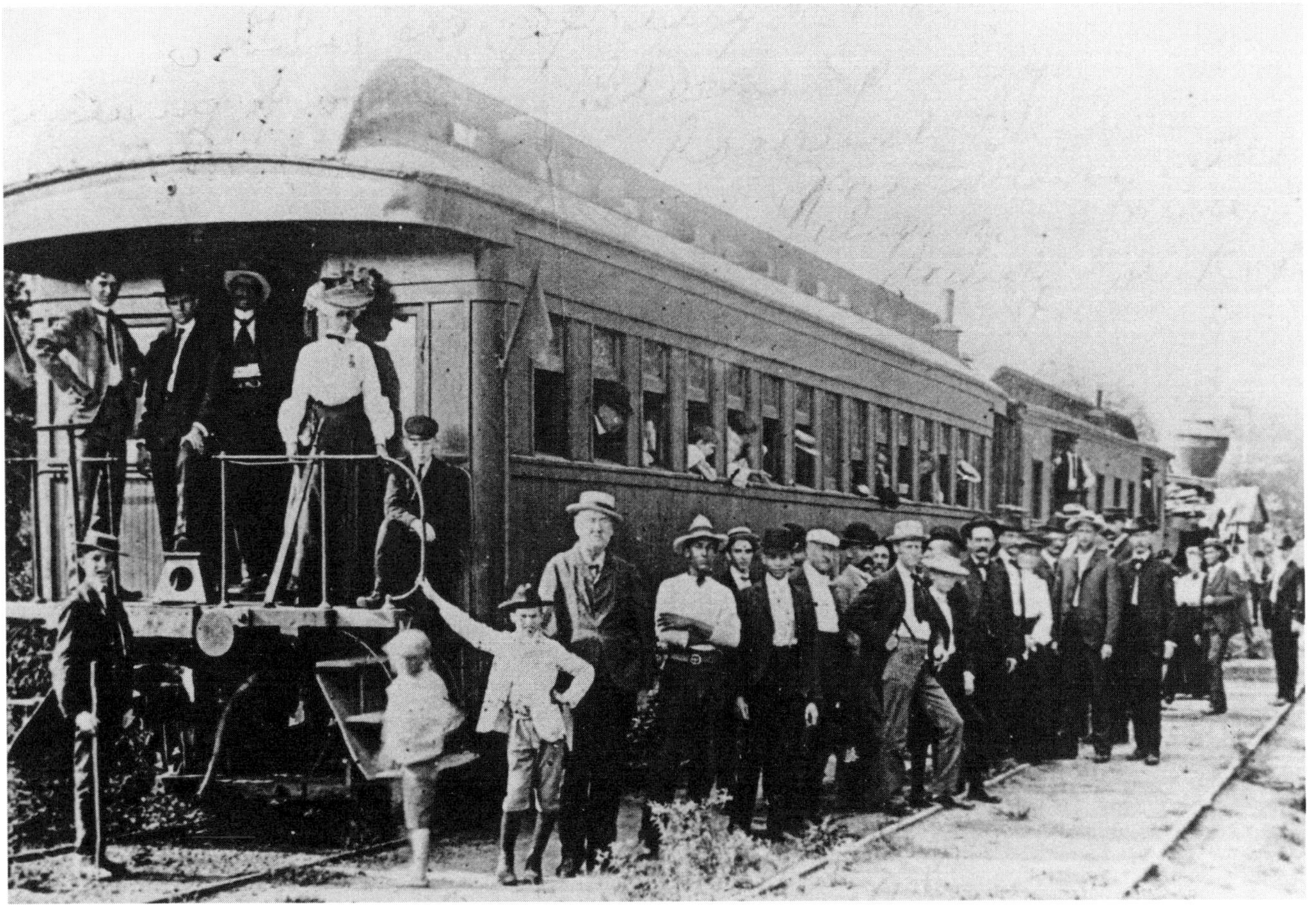

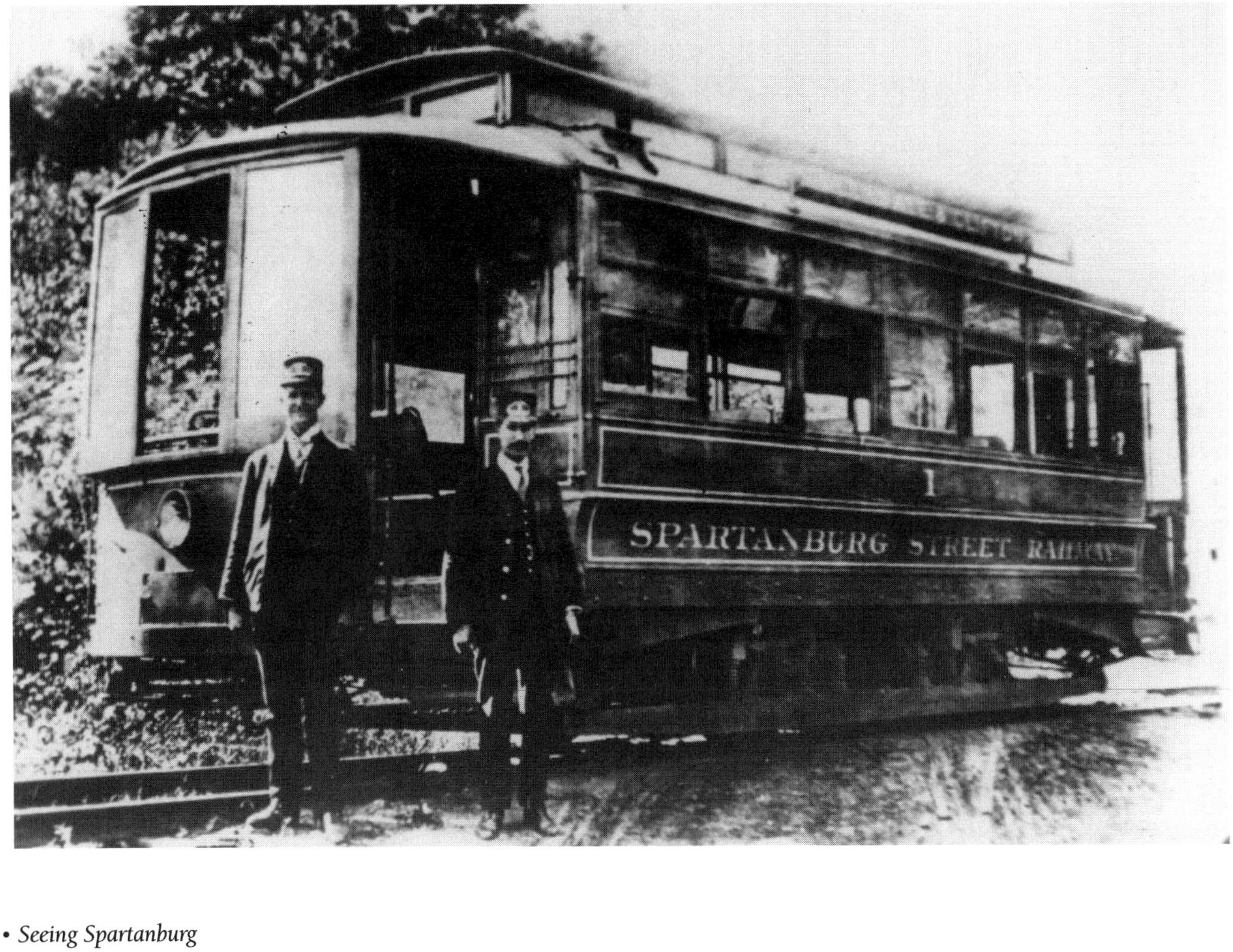
1
SPARTANBURG STREET

ABOVE: Hotel hacks working Union Station about 1910. In the heyday of rail travel, it was customary for hotel porters to pick up passengers and their luggage at the train station.
—*Courtesy of the Spartanburg County Regional Museum*

OPPOSITE PAGE TOP: This 1912 photograph of the Glenn Springs train gives some indication of the popularity of the resort; its rail connection to the city had significantly increased that popularity. The boy standing on the steps is James Zimmerman, a resident of Glenn Springs.
—*Courtesy of the Spartanburg Herald-Journal*

OPPOSITE PAGE BOTTOM: Undoubtedly, the pre-eminent symbol of the modern city was the "Street Railway." Here two conductors pose before the Number 1 car in the Spartanburg system.
—*Courtesy of the Herald-Journal Willis Collection, Spartanburg County (SC) Public Libraries*

1903 RAILWAY ORDER FORM—*Courtesy of Liz and Dwight Patterson*

East Main Street at the intersection with Church Street illustrates the several forms of transportation that coexisted early in the twentieth century: the women walking across the street, the bicycle propped up on the telephone pole, the automobile, the horse and wagon, and the tracks used by the street cars. In the upper right-hand corner of the photograph is the sign for The Carolina Cash Company, a department store that continues to serve the community.
—*Courtesy of the Herald-Journal Willis Collection, Spartanburg County (SC) Public Libraries*

Built in 1850 by Junius Thomson at the corner of East Main and North Church streets, the Palmetto House was long one of Spartanburg's leading hotels. Spartanburg society used it for parties, dinners, and meetings, making it the place to be seen and heard until the late 1870s. Touted, at least locally, as one of the finest hotels in the state, it seemed not to lack for out-of-town guests. But all was not gaiety within its walls, for political meetings were frequently held there. In November of 1860 the Palmetto House hosted the meeting that sent county delegates to South Carolina's secession convention. After the late 1870s the Palmetto retained a shadow of its social importance, thanks largely to the presence of the popular Becker's Oyster Saloon and Ice Cream Parlor. This mid-1880s photograph shows the deteriorating condition of the building. Having outlived its glory, the hotel was torn down in the early nineties and replaced with the Palmetto Building, devoted to stores and offices. —*Courtesy of Wofford College*

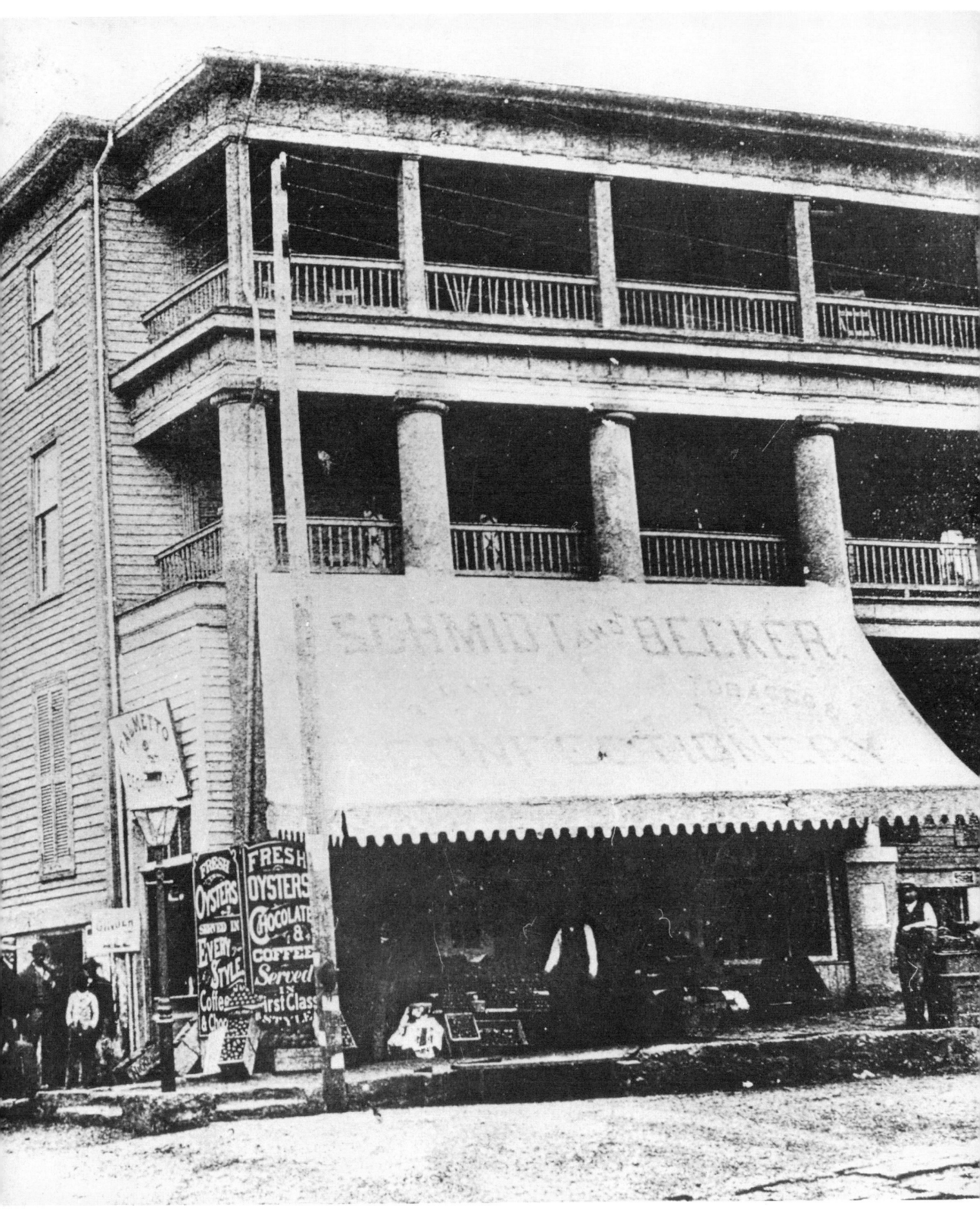

Built on Magnolia Street across from the courthouse in the late 1880s, the Cleveland Building housed law offices and the headquarters of the various business interests of John B. and Jesse Cleveland. The building, commonly called the Cleveland Law Range, has been restored. This photograph dates from the 1940s. —*Courtesy of the Herald-Journal Willis Collection, Spartanburg County (SC) Public Libraries*

OPPOSITE PAGE: After a bitter fight over the destruction of the old courthouse (*shown in the photograph on pages 70-71*), the county's fourth courthouse was built in 1891. It stood on Magnolia Street on the same site as the present courthouse. The bell and clock in the tower were once in the Opera House on the square and now are housed in the special tower erected on the western end of Morgan Square. The fourth courthouse, shown here as it looked at mid-century, was destroyed in 1959. In *South Carolina: The WPA Guide to the Palmetto State* published in 1941, the section on the Spartanburg courthouse reads: "The architecture is typical of the banality of the 1880s. . . . On monthly sales days a portion of the grounds known as the 'the bone-yard' is thronged with rural inhabitants and mountaineers who swap horses, mules, cows, pigs, knives, handiwork, and farm produce. Saturdays also bring many gatherings, when whole families make the grounds their headquarters for the day. They build fires, fry bacon, boil coffee, and exchange gossip. Preachers of strange cults, surrounded by curious or sympathetic hearers, sway with religious ecstasy, their fervor undiminished by the barking of dogs and the crying of babies." —*Courtesy of the Spartanburg County Regional Museum*

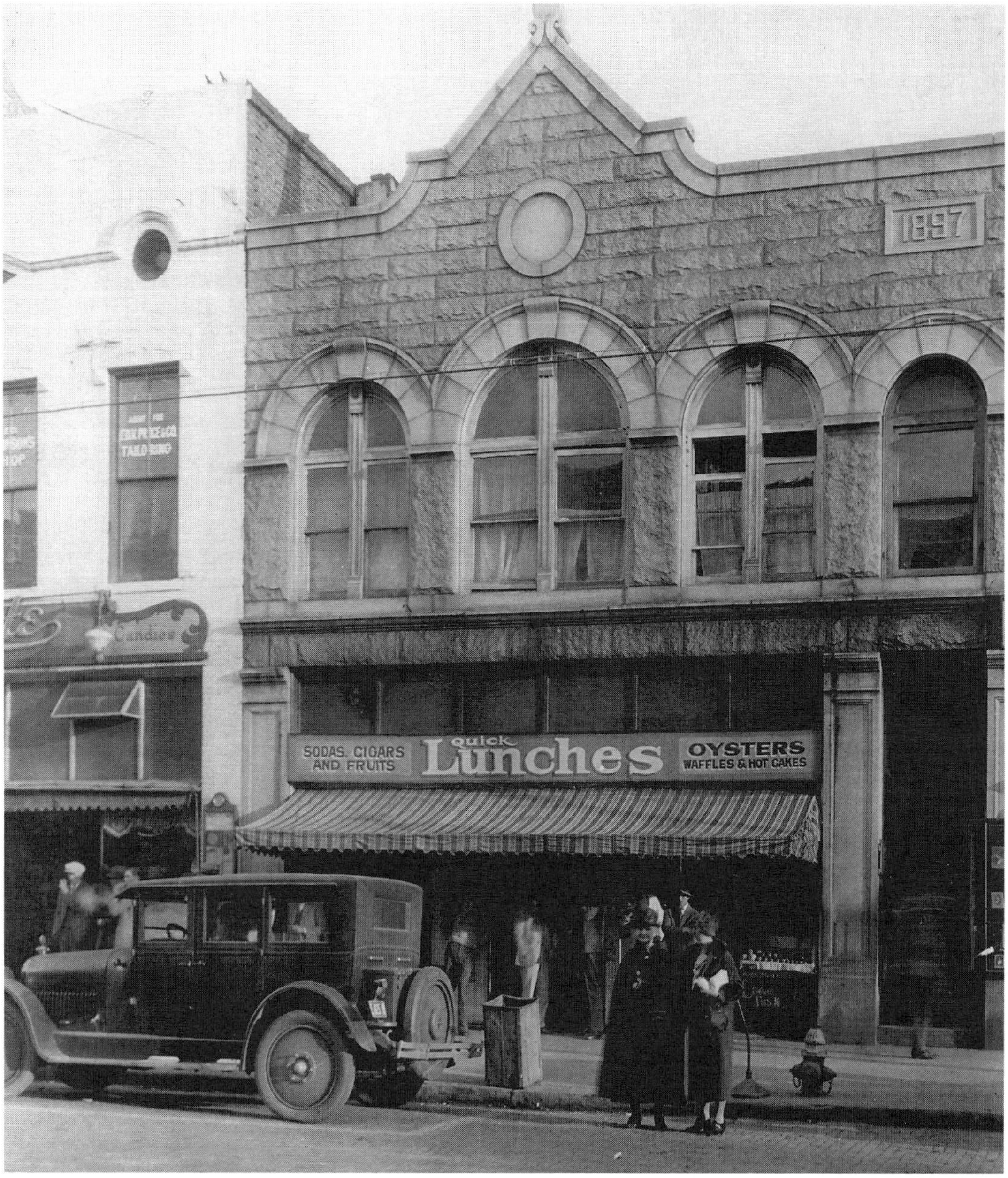
1897
SODAS, CIGARS
AND FRUITS
Quick
Lunches
OYSTERS
WAFFLES & HOT CAKES

In early twentieth-century Spartanburg, people shopped among substantial-looking buildings. This turn-of-the-century citadel of commerce had a fortress look with its stone facade, its ever-popular arched windows reminiscent of Roman bridges, and the solid stone pillars that flank the doorway and display windows. Also notice the brick pavement, the somewhat battered trash container, and the fireplug. With the Elite ice cream parlor right next door, there obviously were sufficient places to eat during a shopping spree.

—Courtesy of the Herald-Journal Willis Collection, Spartanburg County (SC) Public Libraries

Just as Fast as
The Oven Can Bake 'Em
That's Evidence of the
Demand for
Dixie Pies
However, Quality is Never
Sacrificed for Quantity
Production
DIXIE PIES are always
the same standard
quality product
Insist on Dixie Pies
at Your Canteen
DIXIE PIE BAKING CO.
SPARTANBURG, S. C.

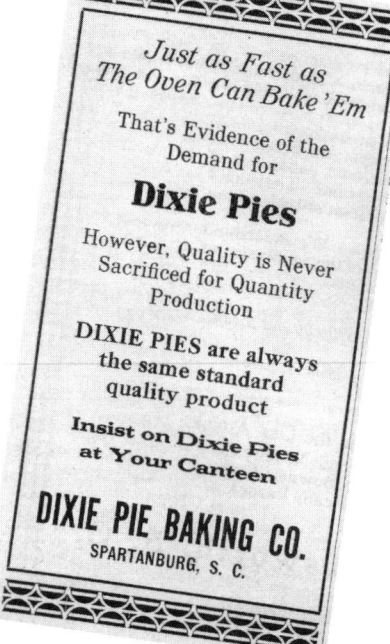

1918 Advertisement
for a Local Bakery

When construction began on the Chapman Building (later known as the Andrews Building), the community bore an air of excitement. Spartans had only read about skyscrapers in the larger cities of the North, yet now they would have one of their own. The anticipation turned out to be fully justified, for the Chapman Building was a beautiful addition to the center of the city and a worthy heir to the grace that had been endangered by the loss since 1890 of many buildings along Morgan Square.

—*Photograph by Alfred T. Willis, courtesy of the Herald-Journal Willis Collection, Spartanburg County (SC) Public Libraries*

When this picture was taken, the arcade of the Opera House had been boarded up in preparation for demolition. The building had red walls and a blue ceiling in its theater, which could seat about 800 people. The demands for entertainment in the city were growing, and the seating capacity was too small to accommodate the crowds. The manager of the theater, Max Greenewald, of Greenewald's clothing store, brought entertainment to the people up to one month before the building was torn down. There was a show almost every night, except Sundays, from the fall through the spring. The shows ranged from "A Message From Mars" (with novel electrical effects) and "East Lynne" (for which the Herald reported standing room was sold, and many were turned away), to "Parsifal" (presumably the opera by Wagner). The structure was demolished in 1906. —*Courtesy of Wofford College*

ABOVE: Harriet Camp Dean graces her home. Note the coal-burning fireplace, the handsome mantle, the tiles around the iron facing of the firebox, the fine rug and chair all set off by Dean's exquisite crocheted collar. —*Courtesy of the Johnson family*

OPPOSITE PAGE: Mary Seay and her sister Sally were direct descendants of the Revolutionary War soldier Jammie Seay and lived in the Seay home on Darby Road. The Seay sisters always referred to themselves as "us gals." Throughout their lives they wore homespun clothing and never went without a bonnet. They never married, were prominent members of Central United Methodist Church and helped to support themselves by lending money at interest. All their furniture, as well as everything else in their house, was made at home. Ann Sanders Fraser remembers visiting the Seay sisters in the early 1890s—always considered a treat by the children—and taking them some gelatin. "Us gals" would not eat the gelatin, however, for when they saw it shake they were convinced that it was alive. The photograph, believed to show Mary Seay, probably dates from the 1890s. —*Courtesy of Ann Sanders Fraser*

TOP LEFT: Elisabeth Emily Cleveland reflects the demeanor of the Victorians of the 1880s, a time when people believed that more was wonderful, thus, the heavy clothes and overstuffed chair. —*Courtesy of Jesse Franklin Cleveland*

TOP RIGHT: Lois Dean, aged three, with her artificial dog.
—*Courtesy of the Johnson family*

LEFT: Donald and David Sanders. Mrs. Sanders badly wanted girls, so until a sister finally came along, the Sanders brothers had to endure a somewhat embarrassing, but not totally out-of-fashion, style of dress and hair.
—*Courtesy of Ann Sanders Fraser*

OPPOSITE PAGE: Sam Orr Black, Sr., sat in his wagon for this photograph taken with an unidentified playmate.
—*Courtesy of Rosa Black*

Dr. Henry Nelson Snyder, on the left, long the president of Wofford College, poses with an unidentified man. This other gentleman in the photograph is often identified as James Carlisle, the former president of Wofford College, but Carlisle died in 1906, at which time Snyder was not this old.

—*Courtesy of the Herald-Journal Willis Collection, Spartanburg County (SC) Public Libraries*

—Courtesy of Dexter Cleveland

—Courtesy of the Charlie Mae
Campbell family

The five Benson sisters gathered for a portrait which, with a single exception, they seemed to take very seriously.

The city of Spartanburg had two schoolhouses by the 1890s. In addition to the Magnolia Street School, the city operated a school on North Converse Street. By 1910 the latter had become a boarding house run by Virginia Brewton, who stands here on the left with her boarders and cook. It was quite common in the nineteenth and early twentieth centuries for widows to take in young ladies to live with them. It helped with expenses, gave the widows company, filled up all the space in those big houses, and prevented a social taboo. Young women were not supposed to live by themselves; they had to be under the protection and guidance of a suitable older woman.
—*Photographs courtesy of Rosa Black*

ABOVE: In a style uncharacteristic of the time, Hattie Gentry let her hair fall to her waist in this formal portrait taken in 1880. She was 16 at the time. A few years later, she celebrates her wedding day in an ankle-length dress with a long, trailing veil. —*Photographs courtesy of Jennie Rhinehart*

LEFT: In 1906 Marie Dean was photographed wearing her hair in the typical high-fashion style known as the "Gibson Girl." The style was popularized by Charles Dana Gibson, whose drawings were evocative of the upwardly mobile middle class and were appealing for their cool self-control and commanding presence. Gibson could also be devastatingly satirical, and both Americans and Europeans loved his work. —*Courtesy of the Johnson family*

Tobe Hartwell was a courier for the First National Bank of Spartanburg around the turn of the century. It was unusual for whites to entrust an African American with that responsibility at that time. Hartwell's leadership within the black community led to the naming of one of Spartanburg's first housing projects in his honor.
—*Courtesy of Silver Hill Methodist Church*

John B. Cleveland was born in 1848 in Spartanburg. He graduated from Wofford College in 1869 and trained as a lawyer. His major success, however, was in business, where he amassed a fortune in land, textiles, and railroads. He was for many years the president of the Whitney Manufacturing Company and the Charleston and Western Carolina Railway. By the turn of the century, John B. Cleveland was Spartanburg's foremost citizen, and the city (as well as private organizations such as Wofford and Converse colleges) was the beneficiary of his generosity. He died in 1928.
—*Courtesy of Wofford College*

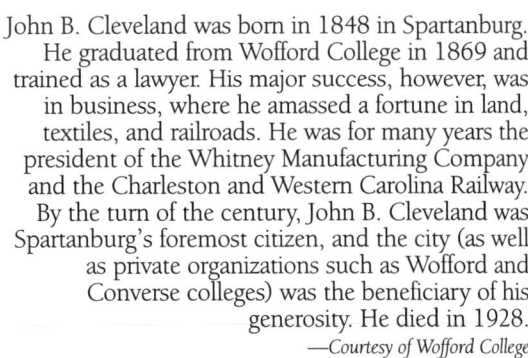

In a photograph from around the turn of the century, Phyllis Goins is seen here with one of the many children for whom she cared. A midwife and informal nurse, Ms. Goins was a leader within the African-American community.
—*Courtesy of Silver Hill Methodist Church*

Dexter Edgar Converse was born in Vermont in 1829 and came south to run the Bivingsville Mill for John Bomar in the 1850s. In the mid-1870s Converse bought the mill and renamed the community in which it was located Glendale. In the following years Converse expanded his operations by building on the Pacolet River three textile mills, which he named Clifton Mills numbers 1, 2, and 3. By the time of his death in 1899, Converse had become the leading textile magnate in the county.
—*Courtesy of Converse College*

Peter Joseph McCauley came to South Carolina from Ireland and settled in Boiling Springs. A Roman Catholic, McCauley took his children to Spartanburg for services in the Catholic church every Sunday, no matter the condition of the roads or the weather. Being a Roman Catholic put McCauley in a small minority in Spartanburg County, but he showed his Irish pluck by wearing a cross around his waist. His seven children (the little girl leaning against the porch was a neighbor) seem to share their father's dash as they pose outside their house about 1910. From left to right: Peter, Bennie, James, Annie, John, William, unknown, Ag, and Mary.
—*Courtesy of Mrs. Maury Pearson*

Snow in 1905 brought out topcoats and furs. The camera also brought out Donald Sanders, the young boy in the background, who, according to Sanders family tradition, managed to get into every picture the family took. From left to right: Ann and Marion Sanders, Mary and Theodore Richardson. —*Courtesy of Ann Sanders Fraser*

The Dean family gathers for a Christmas portrait in 1908. Notice the "Gibson Girl" hairdos (or modifications thereof) on all the ladies.
—*Courtesy of the Johnson family*

These four women have just returned from church at the turn of the century. Going to church has always been an important part of the lives of rural people. In addition to its religious significance, attending church was a time to socialize, to see and be seen, and to dress up, for which people had "Sunday goin' to meetin'" clothes. Although a country phrase, it applied to town people as well. The older woman wears black; around 1900 older women tended to wear black exclusively in mourning for relatives. From left to right: Eliza Sanders, Mrs. Eugene Sanders, Marion Sanders, Toy and May Sanders.
—*Courtesy of Ann Sanders Fraser*

Bored with not much to do in 1904, these children built their own trolley. The boys in the back, from left to right, are Theodore and Robbie Richardson; the girls are Carrie Bell Dawkins, Mar Richardson, and Anna Will Sanders.
—*Courtesy of Ann Sanders Fraser*

EARLY 1900S BILLY CLUB AND HANDCUFFS
—*Courtesy of the Spartanburg County Regional Museum*

Having received their first uniforms in 1881, the Spartanburg City Police lined up on West Main Street in 1885 for a department photograph. From right to left: Chief J. H. Blassingame, Jim Mullinax, Joe B. Bates, John Sprouse, John Jackson and Ed Gentry. In 1889 the uniforms would be changed to those familiar across the nation in that day—the uniform reminiscent of the English "Bobby." Lionel Lawson remembers hearing the city chain gang sing a ditty when John Floyd was mayor and John Hill chief of police: "Chief Hill gave the orders; Chambers rang the bell; Joe Bates brought'em in; and John Floyd gave 'em hell." Joe Bates turned out to be a better policeman than husband; in 1910 he shot and killed his wife. Of course, he was retired by that time.

—*Courtesy of the Herald-Journal Willis Collection, Spartanburg County (SC) Public Libraries*

In 1895 the Spartanburg police once more had new uniforms—the "Bobby" style named after the British Prime Minister, Robert Peel, who had introduced it in the first half of the nineteenth century—and celebrated by gathering to have their photographs taken. In the top image. they chose everyone's favorite setting, the fountain in Morgan Square, once again frozen solid.

—*Courtesy of the Spartanburg County Regional Museum*

ABOVE: In 1904 Drs. Black, Jefferies, and Heinitsh, seeking better places to do surgery than kitchen tables, bought a house on North Dean Street and founded the Spartanburg Hospital. In 1907 they built Spartanburg's first structure specifically designed as a hospital, next door to their building on North Dean Street. Later this hospital was sold to John B. Cleveland, who deeded it to the trustees for the establishment of a home for aged women, known as the Georgia Cleveland Home. This photograph shows the doctors who were stockholders and practitioners in the Spartanburg Hospital along with the head of nursing and her staff. From left to right in the top row: Lena K. Sharp, head nurse; Dr. R. A. Fike; Dr. James L. Jeffries; Dr. George R. Dean; Dr. Hugh Ratchford Black; Dr. George Heinitsh; Dr. W. A. Wallace; Dr. Joe Allen. The young boy is Edwin W. Johnson. —*Courtesy of Marianna Black Habisreutinger*

OPPOSITE PAGE TOP: Spartanburg's first city hospital, now the Georgia Cleveland Home on North Converse Street across from St. Paul's Roman Catholic Church. —*Photograph by Linda Taylor Hudgins*

OPPOSITE PAGE BOTTOM: The nursing program at the old city hospital provided Spartanburg with qualified trained nurses for many years. Here, in this 1917 image, several trainees show that such a life was not all work, although they did have to live in special quarters next door to the hospital (the Georgia Cleveland Home) under rather rigid rules. —*Courtesy of Rosa Black*

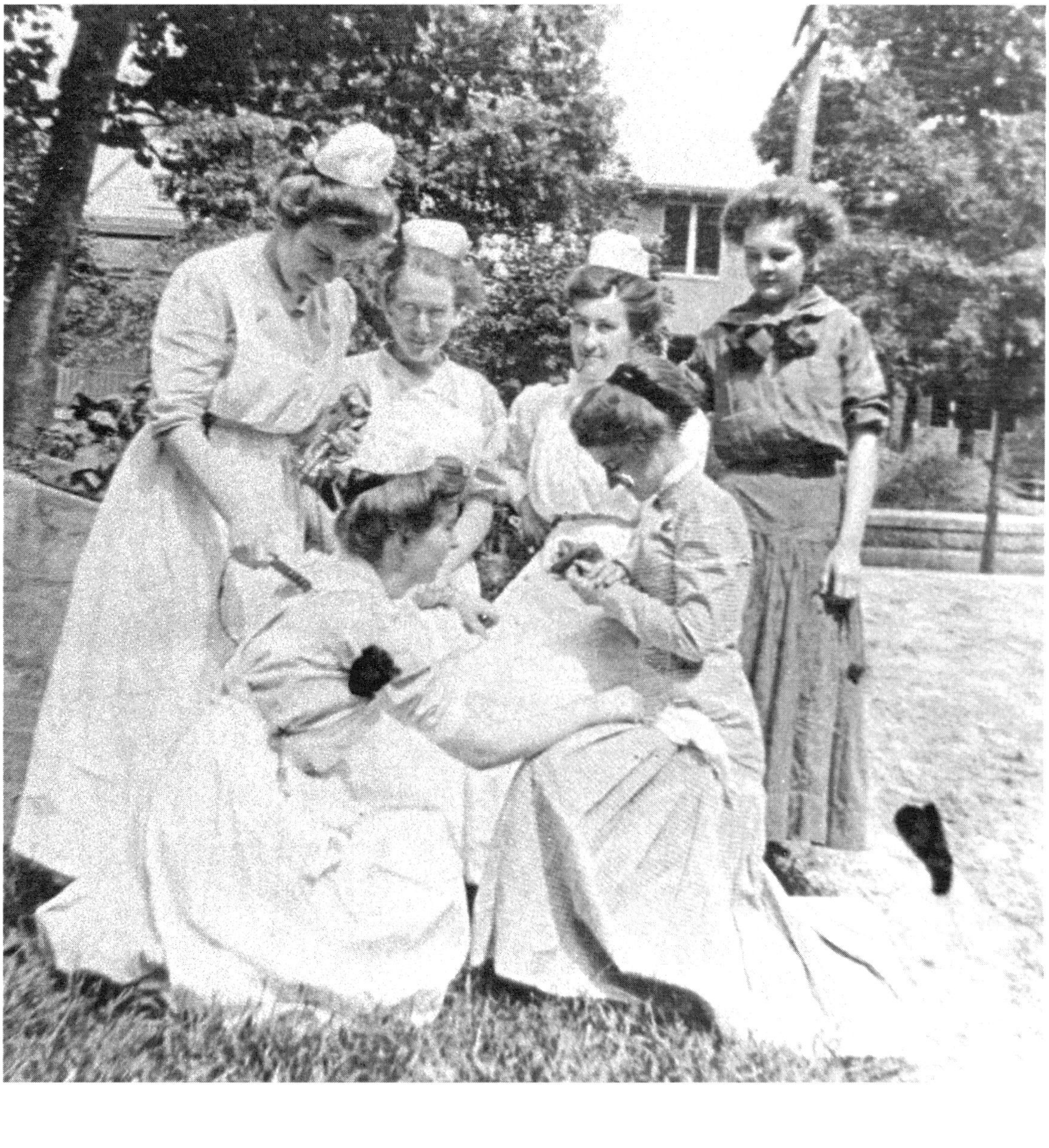

Dr. Benjamin B. Steedly, seen at right practicing in his examination room, built this private hospital in 1916 on the north side of East Main Street between Alabama Street and Oakland Avenue. In the mid-1920s the Young Women's Christian Association took over most of the building because a new city hospital had been constructed on North Church Street. Later the building was turned into apartments, and it was torn down in 1960. —*Courtesy of B & B Studio, the Spartanburg County (SC) Public Libraries*

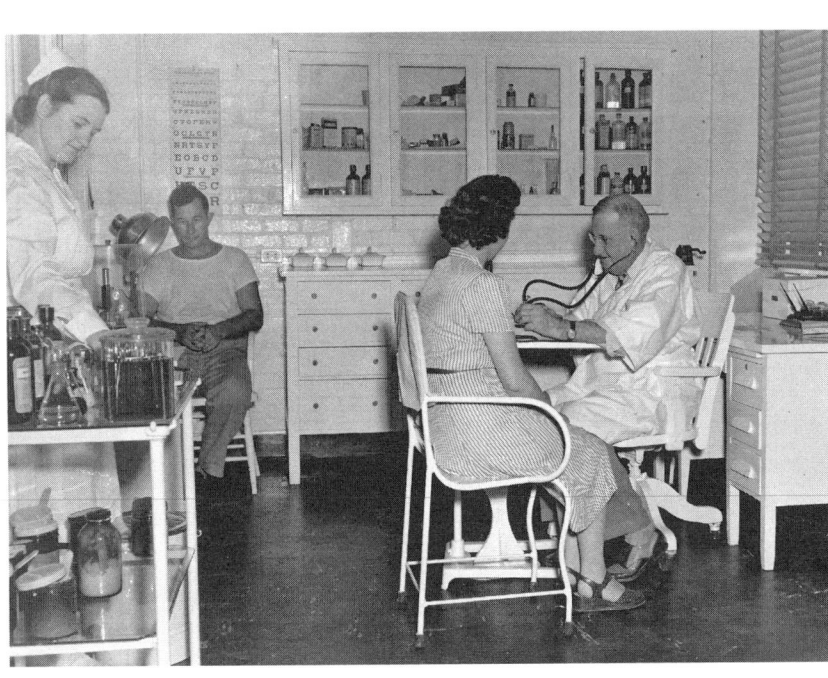

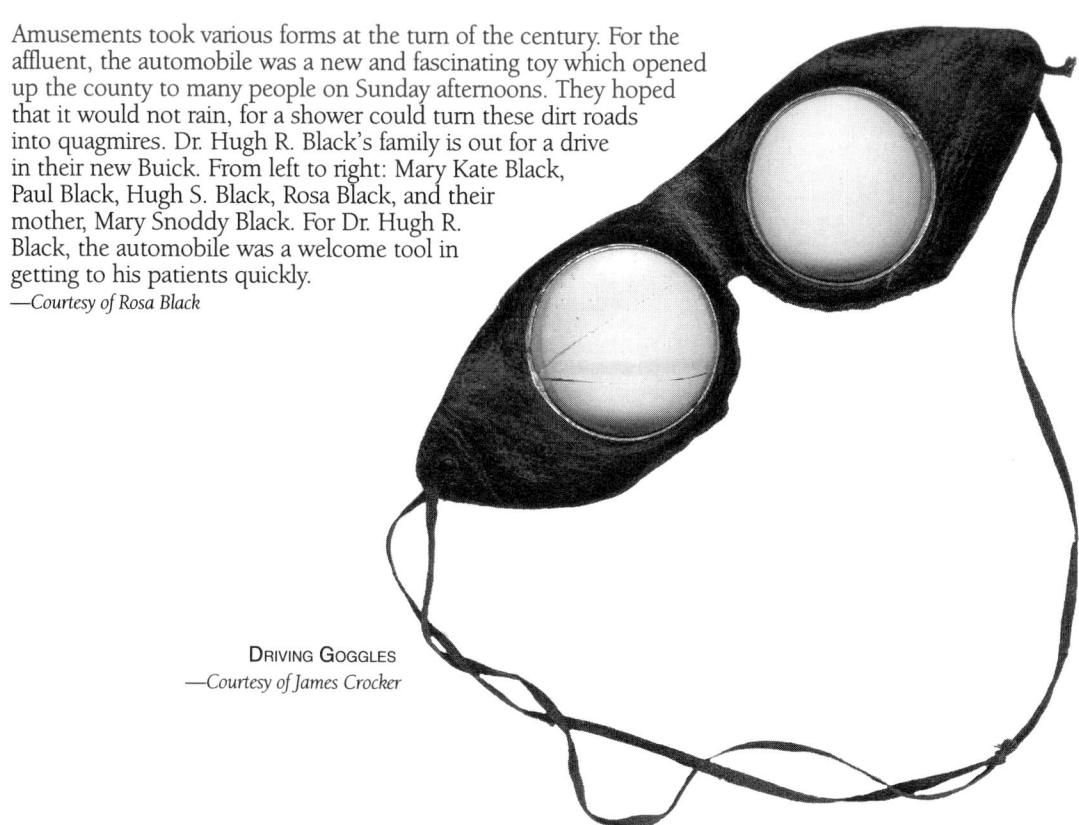

Amusements took various forms at the turn of the century. For the affluent, the automobile was a new and fascinating toy which opened up the county to many people on Sunday afternoons. They hoped that it would not rain, for a shower could turn these dirt roads into quagmires. Dr. Hugh R. Black's family is out for a drive in their new Buick. From left to right: Mary Kate Black, Paul Black, Hugh S. Black, Rosa Black, and their mother, Mary Snoddy Black. For Dr. Hugh R. Black, the automobile was a welcome tool in getting to his patients quickly.
—*Courtesy of Rosa Black*

DRIVING GOGGLES
—*Courtesy of James Crocker*

ABOVE, BELOW & OPPOSITE PAGE TOP: With increasing demand and the help of all these telephone installers, repairmen, and deliverymen (all three photos taken in 1915), Southern Bell expanded quickly. In 1918 it had to move a few doors east of the Elite into its own building in the first block on the southern side of East Main Street. —*Courtesy of the Herald-Journal Willis Collection, Spartanburg County (SC) Public Libraries*

OPPOSITE PAGE BOTTOM: In 1914 the Southern Bell switchboard was located above the Elite on East Main Street.
—*Courtesy of the Spartanburg Herald-Journal*

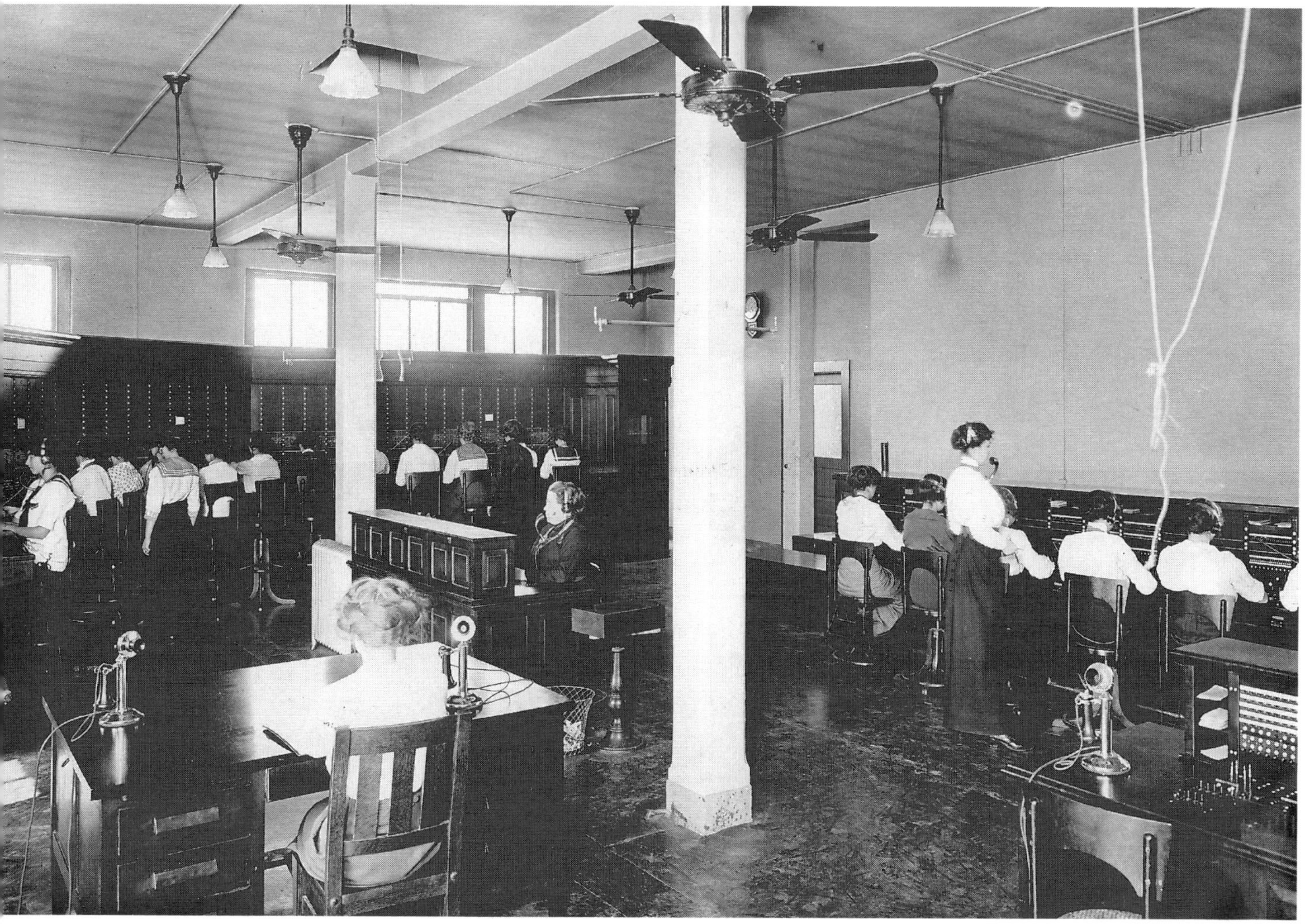

Geo. DEARMAN   O.L. PACE   W. S. YOUNG   LAMBRIGHT   ST. POINIER (POSTMASTER)   SETZLER   GALISEN   Willis

Samuel T. Poinier, right, was a veteran of many heated political contests, all of which he managed to survive. Appointed postmaster during Reconstruction, he was frequently the target of post-Reconstruction efforts to remove him from office. The determination with which he met each challenge shows through in this turn-of-the-century photograph. In the top image, Poinier stands with his staff outside the Opera House, which housed the Post Office for some time. —*Photographs courtesy of the Spartanburg County Regional Museum and the Herald-Journal Willis Collection, Spartanburg County (SC) Public Libraries*

Samuel Poinier's post office in the Opera House looked like it could use some modernization at the turn of the century. He is second from the left.
—*Courtesy of the Spartanburg County Regional Museum*

Spartanburg's smaller fire-fighting wagon was drawn by two horses.
—*Courtesy of the Herald-Journal Willis Collection, Spartanburg County (SC) Public Libraries*

In 1897 the town of Spartanburg employed its first fireman, William Donald Mitchell, for $30 a month. The town owned two pieces of firefighting equipment: a hose and chemical wagon drawn by two horses and a steam engine drawn by three horses. When there was a fire, the bell in the Opera House tolled, and the number of rings told the firemen in which ward the fire was burning. Strips of bacon were used to start the fire under the steam engine. Sometimes the streets were ankle-deep in mud, so the horses had to get to the scene of the fire as best they could. Usually by the time the steam engine got there, the boiler was red hot, but often the fire was already out of control.

Lionel Lawson recalled a tragic story that occurred in the same year this picture was taken, 1912. During the May Day festivities at Converse College, the bell rang out for a fire in Converse Heights. The three-horse engine rushed full speed eastward on Main Street at the same time that a train was heading for the East Main Street crossing. In all the noise neither driver heard the other. Mitchell, the driver of the fire engine, pulled hard enough on the reins to keep the wagon from colliding with the train, but he could not prevent the three magnificent horses from being crushed. According to Lawson the schoolchildren of the town, who had taken great pride in these beautiful horses, were deeply saddened and went by the firehouse the next day to pay their respects to the dead animals. —*Courtesy of Wofford College*

![Streetcars on their way to the County Fair in the late teens.](placeholder)

ABOVE: Streetcars on their way to the County Fair in the late teens.
—Courtesy of the Herald-Journal Willis Collection, Spartanburg County (SC) Public Libraries

RIGHT: These people are waiting in line for the first tickets to the South Atlantic Music Festival in 1912. Patrons spent $6 for five performances, which were held at Twichell Auditorium, whose interior and exterior are shown here. The man in the bowler hat at the front of the line was W. S. Glenn who, for several years, came early to be the first to buy the much-sought-after tickets. The images on these pages illustrate the differing social levels of entertainment available in Spartanburg.
—Courtesy of B & B Studio

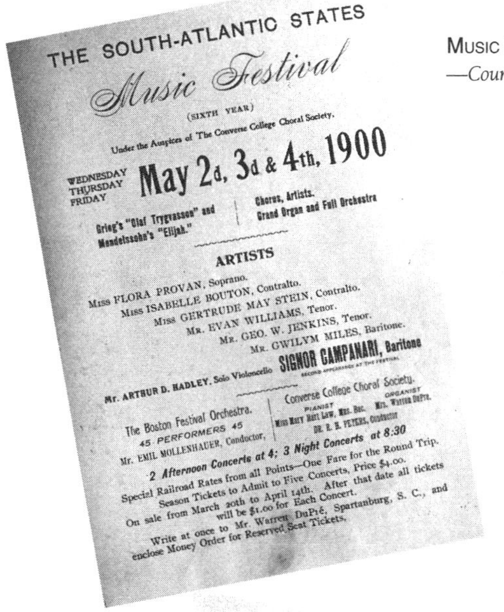

THE SOUTH-ATLANTIC STATES
Music Festival
(SIXTH YEAR)
Under the Auspices of The Converse College Choral Society,

WEDNESDAY
THURSDAY
FRIDAY
May 2d, 3d & 4th, 1900

Grieg's "Olaf Trygvasson" and Mendelssohn's "Elijah." | Chorus, Artists, Grand Organ and Full Orchestra

ARTISTS

Miss FLORA PROVAN, Soprano.
Miss ISABELLE BOUTON, Contralto.
Miss GERTRUDE MAY STEIN, Contralto.
Mr. EVAN WILLIAMS, Tenor.
Mr. GEO. W. JENKINS, Tenor.
Mr. GWILYM MILES, Baritone.
Mr. ARTHUR D. HADLEY, Solo Violoncello **SIGNOR CAMPANARI, Baritone**
SECOND APPEARANCE AT THE FESTIVAL

The Boston Festival Orchestra.
45 PERFORMERS 45
Mr. EMIL MOLLENHAUER, Conductor,

Converse College Choral Society.
PIANIST Miss Mary Hart Law, Mus. Bac. ORGANIST Mrs. Warren DuPré.
DR. R. H. PETERS, Conductor

2 Afternoon Concerts at 4; 3 Night Concerts at 8:30
Special Railroad Rates from all Points—One Fare for the Round Trip.
Season Tickets to Admit to Five Concerts, Price $4.00.
On sale from March 20th to April 14th. After that date all tickets will be $1.00 for Each Concert.
Write at once to Mr. Warren DuPré, Spartanburg, S. C., and enclose Money Order for Reserved Seat Tickets.

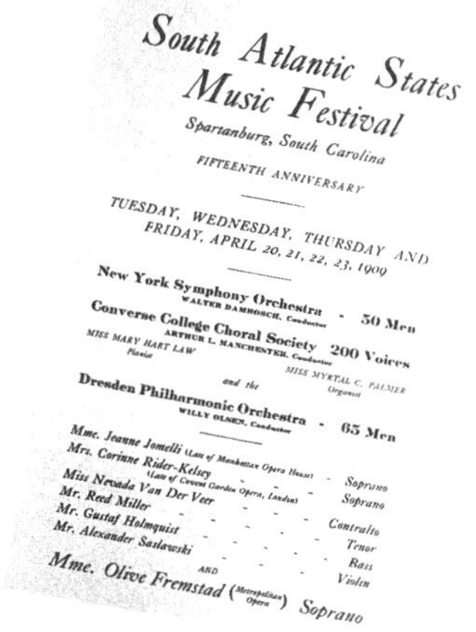

South Atlantic States
Music Festival
Spartanburg, South Carolina
FIFTEENTH ANNIVERSARY

TUESDAY, WEDNESDAY, THURSDAY AND FRIDAY, APRIL 20, 21, 22, 23, 1909

New York Symphony Orchestra - **50 Men**
WALTER DAMROSCH, Conductor
Converse College Choral Society **200 Voices**
ARTHUR L. MANCHESTER, Conductor
MISS MARY HART LAW, Pianist
MISS MYRTAL C. PALMER, Organist
and the
Dresden Philharmonic Orchestra - **65 Men**
WILLY OLSEN, Conductor

Mme. Jeanne Jomelli (Late of Manhattan Opera House) - Soprano
Mrs. Corinne Rider-Kelsey (Late of Covent Garden Opera, London) - Soprano
Miss Nevada Van Der Veer - Contralto
Mr. Reed Miller - Tenor
Mr. Gustaf Holmquist - Bass
Mr. Alexander Saslawski - Violin
AND
Mme. Olive Fremstad (Metropolitan Opera) Soprano

Music Programs
—Courtesy of Converse College

Converse College's Concert Hall and its interior in 1899. This hall was later renamed, Twichell Auditorium, to honor the leader of the Converse College Choral Society, Albert H. Twichell.
—Courtesy of Converse College

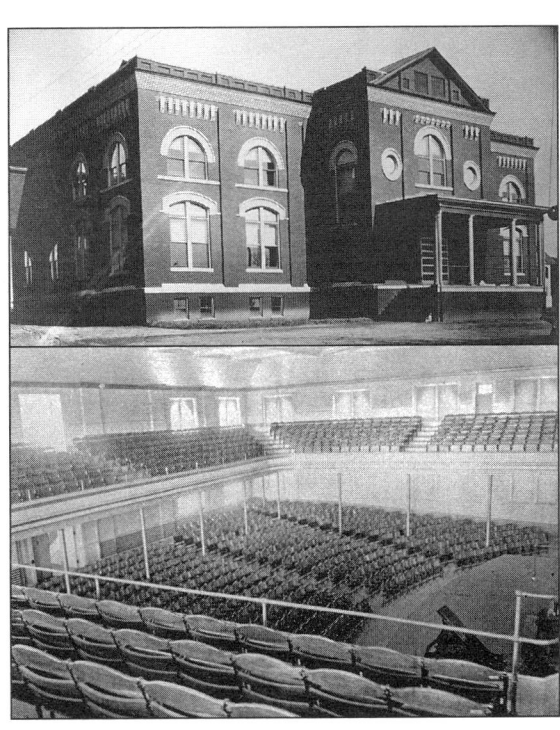

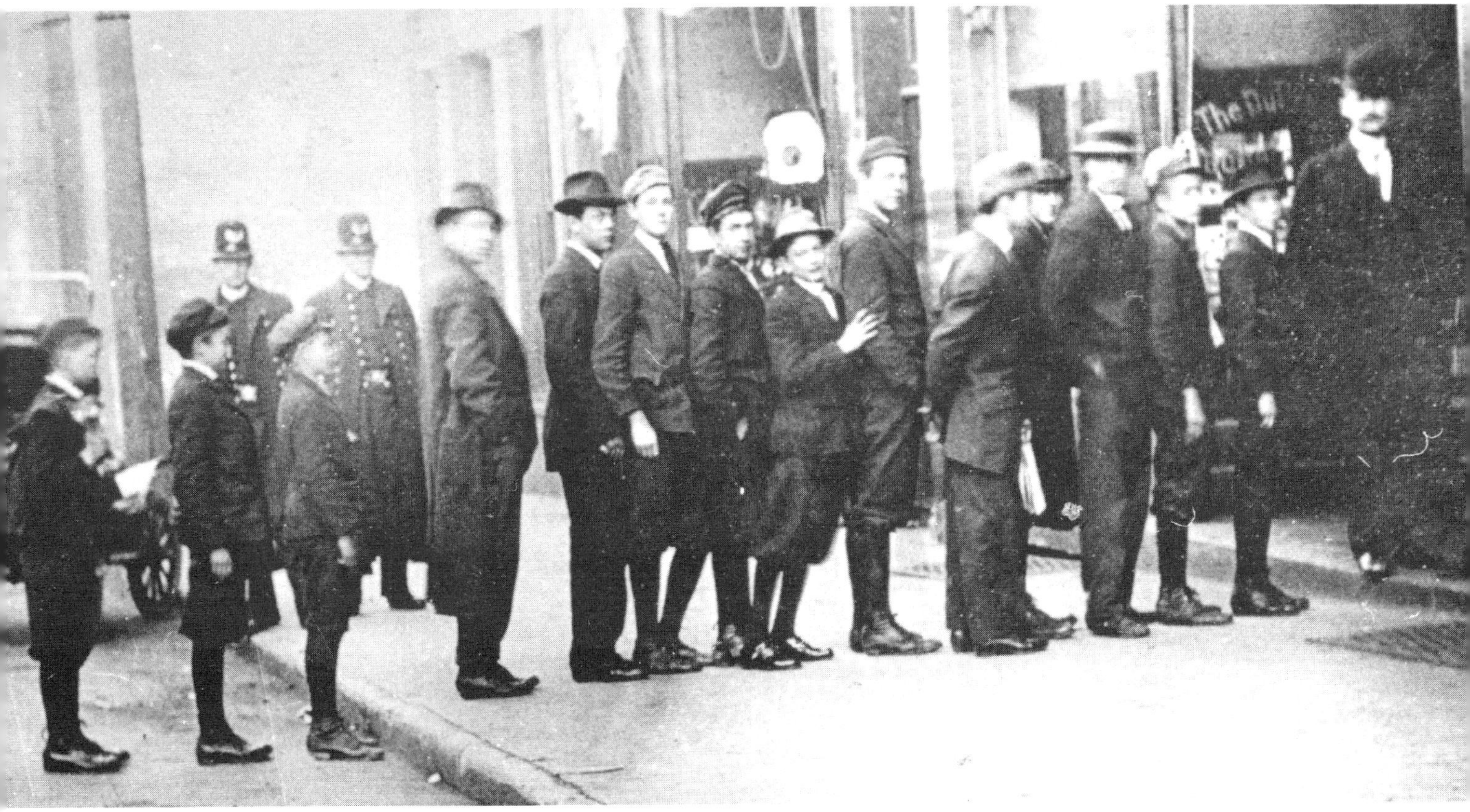

The south side of Morgan Square at Wall Street decorated for a national holiday. On the second floor with the large arched window, in the second building from the right, is W. S. Glenn's Insurance Agency. The building on the far left is the Heinitsh Drug Store. All these buildings still stand.
—Courtesy of George Mullinax

Soldiers of America
ATTENTION

The President of a little lumbering railroad in Michigan once wrote to the President of a big railroad system requesting an exchange of annual passes, and stated that his railroad was not quite as long as his, but was just as wide. Spartanburg is not as large as New York, or the other big cities of the country, but its spirit is just as wide and strong.

In the spirit of such service, we desire to extend to you every banking facility.

Bank of Spartanburg

1918 ADVERTISEMENT IN
CAMP WADSWORTH NEWSPAPER

Above: A Christmas tree decorated in 1910.
—*Courtesy of the Johnson family*

Left: The crowd gathered in Morgan Square may be there for a political rally although there are no signs. There is a group of men on a platform under trees on the left. Whether this particular photograph is of a political rally or not, it does give us an idea of what such a gathering was like in the early part of the century. —*Courtesy of the Herald-Journal Willis Collection, Spartanburg County (SC) Public Libraries*

The lobby and office of the Spartan Inn.
—*Courtesy of Wofford College*

The Merchant's Hotel, later known as the Spartan Inn, was built in 1880. The street floor was given over to shops, and some of the rooms on the upper floors were rented as offices, but most of the upper rooms were used by the hotel. Standing on Morgan Square between the Opera House and the old courthouse, the Spartan Inn was for 30 years the most photographed building in the city. This photograph was probably made in the early 1890s, for the trees that stood in front of the Inn are gone. The hotel had a special carriage, here parked in front of the entrance to the lobby, to carry patrons to and from the railway stations. The "Whitman's" sign belongs to C. D. Whitman, who styled himself Spartanburg's "Iron King" in his ads for iron stoves and other hardware.

—*Photograph by Alfred Willis, courtesy of the Herald-Journal Willis Collection, Spartanburg County (SC) Public Libraries*

ALL LEFT: The Cleveland Hotel was built in 1915 where the west end of the old Spartan Inn had stood. The hotel was named the Cleveland because the property had belonged to John B. Cleveland. The hotel stood directly in front of the site where Jesse Cleveland had built his store in 1810. The Cleveland was the largest of the city's overnight accommodations. In its heyday the hotel was rather posh, as the 1918 postcard of the terrace illustrates. The construction of the Cleveland Hotel added another skyscraper to Spartanburg's skyline; that made two, counting the Chapman Building seen in the background of the first picture. In the teens, Spartanburg was on the move to modernization. —*Photographs courtesy of the Herald-Journal Willis Collection, Spartanburg County (SC) Public Libraries; the Spartanburg Herald-Journal; the South Carolina Historical Museum*

BELOW: Until 1910 hotels in the immediate vicinity of Union Station on Magnolia Street were small and inferior to the larger establishments around Morgan Square. Then the Gresham was built to cater especially to passengers, itinerant salesmen, and other business people seeking lodging near the station. The Gresham (later called the Morgan Hotel) stood directly across the street from Union Station and was one of Spartanburg's finest hotels. It was framed in wood with a brick exterior sheathing. The Gresham eventually fell victim to the decline of rail travel, and it was demolished in the 1980s. —*Courtesy of R. O. and B. R. Pickens*

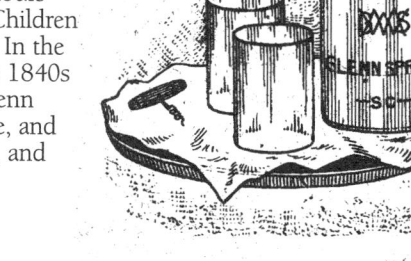

Although the fame of the Glenn Springs area as a summer resort had spread as early as the 1840s, the heyday of the region was in the latter part of the nineteenth and the early part of the twentieth centuries. This photograph of the hotel, its staff, and its guests dates from the 1880s. Whatever fame was achieved by Spartanburg County during this time was the product of either the infamous activities of the Ku Klux Klan in the early 1870s or the praise showered on the beautiful wooded environs of Glenn Springs.

The routine that hotel guests followed seems blissfully dull in our harried age. People used to take the water early in the day, walk along the lovely wooded paths, eat heartily in the well-appointed dining room, take some more water at the spring, and sit and let the hours go by. The hours passed as guests made use of the many rocking chairs provided on the long verandah. Children played under the hotel, which sat up on posts, where the air was cool and comfortable. In the evenings, people played whist or attended parties and danced just as they had since the 1840s when guests had traveled many miles to Glenn Springs' parties. The railroad built to Glenn Springs in the last part of the nineteenth century made all of this leisure more accessible, and thousands took advantage of it. By the 1920s, the resort had diminished in importance, and in 1941 the hotel burned. —*Courtesy of the South Caroliniana Library*

OPPOSITE PAGE: Of the places to go at the turn of the century, perhaps the most exciting was a trip to Glenn Springs. Getting there was made much easier after 1894 when the picturesque Glenn Springs Railroad opened. The train ran from Roebuck to Glenn Springs, a nine-mile trip. Coming from Spartanburg, passengers boarded a Charleston and Western Carolina train at the Union depot and rode out to Roebuck where they connected with the little two-car Glenn Springs train. Many people came to the resort every summer, and the train service was first rate. The conductor, Captain Tom Smith, stood about six feet, three inches, and drove a two-horse carriage to work every day. In this photograph he is leaning out the doorway of the baggage car, immediately behind the engine. The engineer was Giles Templeton and the fireman was Mr. Miller, both of whom are standing in the engine compartment. The porter, Joe Clark, stands just to the left of the man leaning against the train. The train from Roebuck cost adults 75 cents and children 35 cents. The Captain was known to "neglect" to collect from children who were residents of Glenn Springs and who often liked to ride the train.

1904 STOCK CERTIFICATE

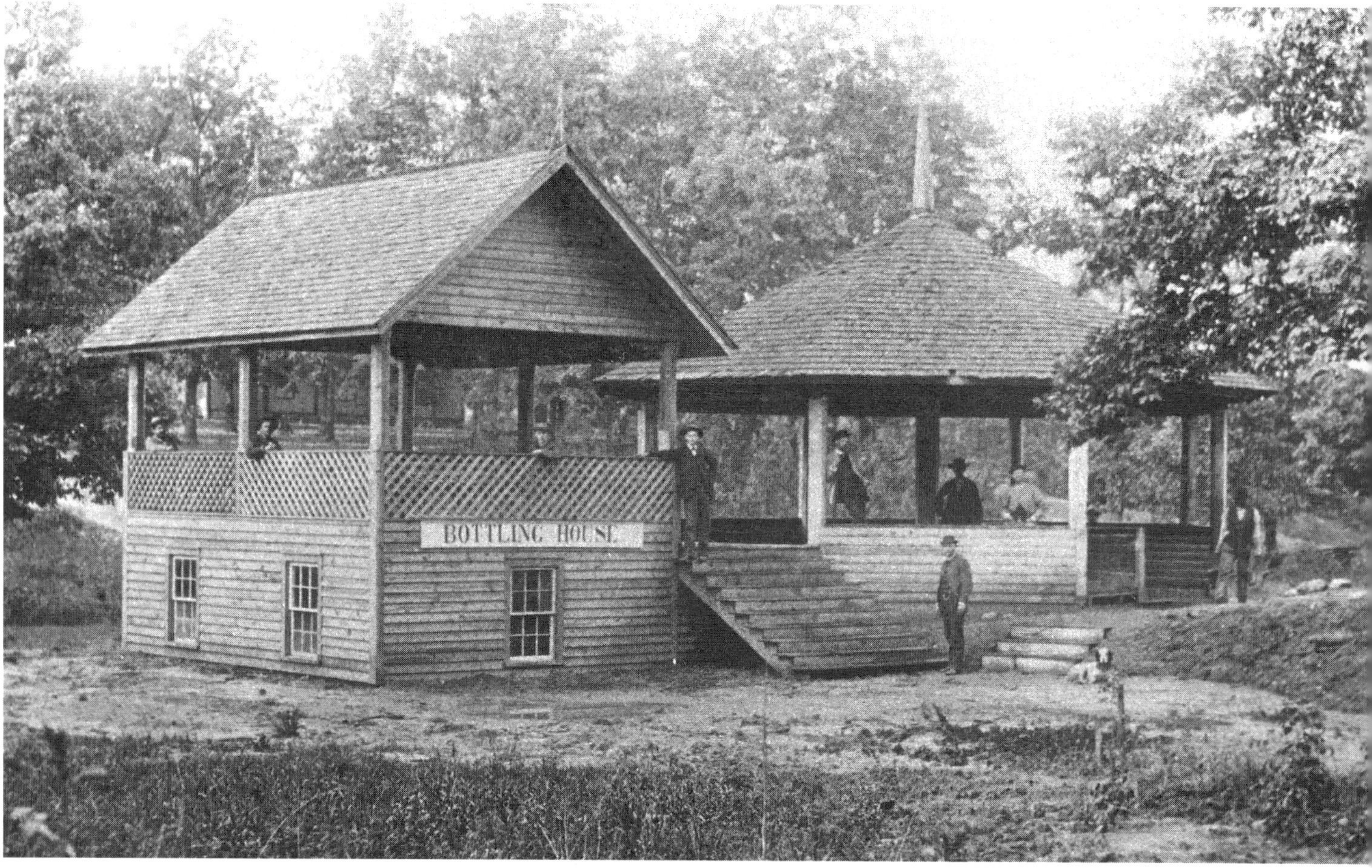

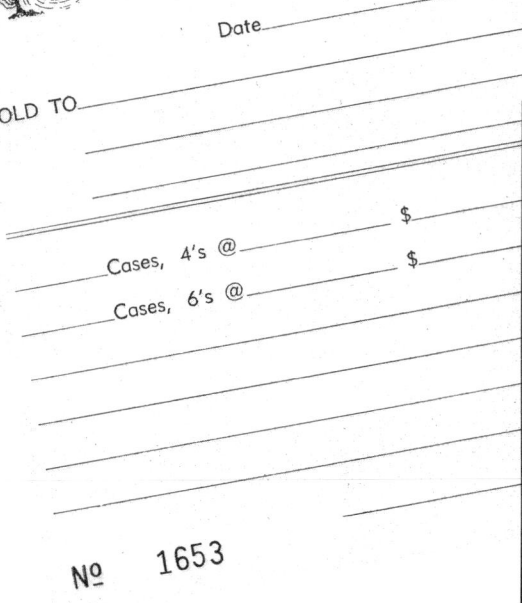

Glenn Springs got its fame from its spring water, which was bottled in this plant and sent all over the world. This image dates from the 1880s.
—Courtesy of the South Caroliniana Library

"Nature's Formula"
ACTIVELY PATRONIZED for OVER 125 YEARS
Glenn Springs
Mineral Waters
GLENN SPRINGS, S. C.
Date
SOLD TO
Cases, 4's @ $
Cases, 6's @ $
№ 1653

EARLY ORDER FORM & LABEL DESIGN
—Courtesy of the Spartanburg County Regional Museum

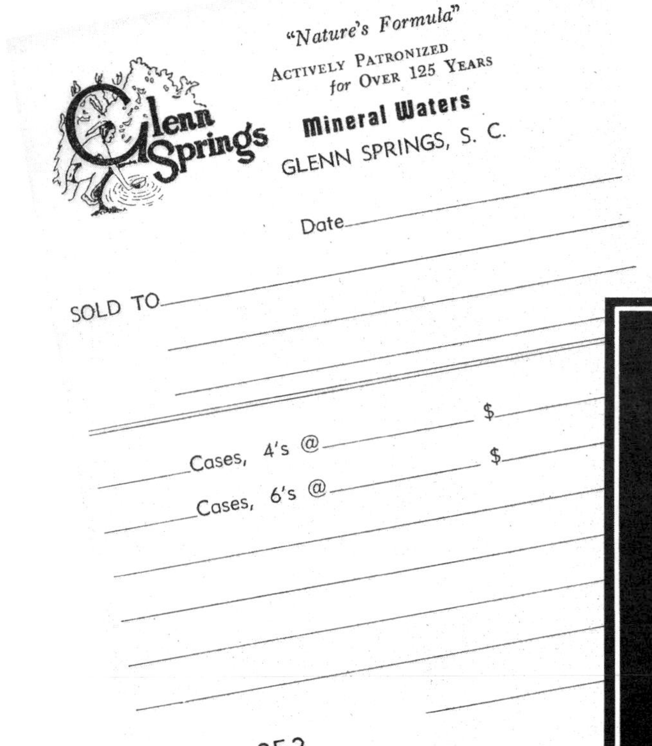

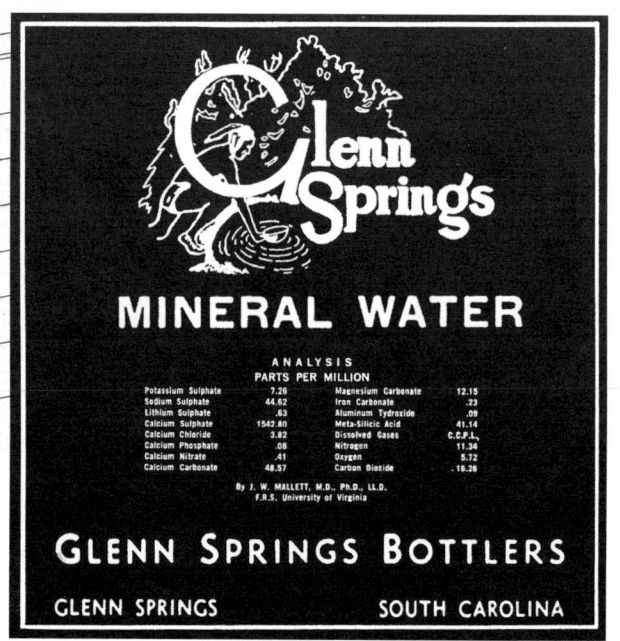

Spartanburg people visited local springs for relaxation, for walks on wooded paths, and sometimes for medicinal qualities attributed to the water. One such place was Kirby Springs, later known as White Stone Spring because of the white mineral coating on the exposed rock. Note the continuously flowing water to the left in this circa 1900 photograph of a Sunday outing. From left to right: Jones Foster, James C. Foster, Lula Foster, Neynon Fowler, and Lloyd Dillard. —*Courtesy of the Spartanburg Herald-Journal*

Like most residents of Glenn Springs, the Chapmans took in boarders in the summer. This picture, taken in the early 1890s, shows the Chapman children with their boarders of that season. Second from the left in the second row is Florence Chapman; her brother Jeff and her sister Rosa stand second and third from the left in the back row. The girl in the window, coquettishly hiding most of her face, was Susan. Although too shy to stand with the others, she consented to peek out of the window. Although the Glenn Springs Hotel accommodated the largest number of summer guests, so many people wanted to summer here that private houses rented out rooms.
—*Courtesy of Russell Stevenson*

Glendale Park was part of the mill community of Glendale. Its woods and pond were a pleasant place to picnic and to spend an afternoon. In 1900 a trolley line (seen here in the upper left corner of the photograph) was opened from Spartanburg through Glendale to the Clifton Mills. The line ran up East Main Street down Pine Street to Country Club Road, where it turned off to Glendale. After 1900 a trip to Glendale Park was often part of a city schoolteacher's reward to her students for a job well done. A family outing to Glendale Park was an inexpensive and pleasant activity for mill worker and executive alike.

—Courtesy of the Spartanburg County Regional Museum

1911 HORSE SHOW MEDAL
—Courtesy of Bill Littlejohn

In 1903 the Barnum and Bailey Circus, after five years in Europe, came to Spartanburg for the first time in 15 years. The circus started with a grand parade, which featured "elegant novel allegorical chariot and floats, living tableaux, Horses, Elephants and a 40-horse team driven by one man." Thousands of people from all over the piedmont came to Spartanburg to see this truly spectacular show, which boasted over 1,000 performers and animals. So large was the circus that it took 86 railroad cars in five trains, each about a half mile long, to transport it. Performances were held just south of Hampton Avenue between South Church and Liberty streets. The photograph gives some idea of the crowds that came into town to see the show. People were hanging out of the windows. Even the customers of Bishop's Cafe took time out from their "strictly American" food, considered among the best in town, to gape at the spectacle. Bishop's had a marble floor and the reputation to go with it. *—Photographs courtesy of H. W. Cudd*

ABOVE: Rock Cliff Park opened in 1910. It was located at what used to be called Garrett Springs, close to an old mill. The park stood off Heywood Avenue near the bridge over Lawson's Fork, and unlike other parks of the time, it provided a Ferris wheel, a merry-go-round, and a ride called the "ocean wave." This latter contraption turned around while lifting and dropping the occupant much like a wave would do. For the adults there was a bowling alley, a dance pavilion, and facilities for swimming and boating. The trolley ran up East Main Street to the park. Nothing remains of the park today except the end of the trolley tracks.

LEFT: Beginning in 1890 the Woodruff Fair drew people from the southern half of the county for 20 years. The fairs lasted three days and were held in the fall when the weather was cool. There were exhibits, a grandstand, and, most popular of all, a racetrack. The half-mile track provided spectators not only with the fast sulky races shown in this photograph made about 1907, but also with riding contests for women riders, which were held in a ring in the middle of the track. Riding sidesaddle, the ladies paced their horses at a walk, hoping to impress the judges with their ability and style. —*Courtesy of Ron Lanford*

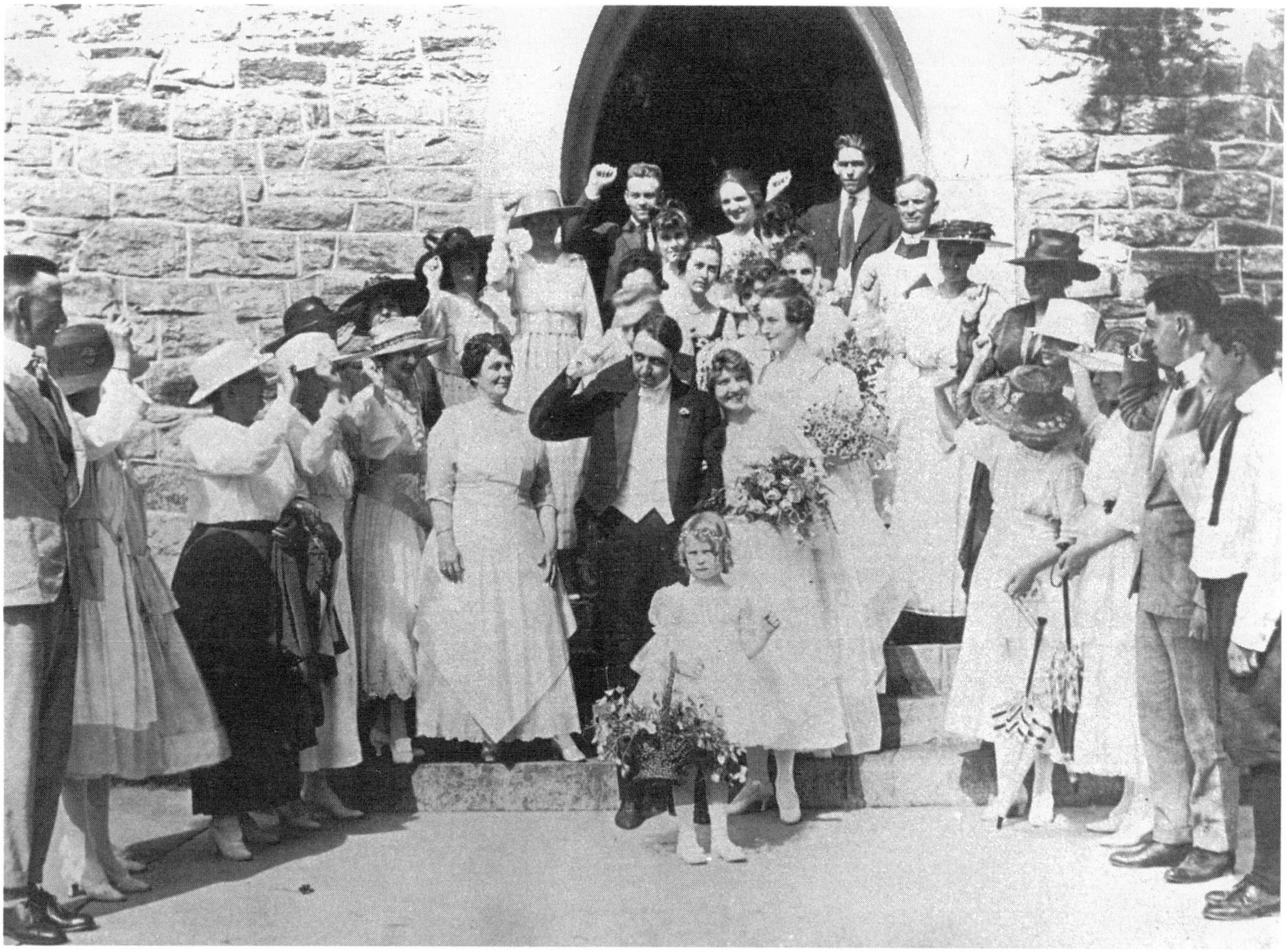

In 1917 the Rex Theater featured a movie made in Spartanburg entitled "The Wrecker." The plot was a typical one in which poor boy falls in love with rich girl. When the boy asks the girl's father for permission to marry his daughter, the father tells him that he cannot support the girl in her accustomed manner. But if the boy—a crack engineer—will win the railroad race, he'll become an assistant superintendent and can marry his sweetheart. A jealous rival, wishing to cause a wreck and delay the hero, throws a switch, putting both north and south bound trains on the same track. According to the preview, "the steel monsters crash together in a head-on collision and a terrible catastrophe is revealed to our view. The scenes are of an actual wreck, and at the time the pictures were taken, the fireman of one of the engines lies buried beneath his engine." After seeing this bloodletting, the audience witnessed a "spirited pistol battle on Main and Magnolia streets with the Spartanburg policemen." But all turns out well and our hero, who wins the race in spite of the awful delay, marries his girl in the Church of the Advent. The wedding scene, captured in the photograph above, featured Mrs. Walter Montgomery on the groom's right; Tom Calvert as the groom; Beth Green as the bride; and the Rev. W. H. K. Pendleton as the minister. The little bridesmaid in the front is Peggy Gignilliat. All this for 20 cents. The show was a big hit.

—*Photograph and movie program courtesy of Kate M. Ward*

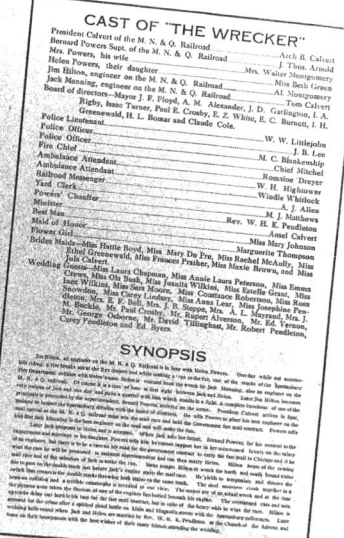

In Spartanburg, as well as in the rest of the country, movie houses began to drive out live entertainment around 1910. In a few years the Bijou, the Grand, the Strand, and in 1917 the Rex all were operating on East Main Street. Of all these theaters, the Rex was the finest. In addition to special features like "The Wrecker," the Rex luridly advertised such stars as Adolphe Menjou, Conrad Nagle, and Hedda Hopper in "Sinners in Silk," a 1925 feature that brought out the crowds. The interior of the Rex was photographed in the mid-1920s. —*Courtesy of Wofford College*

Just after the turn of the century, Spartanburg was the site of many conventions, and one of the largest was that held for Shriners from the southeastern states in 1911. For the occasion Robert Olin Pickens built this marvelous camel based on the Dromedary date package. Some boys pulled the animal along the street on bicycle wheels. Pickens constructed the camel out of copper, angle irons, and cowhide; it took him two months to build, and he was paid $186 for the job. The best part of the construction was the special use to which it was put. Pickens made the hump removable, and a keg of beer could be placed inside with 250 pounds of ice. The saddlebags held paper cups, and when the faucet connected to the udder was turned, the red light bulbs in the eyes would light up. After the convention the camel went on display in the Harris Theater and was then shipped to the West Coast for another convention. It never came back.
—*Courtesy of R. O. and B. R. Pickens*

ABOVE: The Hampton Guards. —*Courtesy of the Spartanburg County Regional Museum*

OPPOSITE PAGE TOP: South Carolina has a long tradition of local militia. In the antebellum period many such military companies sprang up within the state. Some were mostly interested in socializing, but others actually drilled weekly and took the military aspect seriously. One of the best-known of the latter was the Washington Light Infantry from Charleston. In 1856 this company came to Spartanburg to commemorate the Battle of Cowpens. The presence of this fine military encampment on the grounds of Saint John's School, where Converse College now stands, inspired some villagers to form a company of their own; thus, the Morgan Rifles were born. They drilled, paraded, and often held shooting exhibitions where rather elaborate prizes were awarded. As local entertainment, such affairs struck the fancy of the population. This 1887 photograph with the snappy uniforms and serious demeanor testifies to the vitality of the organization and the continuing belief among Spartans in a reliance on local militia. The other two photographs, the one with the Stetson-like hats from the period of the Spanish-American War in the late '90s and the other with the caps from an even later period, testify to the continuing interest in military organizations. —*Courtesy of the Spartanburg County Regional Museum*

OPPOSITE PAGE BOTTOM: The Spartan Rifles.
—*Photographs courtesy of the Herald-Journal Willis Collection, Spartanburg County (SC) Public Libraries*

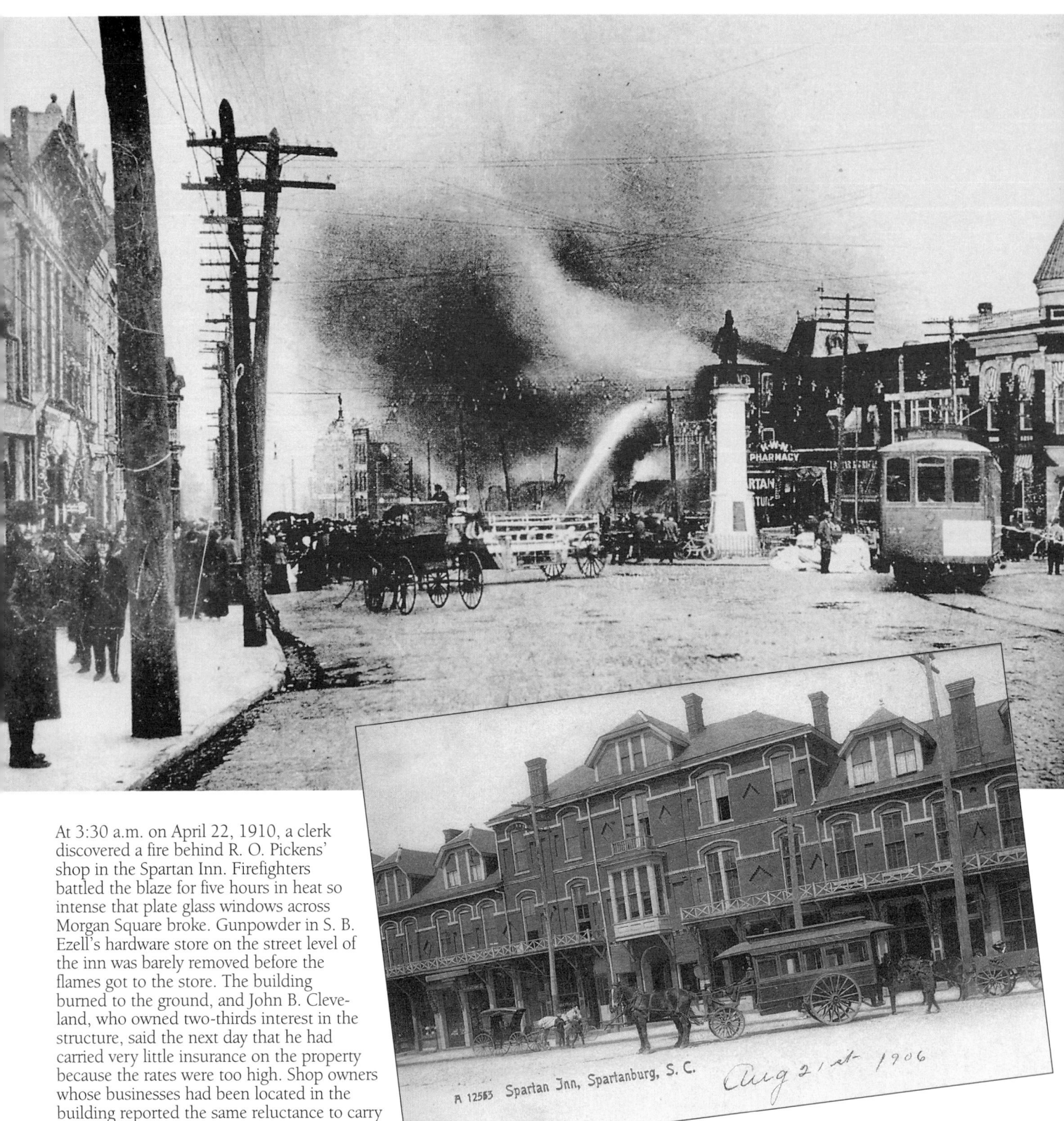

At 3:30 a.m. on April 22, 1910, a clerk discovered a fire behind R. O. Pickens' shop in the Spartan Inn. Firefighters battled the blaze for five hours in heat so intense that plate glass windows across Morgan Square broke. Gunpowder in S. B. Ezell's hardware store on the street level of the inn was barely removed before the flames got to the store. The building burned to the ground, and John B. Cleveland, who owned two-thirds interest in the structure, said the next day that he had carried very little insurance on the property because the rates were too high. Shop owners whose businesses had been located in the building reported the same reluctance to carry the expensive coverage. The fire deprived the city of Spartanburg of one of its most picturesque buildings and one of the very last structures that had made up the "old Morgan Square."

—*Photograph by Alfred T. Willis, courtesy of the Herald-Journal Willis Collection, Spartanburg County (SC) Public Libraries*

A 12563 Spartan Inn, Spartanburg, S. C. Aug 21st 1906

A POSTCARD IMAGE OF THE SPARTAN INN BEFORE THE FIRE.

In 1907 an entire block of houses burned in the Spartan Mill Village, leaving only chimneys. In the top image is the wooden structure of Duncan Memorial Methodist Church, which was left unscathed. In his book *Spartanburg*, Vernon Foster tells the story that when Walter S. Montgomery visited the site after the fire and stood on the church grounds, he was heard to say: "This must indeed be holy ground."

—*Photographs courtesy of the Herald-Journal Willis Collection, Spartanburg County (SC) Public Libraries*

In June 1903 gentle rains fell for nearly five days prior to the torrential downpour on the night of June 6. A worker at one of the Clifton mills became alarmed during the early morning hours at the rapidly rising waters of the Pacolet River, and he gave the alarm. By six o'clock that morning, Clifton Mill No. 3 was swept downstream against Clifton Mill No. 1. In the chaos more than seventy people died. This 1882 photograph of the Pacolet Mill illustrates why the flood of 1903 was so devastating by showing how close to the regular level of the river most mills were built. Just to the right of the mill, cotton bales await processing. The lower photo shows the aftermath of the flood at Pacolet Mills. *—Photographs courtesy of Lockwood Greene, Spartanburg County Regional Museum*

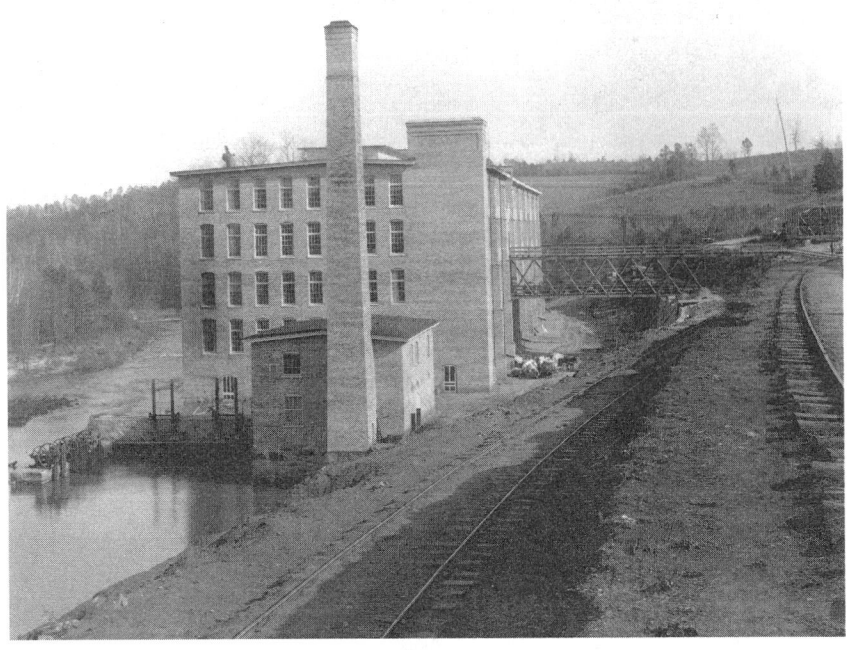

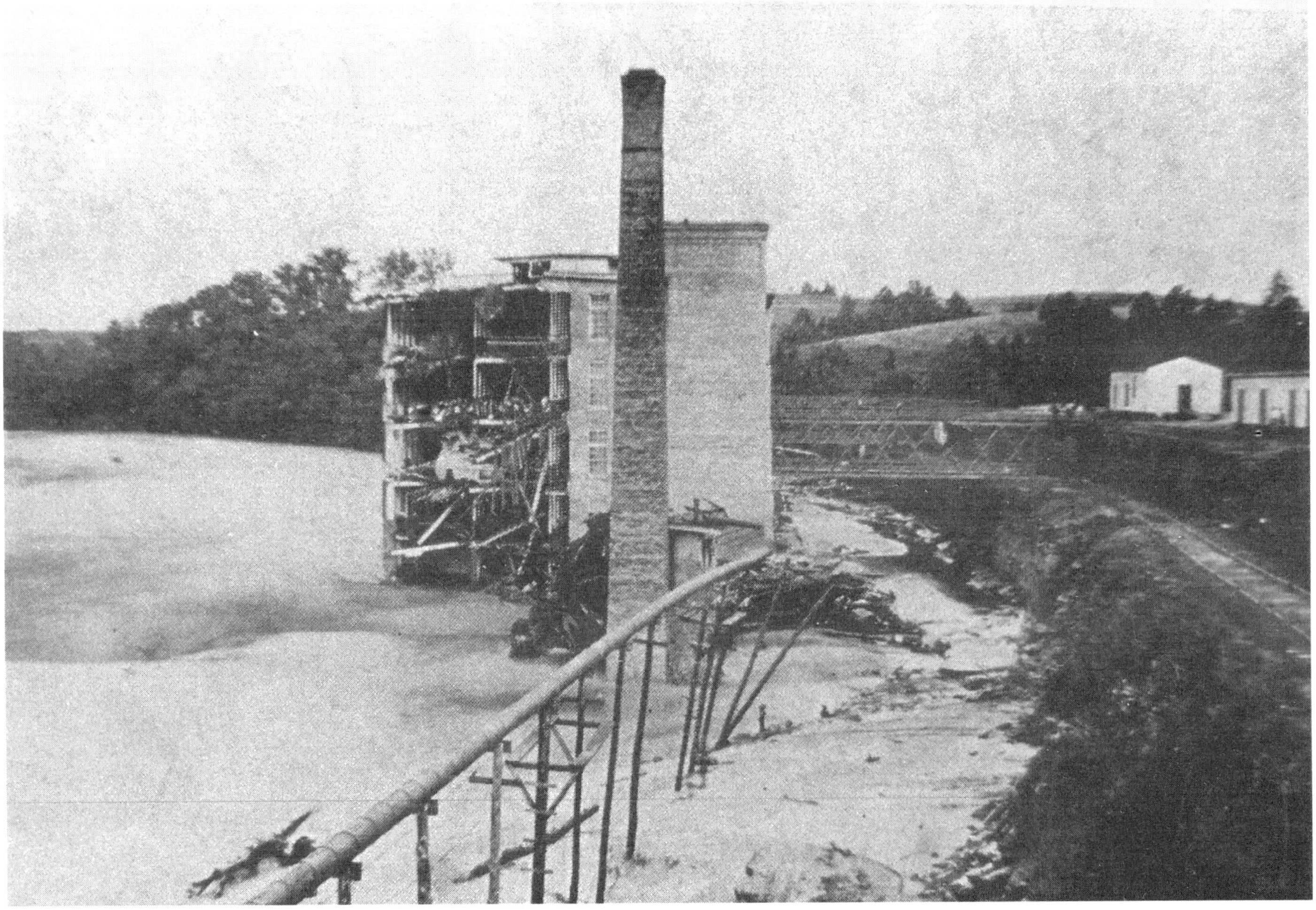

OPPOSITE PAGE: Scenes at Clifton Mill No. 3
—Photographs courtesy of Spartanburg Regional Museum, Marjorie Atkins

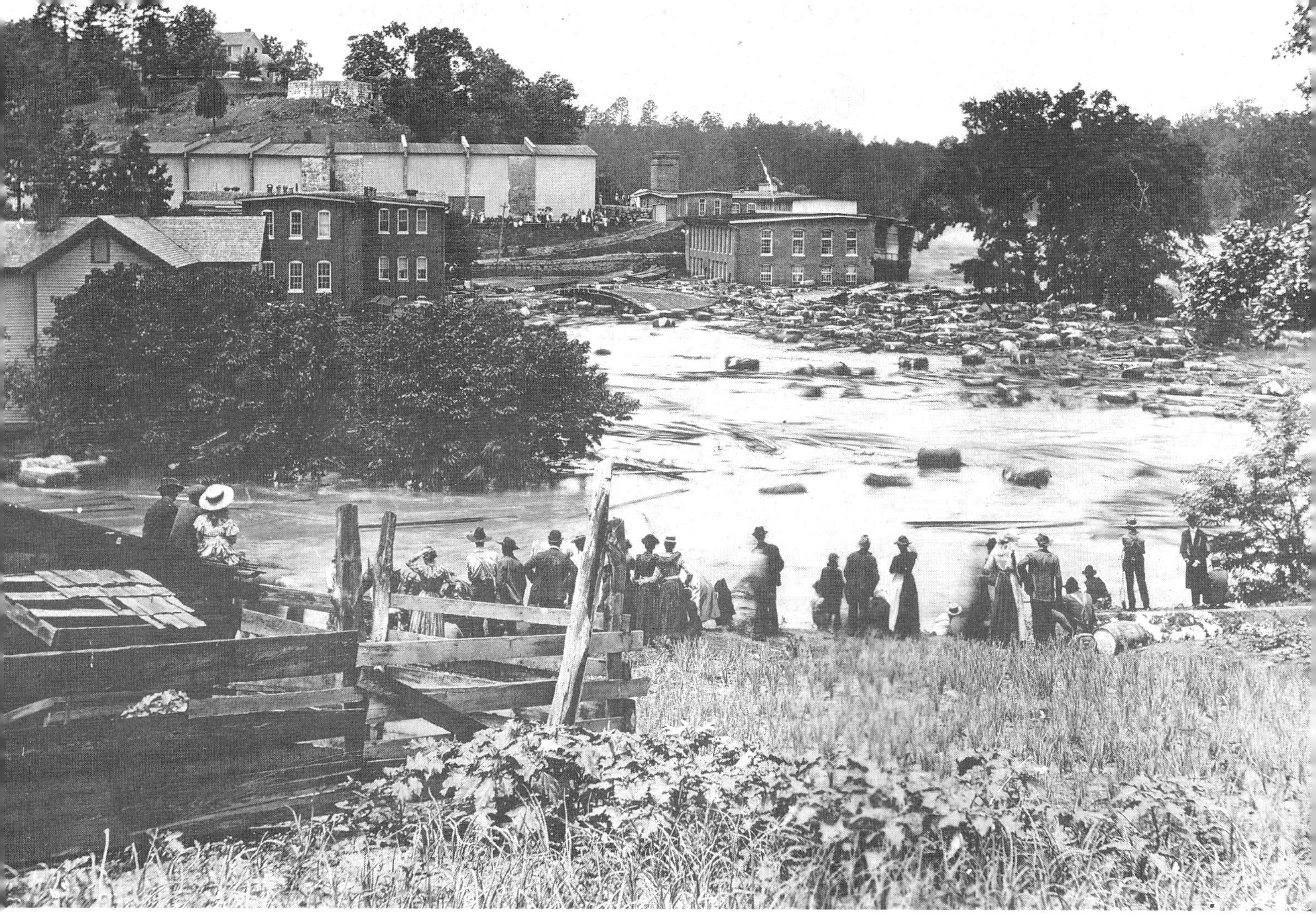

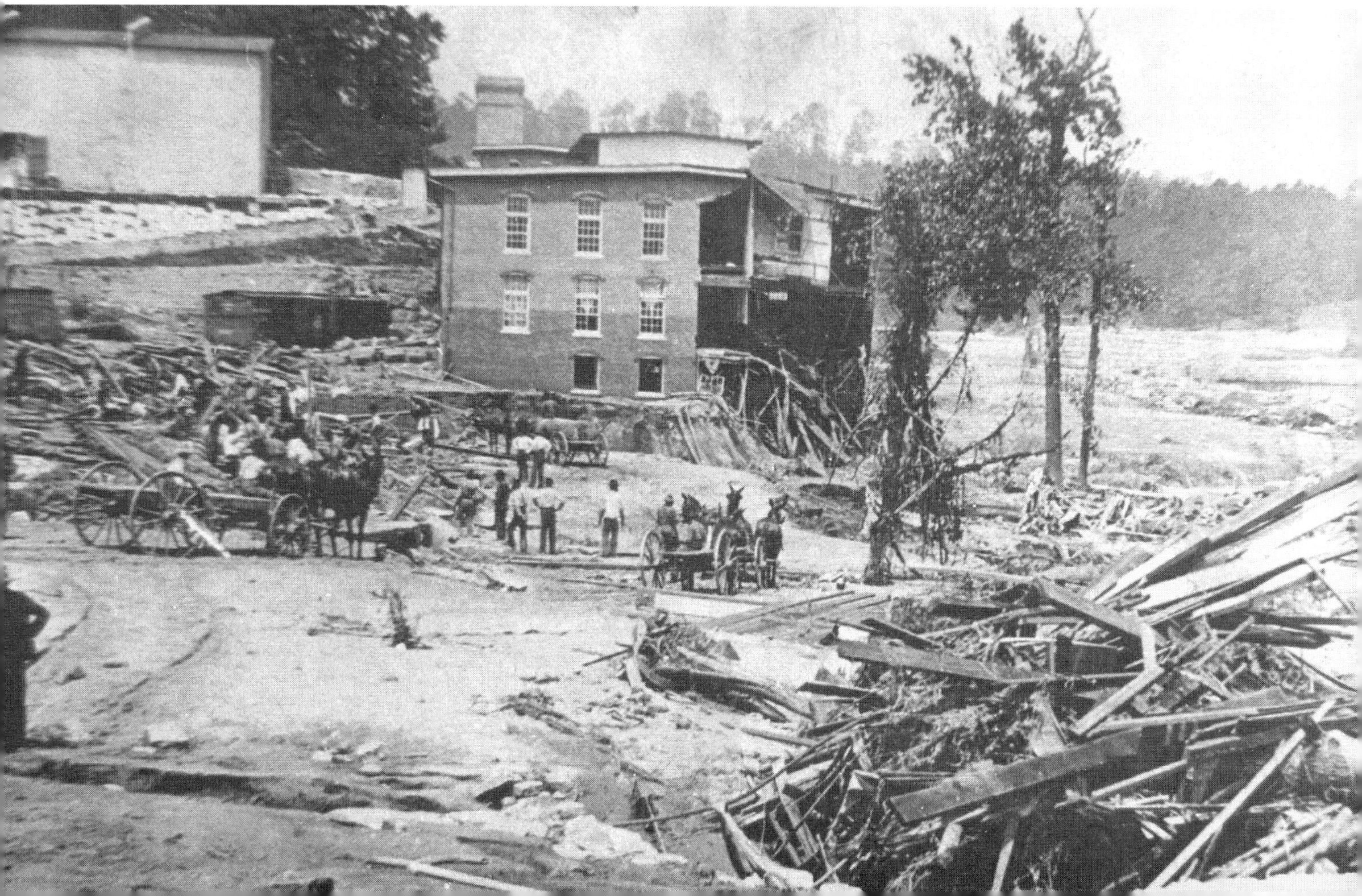

The flood swept away bridges, roads, and houses and cut these communities off from the rest of the county. The trolley tracks to Converse were destroyed and were never rebuilt. Other rivers in the county, the Tyger and the Enoree, also flooded. The top image shows damage at Clifton No. 1, while the bottom shows Clifton No. 2. —*Courtesy of Converse College*

OPPOSITE PAGE: The flood wreaked havoc on the rail transportation system.
—*Photographs courtesy of Converse College, the Spartanburg County Regional Museum*

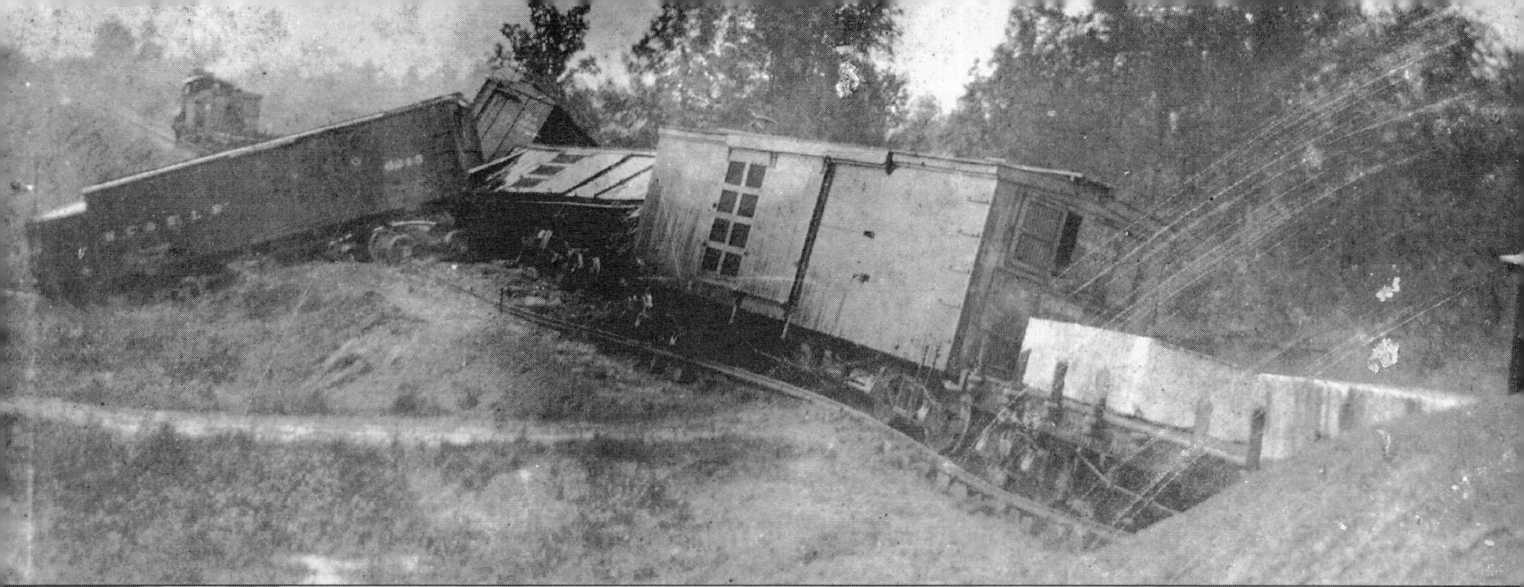

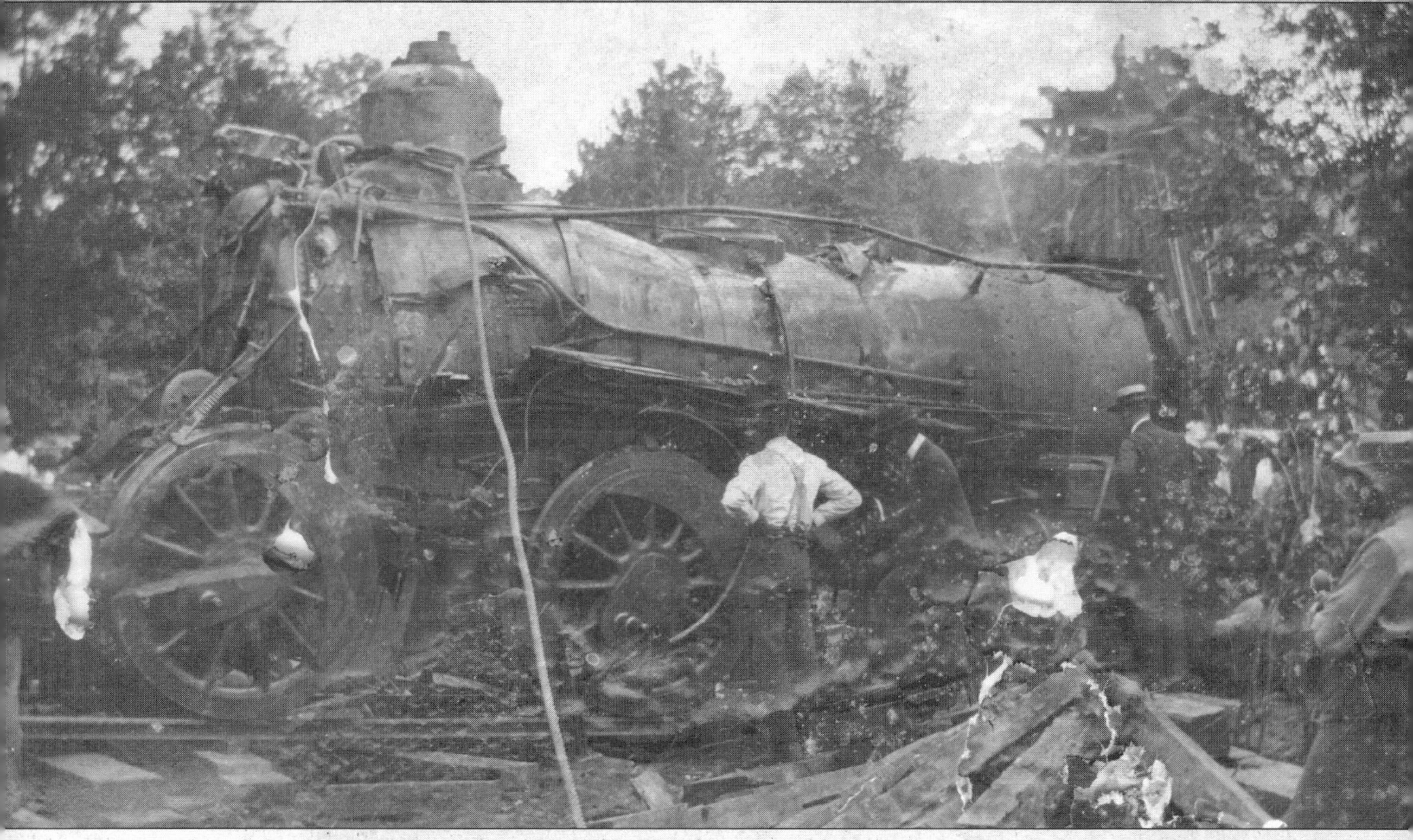

SOUTHERN
9412
SOUTHERN
41099

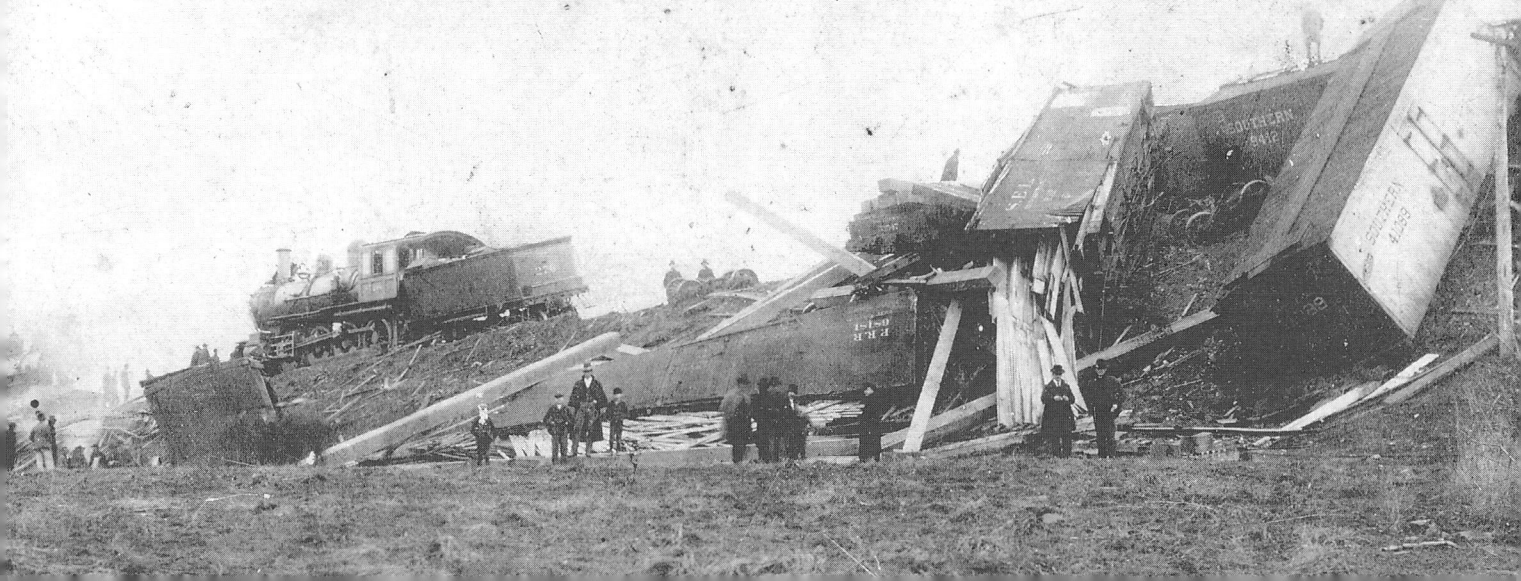

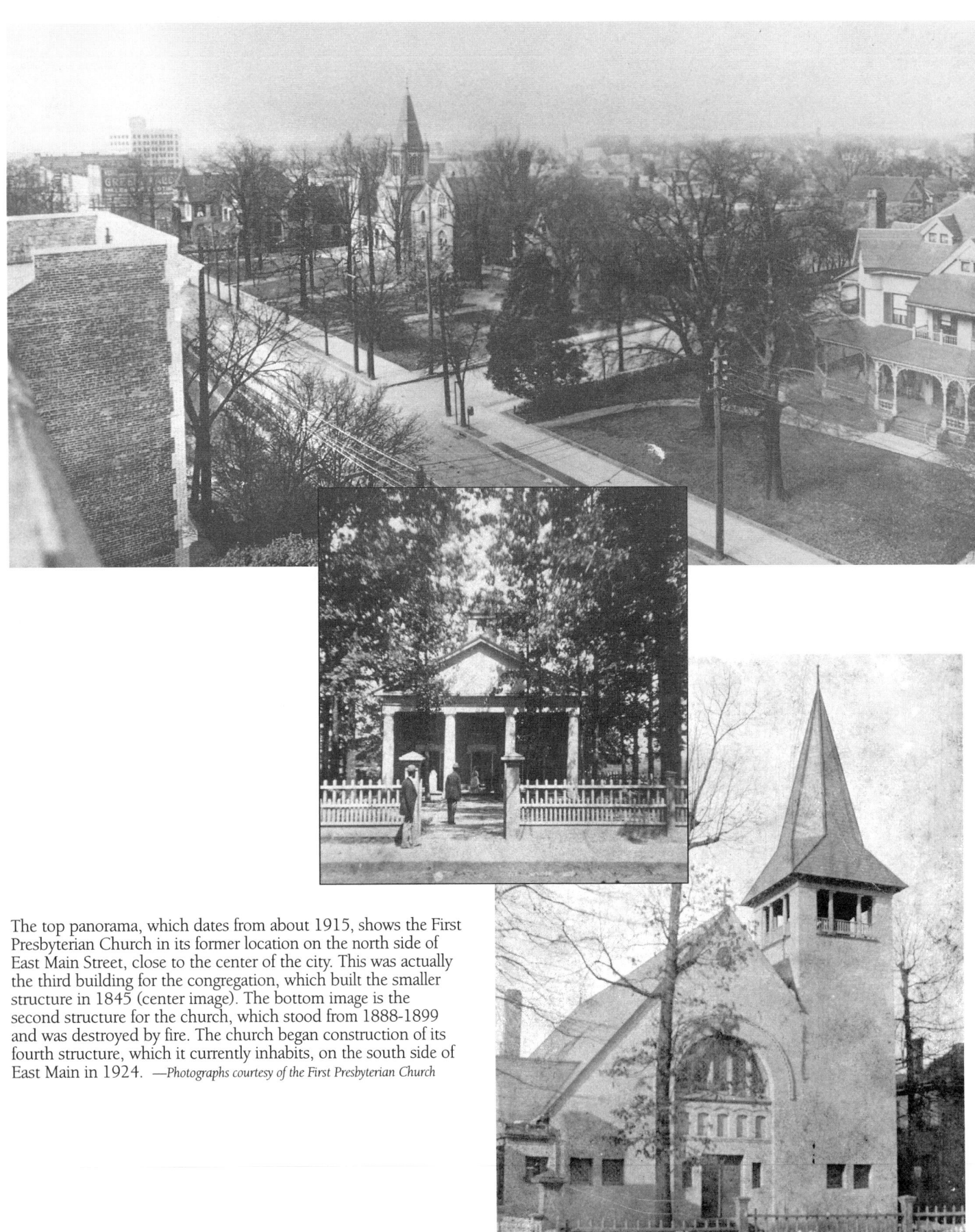

The top panorama, which dates from about 1915, shows the First Presbyterian Church in its former location on the north side of East Main Street, close to the center of the city. This was actually the third building for the congregation, which built the smaller structure in 1845 (center image). The bottom image is the second structure for the church, which stood from 1888-1899 and was destroyed by fire. The church began construction of its fourth structure, which it currently inhabits, on the south side of East Main in 1924. —*Photographs courtesy of the First Presbyterian Church*

SILVER HILL METHODIST EPISCOPAL CHURCH, SPARTANBURG, S. C., REV. JAMES F. PAGE, PASTOR 1902-1905

Top: Silver Hill Methodist Church is the oldest African-American Methodist congregation in the city of Spartanburg. —*Courtesy of Silver Hill Methodist Church*

Lower Left & Right: Construction of the Episcopal Church of the Advent began in the 1850s and continued throughout the nineteenth century. These interior and exterior images were taken in 1893. —*Courtesy of Church of the Advent*

Church picnics are traditional ways to celebrate fellowship in the South. The ladies of Spartanburg's First Baptist Church are setting up their tables for such a picnic on the church grounds. On the far left is the Reverend William Ball Sr., who served the church from 1919 to 1932.

—Courtesy of the Herald-Journal Willis Collection, Spartanburg County (SC) Public Libraries

LEFT: Roman Catholics seem to have moved into Spartanburg County in the middle of the nineteenth century, but not until 1883 were there a sufficient number of Catholics and sufficient funds to build a church of their own. In that year local Catholics built Saint Paul the Apostle Church on North Dean Street. The building was an American Gothic miniature, built along the lines of Saint Patrick's in Charleston. The building was extensively renovated in the late 1930s. This photograph dates from about 1900.
—*Courtesy of Saint Paul the Apostle Church*

OPPOSITE PAGE: After the turn of the century, members of the congregation of Bethel Methodist Church became aware that people who lived farther down South Church Street had difficulty in coming to services. Although there had been much talk, no action had ever been taken. In 1912 furniture store owner Charles P. Hammond decided that a new church must be built to serve the South Church Street population. Hammond arranged for carpenters, plumbers, roofers, painters, and brick masons to arrive at the site for the new church on the first day of May at 7:00 a.m. The men worked furiously throughout the day, with no pay, and by evening the new congregation held its first service in the completed church. Although it had been known ever since in the community as the "One-Day Church," the building was officially named El Bethel after its parent congregation. The structure was replaced in mid-century. —*Courtesy of B & B Studio*

The Jewish Temple, B'nai Israel, was built in 1916 at the intersection of Dean and Union streets opposite Evans High School. The building was sold about 1960 and a new temple built on Heywood Avenue.

In 1889 the city of Spartanburg built its first public school on Magnolia Street on the north side of the courthouse. Today the courthouse occupies the entire block.
—*Courtesy of the Herald-Journal Willis Collection, Spartanburg County (SC) Public Libraries*

Dr. Frank Evans and Mrs. Tenant stand with their pupils in one of the city's most popular schools. In 1895 Dr. Evans became Spartanburg's sixth superintendent of public schools and served in that capacity until 1934. —*Courtesy of the Johnson family*

ABOVE: Children attending the Magnolia Street School posed for this class photograph in 1901. —*Courtesy of the Spartanburg County Regional Museum*

LEFT: Following the construction of the Magnolia Street School in 1889, the city struggled valiantly to provide enough space to educate all its children. The attempt was marked by the construction of buildings so formidable that they looked as if they would keep the children in and the parents out. They were like fortresses—veritable "citadels of learning." The old Southside School, built in 1906, eventually became Jenkins Junior High School, which was torn down in the 1970s. —*Photograph by Alfred T. Willis, courtesy of the Herald-Journal Willis Collection, Spartanburg County (SC) Public Libraries*

Under the leadership of Dexter Converse, several Spartanburg businessmen subscribed funds to found Converse College in the late 1880s. While the Main Building was under construction, these same men founded a private school to prepare the girls for the rigors of college work. Mattie B. Gamewell, who had been teaching in the public schools, accepted the position of teacher in the Converse Fitting School, and Dexter Converse provided a small house on Kennedy Street (directly behind the Piedmont Club) for the school. Miss Gamewell is seen here with her first class of students in 1889.

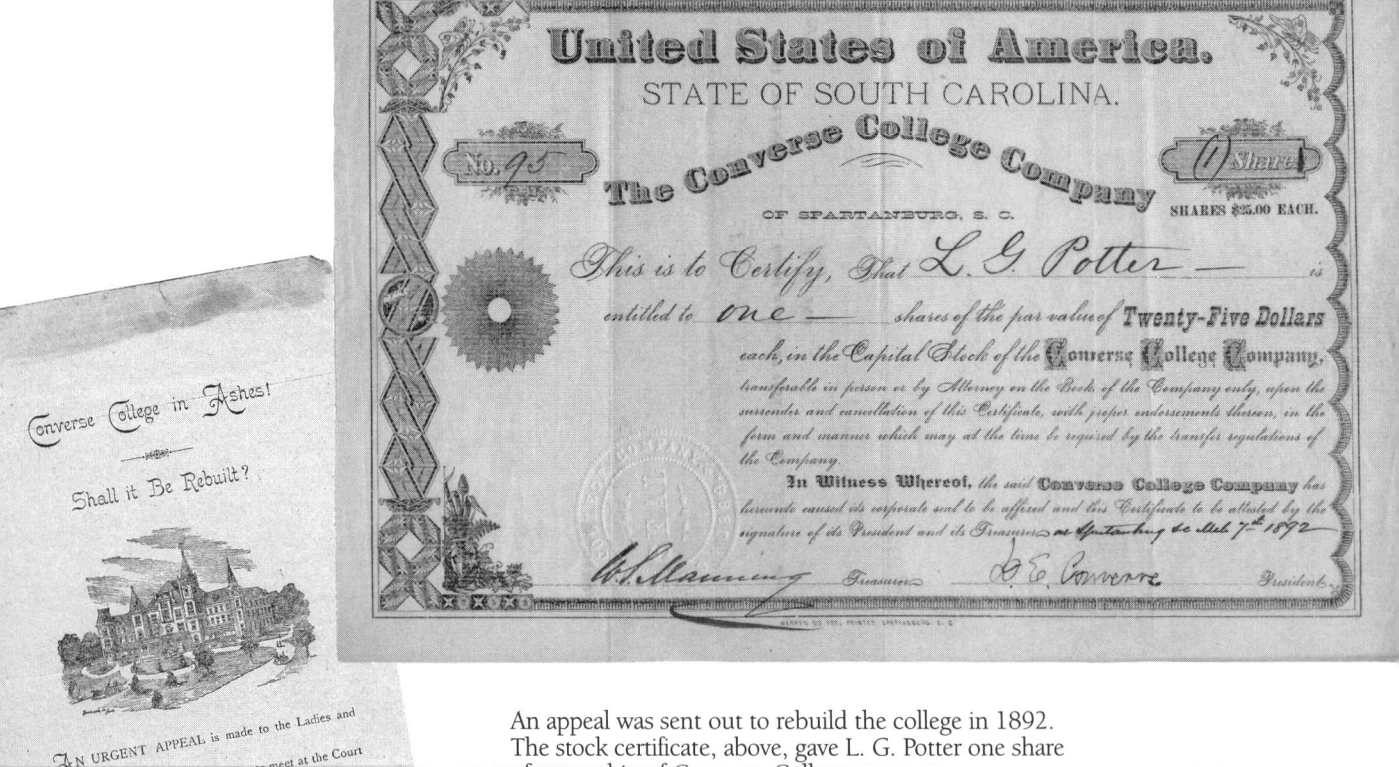

An appeal was sent out to rebuild the college in 1892. The stock certificate, above, gave L. G. Potter one share of ownership of Converse College.

At about midnight on January 2, 1892, a cry went up in the Main Building at Converse College that the kitchen was on fire. The girls lined up with pitchers in hand to try to quell the blaze. Volunteer firemen from Spartanburg arrived on this bitterly cold night to find that their hoses were too short to reach the college from the nearest fire hydrant. When the hoses from all three volunteer fire-fighting groups were linked, they barely reached the building. Then the final disappointment: the water pressure was only sufficient to throw water ten feet into the air. In dismay the men rushed to the annex and hosed it down so the fire would not spread; meanwhile, they watched helplessly as the Main Building was engulfed in the flames. Many citizens rushed through the building as the flames spread, saving all they could, but most of the college's equipment, books, and the personal belongings of the students were lost. This photograph, taken the morning after the fire, shows how little remained. Fortunately, the college's supporters rallied to resume classes, house the students, and begin a subscription to rebuild. The bottom postcard image illustrates the success of the college and its supporters.

—*Photographs courtesy of Converse College*

In 1897 the Converse yearbook, "Y's and OTHER Y's," included a picture of the custodial staff. The caption of that day —"Our Servants"—says a great deal about that era.

In the early 1900s, Converse girls, when not in class, lived in surroundings reminiscent of Sarah Bernhardt's. This ornate dormitory room was obviously tidied up for the picture, or students of that day were very unlike students of our own. At least there is a picture of college-aged men on the table, showing that interests haven't changed much.

These young women made up the first graduating class from Converse College when they sat for their portrait in 1897.

Converse College students boarding the streetcar for an outing in 1906.
—*Photographs courtesy of Converse College*

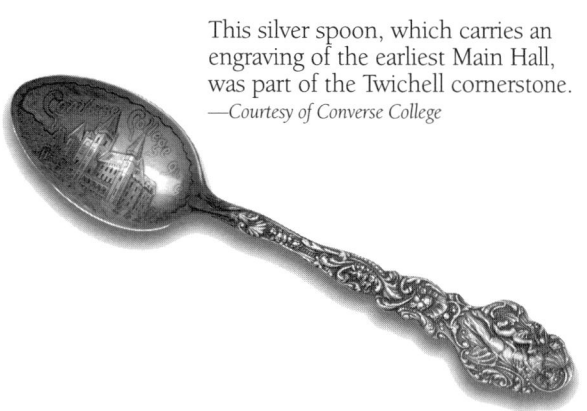

This silver spoon, which carries an engraving of the earliest Main Hall, was part of the Twichell cornerstone.
—*Courtesy of Converse College*

Rɪɢʜᴛ: Mary Elizabeth Patterson of Bellefontaine, Ohio, had her photograph taken the year she entered Converse in 1910. The elegance of her hat and dress epitomized the "ladies of quality" the women's college hoped to educate. The Yankee girl married Lewis W. Perrin of Spartanburg in 1915 and resided here until her death in 1962.
—*Courtesy of the Perrin family*

Bᴇʟᴏᴡ: The athletic association of Converse College inaugurated May Day festivities in 1910. The pageant included dancing, singing, and a drama, all centered on a special theme. A May queen was crowned, and people came from the city to watch the festivities. This image was taken in 1916.
—*Courtesy of Converse College*

Wofford's graduating class of 1897 on the steps of Old Main.
—*Courtesy of Jesse Franklin Cleveland*

BELOW: Wofford organized its first football team in 1889. After two successful contests against Furman, the Wofford faculty criticized the game, and the program languished for a few years. By 1893 Wofford was at it again, playing both Furman and the University of South Carolina. Then came an invitation to play Athens (the University of Georgia) in Spartanburg in 1895. This photograph, taken during that game, shows Athens in the dark jerseys heading for the Wofford goal. Athens won the game 10 to 0, and Wofford moved to hire a regular football coach. Football in those days was so rough that broken bones were not uncommon, and the Methodist Conference of 1896 denounced the game as brutal, criticized it for interfering with scholarship, and forbade it at Wofford. It was not until 1914 that Wofford fielded another football team.
—*Photograph by Richard F. Peterson, courtesy of Wofford College*

TOP: A panoramic view of Wofford College taken in 1909. On the left is "Old Main" and on the right is the Cleveland Science Hall, constructed with a gift from John B. Cleveland.
—*Courtesy of the Library of Congress*

CENTER ROW: The Calhoun and Preston Literary Societies dated from the 1850s and were the most prestigious groups to which a Wofford student could belong. In 1872 the board of trustees made membership in one or the other compulsory. The societies engaged in long debates, some of which became quite acrimonious. Although for a time some students treated membership with indifference, for the most part students took the activities of the societies seriously. The halls seem to invite the serious, if not the contemplative. Both photographs date from 1909; the left photograph is of the Calhoun Society Hall and the right is of the Preston Literary Society Hall.
—*Photographs courtesy of Wofford College*

1907 POSTCARD VIEW OF OLD MAIN

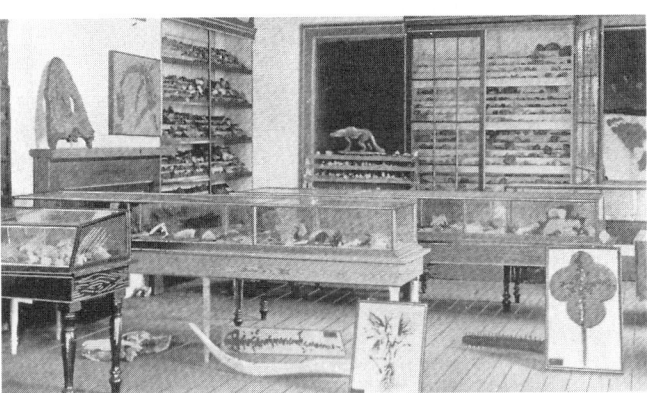

Chemistry lab and geology classroom from 1898.
—Photographs courtesy of Wofford College

Wofford students traditionally have rubbed the misspelled word on this plaque in the Old Main building, seeking good luck on examinations and protection from the spelling gremlin. *—Courtesy of Mark Olencki*

TEXTILE INSTITUTE. SPARTANBURG. S. C.

SAMPLE BOOK No. 4
ADDRESS MODEL MILL
SPARTANBURG, S. C.

THIS BOOK CONTAINS SAMPLES
OF
"CHARACTER CLOTH"
(Trade Mark Reg. March 9, 1920)

"CHARACTER CLOTH" IS 30 INCHES WIDE
UNLESS OTHERWISE STATED
ALL STYLES IN THIS BOOK 7½c PER YD.

MADE IN THE MODEL MILL
BY TEXTILE INSTITUTE STUDENTS
EARNING AN EDUCATION

In 1911 David English Camak, a Methodist preacher, opened a school primarily for mill workers. Under the Camak plan people worked two weeks and used their earnings to attend school for two weeks. The workers were paired so that work in the mill could continue uninterrupted. By 1913 Camak's success was assured with the building of Hammond Hall, (inset image), which is currently in use as a men's dormitory. The top photograph was taken at the opening of the model mill that was built to train mill workers at Textile Industrial Institute. Workers at the model mill produced fabric called "character cloth," a name that reflected Camak's intent to develop not only his workers' skills but also their minds and hearts. The college sold the model mill to Powell Knitting Company in the 1920s, and the mill closed in the 1990s. The college is now known as Spartanburg Methodist College.

—*Photographs courtesy of Lockwood Greene, Wofford College*

CHARACTER CLOTH
—*Courtesy of Spartanburg Methodist College*

Samuel B. Ezell, the bearded man, stands before his hardware store with his employees. Ezell operated his store in the Spartan Inn, so this photograph was taken before 1910. A chilled plow is one that has been hardened by a special foundry process. Also shown here is the interior of Ezell's hardware store around 1900.

—*Courtesy of B & B Studio*

Top Center: The United States mail service in the 1880s.

—*Courtesy of the Herald-Journal Willis Collection, Spartanburg County (SC) Public Libraries*

Center: The interior of the Dunbar Brothers' Carriage Shop on East Main Street looked like this in 1900.

—*Courtesy of Ned Austell*

John A. Henneman stands before his jewelry store on Morgan Square in the 1880s. Henneman came to Spartanburg in 1859 and served as mayor in the late 1880s. He proved himself feisty when he braved the anger of a mob and spiked a cannon they had wheeled before the city jail in an effort to remove and hang a prisoner. By driving a spike into the fuse hole at the top of the cannon and breaking off the spike with a side blow of the hammer, Henneman made it impossible to remove the spike and rendered the cannon useless. On September 27, 1891, Henneman heard a man and woman quarreling in a house and went in to quiet them. Henneman and the man came out of the house shouting at each other. When the man went back inside, Henneman said, "You are going after your pistol, are you?" and drew his own and also went into the house. A shot was heard, and the two men came rolling out of the door. The other man had Henneman's gun and shot him with it. John Henneman died a few minutes later.

RIGHT: The first telephone in Spartanburg County ran from this store in the city to Cate's store in Glenn Springs. The photograph was taken in 1888.
—*Courtesy of Mrs. W. C. Cannon*

BELOW: R. O. Pickens came to Spartanburg and started his roofing business in the old Spartan Inn in 1904. Pickens, second from the left, and his crew set out on a job. —*Courtesy of R. O. and B. R. Pickens*

OPPOSITE PAGE TOP: The Herring Furniture Store in 1905.

OPPOSITE PAGE BOTTOM: The Chero-Cola Company bottled its drink in Spartanburg to compete with Coca-Cola before that company had its own local bottling plant. Chero-Cola played on local pride in its advertisements: "Insist on having your drinks made by recognized bottlers–it costs YOU no more."
—*Photographs courtesy of the Herald-Journal Willis Collection, Spartanburg County (SC) Public Libraries*

C.D. KENNY CO.
TEAS
COFFEE & SUGAR
THIS WILL BE THE NEW HOME
OF WESTERN UNION TELEGRAPH CO.
Chero-Cola
DRINK
Chero-Cola
THERE'S NONE SO GOOD
5¢
DRINK
Chero-Cola
THERE'S NONE SO GOOD
5¢
No. 1.
Chero
Cola

Dupre's Book Store was founded in 1852 and was long a part of the intellectual life of the county. In this mid-1890s photograph the store is on Morgan Square; it later moved to East Main Street. Dupre's offered new and used books, stationery, prints, pens, and other office supplies. It was also a place where people gathered to gossip, browse through books, and generally wile away the hours. Warren Dupre, who assumed control in 1887, stands in the doorway with his son Wallace; to his right is Gabriel Cannon and to his left is a clerk, Samuel L. Cavis, and a porter whose name is unknown.
—Courtesy of Mrs. W. C. Cannon

Harry Price opened his store for men in 1903 in the east half of the building on the corner of West Main and South Church streets, Price catered to a middle-class trade, advertising that he sought to fill the "wants of every gentleman so far as they pertain to Man's Furnishings." He did so by offering shirts from 50 cents to a $1.50, neckwear from 25 cents to 75 cents, and men's straw hats from 35 cents to $3.00. Harry Price, third from the left, stands before his store in 1904 with staff and his dog Lucille. —Courtesy of Harry Price

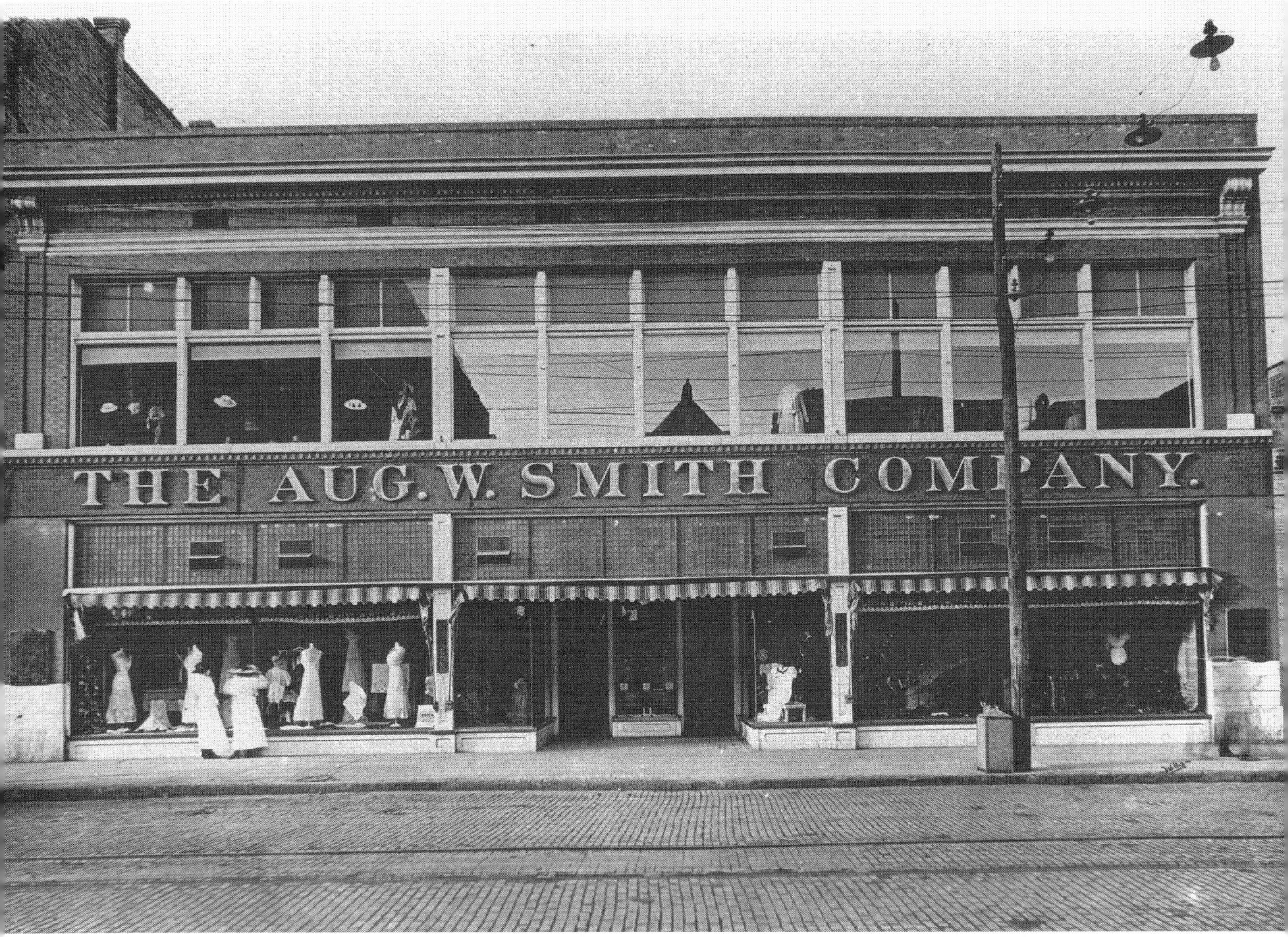

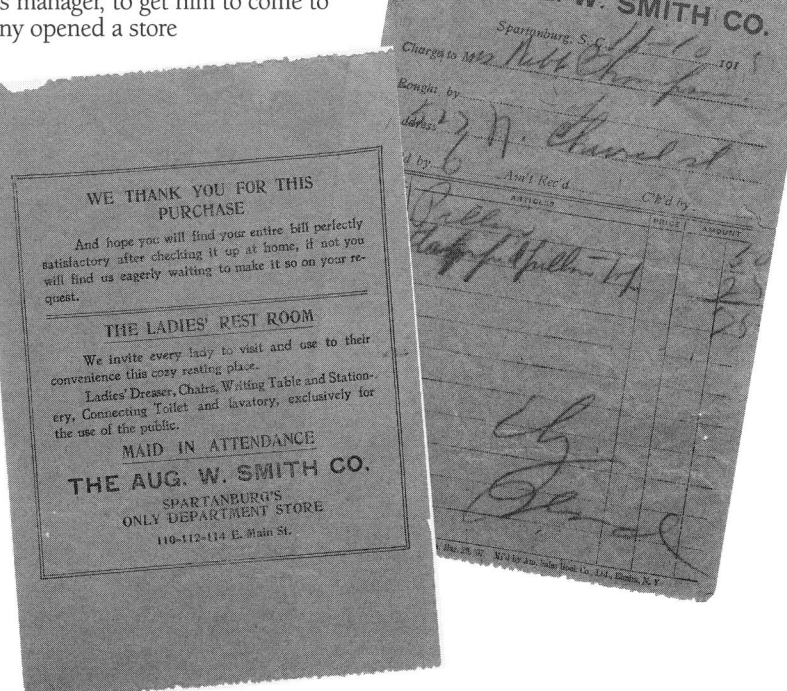

In 1890 Augustus W. Smith, a textile executive living in Woodruff, bought a store in his hometown of Abbeville. By 1901 he decided to move the store to Spartanburg and sold a half interest in the business to Frank McGee, the store's manager, to get him to come to Spartanburg as its manager. The Aug. W. Smith Company opened a store on East Main Street. In 1925 McGee and city officials made a deal that if the store were to move farther east on Main Street, the city would widen the roadway from Liberty to Pine. So the Aug. W. Smith Company purchased the Chapman property and built its new store. Meanwhile Smith had moved to Spartanburg and built a house at the corner of East Main Street and Mills Avenue, which now serves as the Converse College Alumnae House. In later years, Smith moved to Greenville to pursue his primary career in textiles.

—Photograph by Alfred T. Willis, courtesy of the Herald-Journal Willis Collection, Spartanburg County (SC) Public Libraries

WE THANK YOU FOR THIS PURCHASE

And hope you will find your entire bill perfectly satisfactory after checking it up at home, if not you will find us eagerly waiting to make it so on your request.

THE LADIES' REST ROOM

We invite every lady to visit and use to their convenience this cozy resting place.

Ladies' Dresser, Chairs, Writing Table and Stationery, Connecting Toilet and lavatory, exclusively for the use of the public.

MAID IN ATTENDANCE

THE AUG. W. SMITH CO.

SPARTANBURG'S ONLY DEPARTMENT STORE

110-112-114 E. Main St.

THE AUG. W. SMITH CO.

Spartanburg, S.C. 191

Charge to

Bought by

Address

Acc't Rec'd

Cr'd by

ARTICLES | PRICE | AMOUNT

Back & Front of an Early 1900s Receipt

—Courtesy of the Spartanburg County Regional Museum

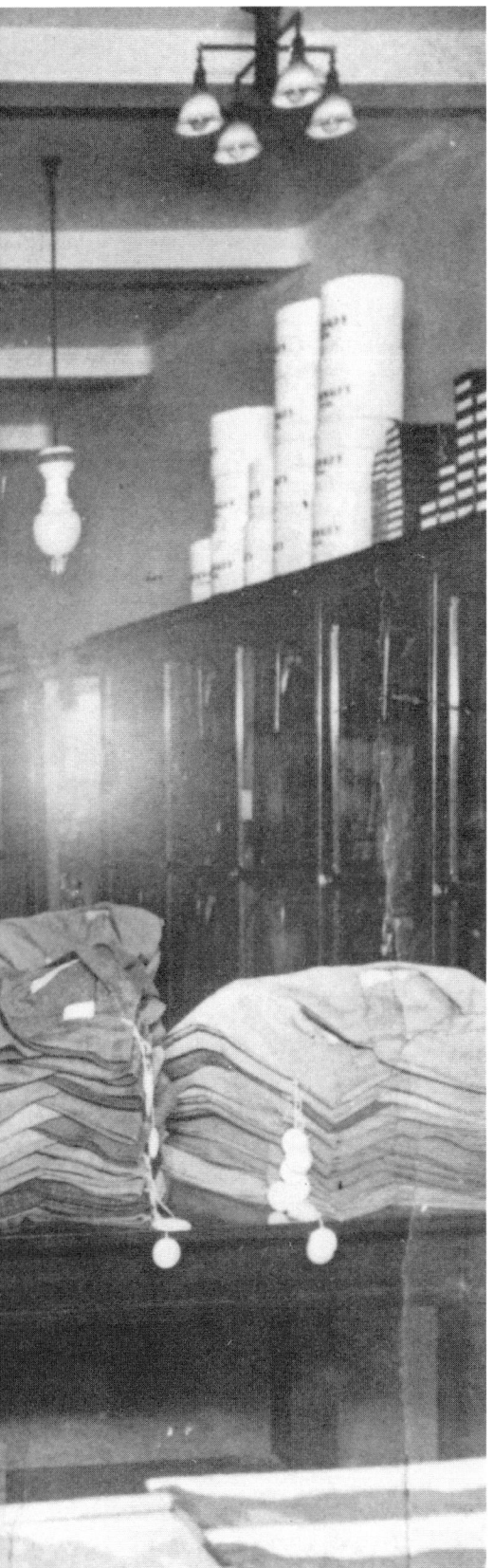

Established in 1886, Greenewald's served the clothing needs of the men of Spartanburg through the 1980s. Shortly after 1892, Greenewald's located in the Duncan Building on the north side of Morgan Square at the corner of Magnolia Street, but it soon moved over to the south side of the square. In 1910 it moved to the corner of South Church and West Main streets, where it remained until it closed. At the time this picture was taken in 1911, Greenewald's was the second store west of Church; part of the building was later removed to widen South Church Street. Max Greenewald, on the extreme left, was an active citizen, for he was involved both in volunteer firefighting and in running the entertainments at the old Opera House. Note the suitcases in the upper left, the splendid double staircase in the back of the store, the criss-crossed piles of trousers on the front table, and the hat boxes piled on top of the hat display cases with glass doors on the extreme right. Also notice the small travel trunk beneath the front table. Such sturdy trunks were a necessity for touring in that day. —*Courtesy of James D. Cobb*

RIGHT: African-American tenant farmhouse, 1913. Note the cotton grown up to the house; land owners insisted that tenants grow as much cotton as possible since the land owner was most often paid for the use of the land with a percentage of the crop. The tenant's dress is in sharp contrast to the structure of his house.

BELOW: Typical farmhouse and well, 1913.
—*Photographs courtesy of the South Caroliniana Library*

Agriculture remained the economic backbone of the county into the twentieth century. This photograph, taken in 1895, is typical in many ways. This photograph is of John M. Turner and his wife, Sara (seated), with their eight children. Eldest son, Will, stands next to the horse. The family is being photographed in front of their home. Rural people took pride in where they lived, as proof of what they had accomplished. Note the rough stone chimney topped by a brick flue; the fireplace has both interior and exterior fireboxes. Scenes similar to this were often duplicated in the western plains and rural East. —*Courtesy of the Spartanburg County Regional Museum*

This Spartanburg County cotton field was photographed about 1900. Although many African-American residents of the county, both during and after slavery, were skilled artisans, the majority worked in agriculture.
—*Courtesy of Ned Austell*

7. COTTON READY FOR SHIPMENT.

ABOVE & LEFT: The cost of shipping cotton was determined both by the bulk and the weight of the bale. It was important, therefore, to compress as much fiber into a bale as possible. This contraption pressed a bale of about 500 pounds, which became the standard weight toward the end of the nineteenth century. The old screw cotton press shown in this photograph was already outmoded at the time this postcard appeared in 1908.
—*Courtesy of the South Carolina Museum Commission*

OPPOSITE PAGE BOTTOM: Family and employees pose before the McMillin cotton gin in 1904. The girl sitting on the horse in the middle of the picture was the daughter of a Yankee soldier who was part of the Union army stationed in Spartanburg County during Reconstruction. Like so many other Yankees through the years, he had fallen in love with a Southern belle, married her, and settled at Fingerville. This photograph was taken only two years after a tragedy occurred at this gin. James Henry McMillin, the owner of the gin, was dressed up to go to town but stopped off at the gin to check on the work. When he looked at the gin, he saw a piece of lint caught in the blades of the saw, and he could not resist reaching over to snatch it up. As he did so, the blades of the saw caught his cuff link and cut off his arm. He soon died from the accident. Had he been wearing his work clothes he might not have been caught. One of McMillin's descendants comments, "There's such a thing as being too neat." —*Courtesy of the J. H. McMillin family*

In 1791 the state of South Carolina had granted Andrew McMillin 394 acres of land in the Fingerville area. Over the years the McMillins started various businesses, most of which were located just southeast of Fingerville on the North Pacolet River. Early in the nineteenth century, they built a small building, attached to the three-story structure to the left of the picture, as a gristmill powered by Obed Creek, which runs under the bridge shown here. Later, the three-story structure was built as a wheat mill, but Obed Creek did not provide the necessary power to drive the large water wheel. Therefore, the McMillins dammed the North Pacolet River, which was off to the top right of the picture, and built a sluice to the wheat mill to power the wheel. By the time this photograph was taken in 1910, neither mill was in operation. The building behind the wheat mill was a cotton warehouse, but it was not large enough to store all the bales, and the overflow can be seen in the yard. Leaving cotton out in the weather was common among Southern ginners. The house was the McMillin residence at the time, and the small cabin to the extreme right of the picture was an old blacksmith shop. This picture is a miniature history of the activities of ambitious Spartanburg farmers. Corn and wheat mills, cotton gins, and blacksmith's shops were the mainstays of much of the county's economy in the nineteenth century. —*Courtesy R. H. McMillin family*

Next to agriculture, cotton mills provided county residents of the last 20 years of the nineteenth century with their most common form of employment. Indeed, during the 1880s and 1890s mills went up in the city of Spartanburg and all over the county. Fingerville Manufacturing Co., a cotton mill, was begun in July 1888. Note the wagonload of cotton bales arriving on the right of the photograph.
—*Courtesy of the Herald-Journal Willis Collection, Spartanburg County (SC) Public Libraries*

BELOW: Mills were dependent on water power. Most of the rivers and streams that flowed through Spartanburg County did not carry enough water nor have a steep enough drop to create the power needed. Mill owners built dams, creating ponds with spillways that served the purpose. Many youngsters, wanting to escape the summer heat, swam in these ponds unattended by adults, and some, unfortunately, drowned.

LEFT: After the phenomenal success of the Glendale Cotton Mill, D. E. Converse wanted to expand his textile manufacturing interests. He bought the site of the South Carolina Iron Works at Clifton in 1880 and built the first of the Clifton Mills. The bridge to the extreme left of the photograph served the workers who lived in the mill village located across the river from the plant. The neat rows of houses above the mill constituted the other half of the village that housed the company's workers.
—*Courtesy of Stanley Converse*

BELOW: James Alfred Chapman came to Spartanburg from Kentucky in 1899 and built Inman Mill in 1902. The mill contained 15,000 spindles and 400 looms. The mill village was constructed to house workers who came from the mountains of North Carolina and Tennessee and from surrounding towns. The building to the left with the white porch was the company store. Lined up between the houses were the outhouses—the common sanitary facilities of the day. The two boxcars in the photograph illustrate the economic position of the Southern textile industry. The boxcar in the middle, partially hidden by a building, is from the Southern Railroad and may have just delivered the cotton stacked on the platform behind the mill. The boxcar in front of the company store is part of the Boston and Maine Railroad and is waiting to take finished goods to New York. The textile mills of the South bought their raw materials from their region but sold their manufactured goods to Northern capitalists. Most of the machinery used in the mills also was purchased in the North.

Here is a sample of workrooms of early twentieth-century mills.

The stitching room. Notice the double stacks of windows, all open, to provide as much natural light and air circulation as possible. The small and very high electric lights could not have been very helpful.

The washer-bleacher room.

Humidifiers were important to keep the cotton fibers from drying out and easily breaking. —*Photographs courtesy of Lockwood Greene*

A shift in a cotton mill had its photograph taken in 1915. Notice that the children are barefoot, the cause of the rampant spread of hookworm. Some of the mill workers look debilitated because of long working hours, poor diet (the cause of pellagra), and the frequent infestation of hookworm brought about by filthy outhouses and the lack of shoes. Around 1910 Walter Hines Page of North Carolina waged a newspaper war against two ever-present conditions of life for poor Southerners—poor sanitary conditions and bare feet. He wanted to rid Southerners of hookworm, but their politicians and newspaper editors became defensive and attacked Page as a traitor to the region for even suggesting the presence of the parasite among them.

The presence of so many young children seems striking in our age, but it was common in that day. Serious efforts to curb child labor began in the 1890s, but were resisted both by management and by many workers. Management profited from the lower wages they could pay children, while many parents would have suffered from the decrease in income that child labor legislation would have caused. The children, of course, were not consulted. Some child labor legislation was passed in the first two decades of the century (notably a 1917 law prohibiting employment below the age of 14), but the laws were often violated. In 1930 national and state laws set the minimum age at 16. —*Courtesy of Elisabeth Bridgeman Jones*

Mill supervisors in 1902.

Cotton from the fields begins its journey through the mill. The photograph obviously was staged for the grand opening of this new plant. Notice there is only one actual worker in the picture.
—*Courtesy of Lockwood Greene*

Except for the organ on the right, the interior of this mill village house was typical. The photograph was taken in 1913.

Pellagra, a chronic disease that was the scourge of thousands of Spartanburg County residents early in this century, was characterized by boils, stomach trouble, and general listlessness. There were two schools of thought in the scientific community on the cause of the problem: some believed that the cause was poor sanitary conditions, but others believed that it was inadequate diet. Diet was largely discounted because the disease occurred in the summer when a variety of foods was available, but few suspected that it took some six months for a dietary deficiency to manifest itself. In 1913 the United States' Public Health Service chose Spartanburg County as one of the areas in which to conduct studies of the disease. These pictures of typical mill village and farm dwellings were taken by the investigators in 1913 to illustrate sanitary and general living conditions among those people in the county most prone to contract the disease. Eventually, doctors discovered that diet was the cause of pellagra; in the winter months people ate white corn meal, sow belly, molasses, grits, and rice. White gravy and biscuits were a must with almost every meal, but people ate few vegetables and got few vitamins. —*Photographs courtesy of the South Caroliniana Library*

Camp Wadsworth

Photograph taken May 6, 1918, at Middletown, New York, showing the departure of a contingent of conscripts for Camp Wadsworth, South Carolina. Relatives and friends have gathered around the train to bid the future soldiers goodbye.
—*Courtesy of the Still Pictures Branch, National Archives II, College Park, Md.*

Airing tents. —*Courtesy of the Spartanburg County Regional Museum*

WADSWORTH FIELD MUSIC GUIDE—*Courtesy of James Crocker*

The Camp Wadsworth quarters of Capt. Dieves. The New Yorkers did not lack for imagination or playfulness in their Southern environment.

Soldiers were issued these cards upon arrival in Spartanburg. —*Courtesy James Crocker*

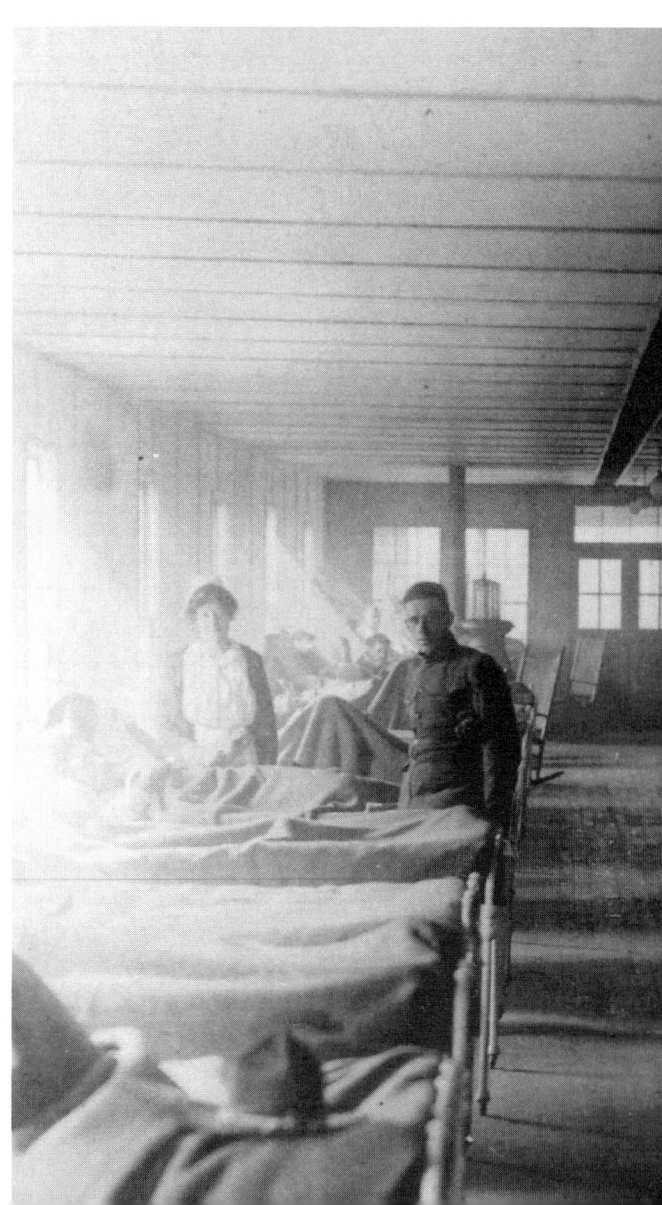

With training and constant drilling, civilians were turned into soldiers, but, as in every military camp in world history, the hospital ward was one of the most used facilities. This was Camp Wadsworth's Hospital Ward. The men do not look too bad and the nurse, holding one soldier's wrist as if she was taking his pulse, looks kind.

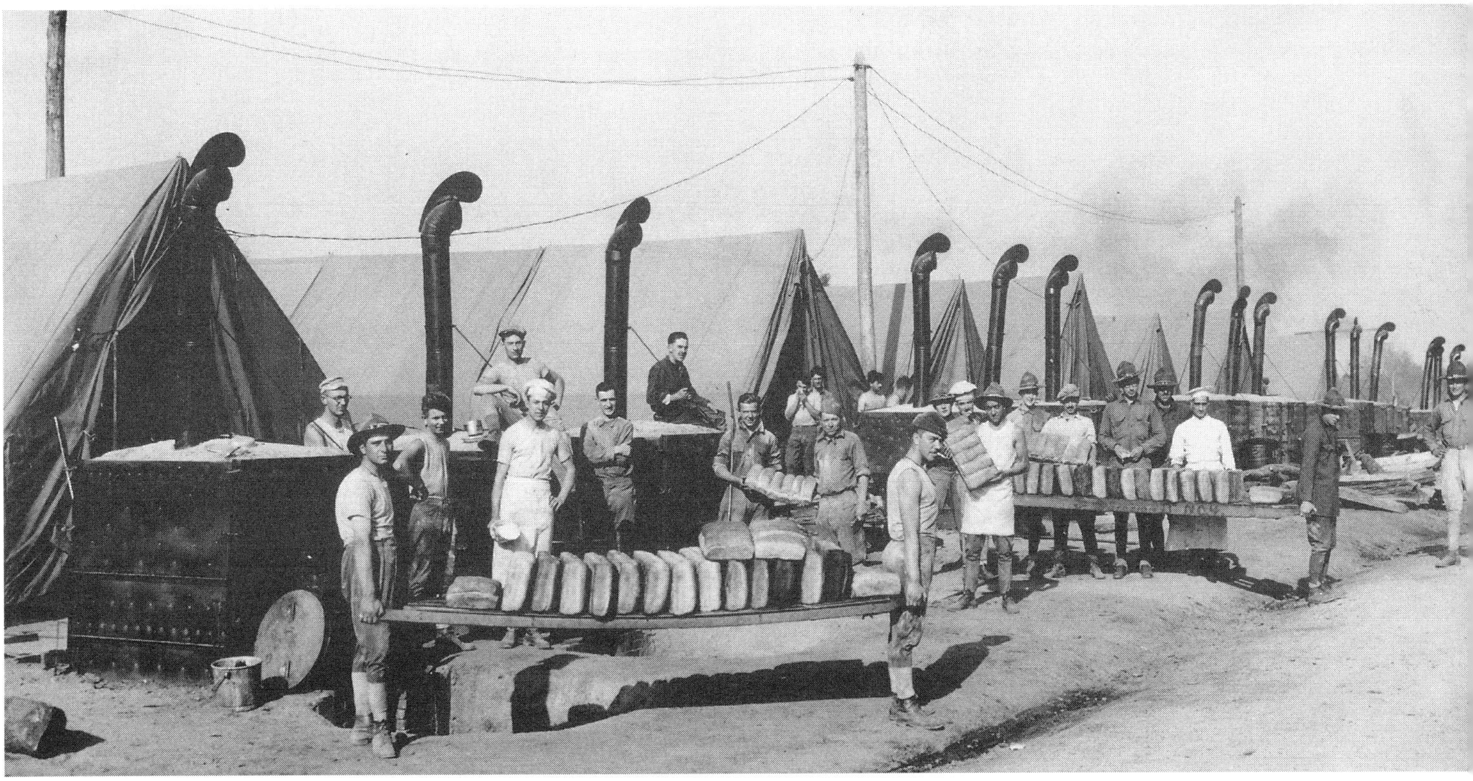

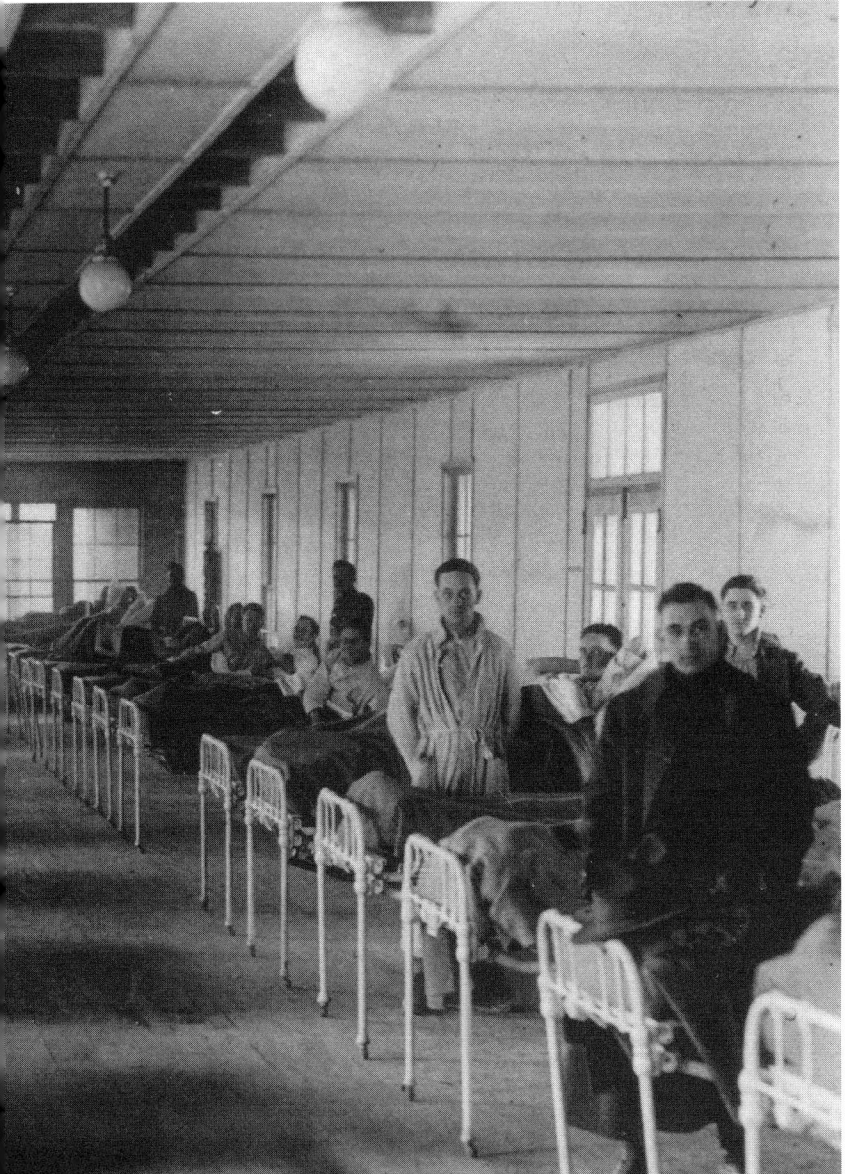

Above: Providing bread for the thousands of soldiers in the American camps became quite a problem, and this is one of the bread baking units that helped solve it.
—Photographs courtesy of the Still Pictures Branch, National Archives II, College Park, Md.

"MESS CALL" Means

C. D. Kenny Co.

BEST COFFEE AND TEAS

Scented blends 18c. to 28c.
Rio blends . 15c. to 20c.
Kenny special
MESS coffee 21c. wholesale

Only exclusive wholesale tea and coffee house in the city

127 Morgan Square
SPARTANBURG

Phone 747

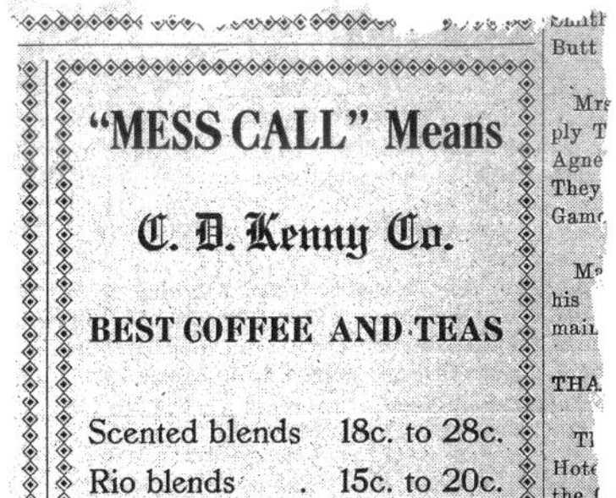

1918 Advertisement from the Wadsworth Newspaper *Gas Attack*

TOP: When America entered World War I, the army picked Spartanburg as a training camp for troops. In 1917, in less than a year, over 900 buildings were built and over 20,000 troops were encamped a few miles west of the city. All of the buildings shown here are either officers' quarters, quartermaster buildings, offices, or other storage, processing, and medical facilities. The soldiers slept in the tents. The presence of almost 27,000 men just on the outskirts of the city proved challenging and troublesome. Prices shot up, everything became crowded, and the city began to realize in some ways what a small place it actually was. But the strain did not last long; in two years it was all over, and the camp was empty.
—*Courtesy of the Spartanburg County Regional Museum*

CENTER ROW: The black soldier was photographed by P. A. Gadsden of Spartanburg. These three other Wadsworth soldiers enjoyed an afternoon at a waterfall next to a Spartanburg mill. On the far right, two soldiers pose in a local cotton field for a photograph to be sent home to their families —*Photographs courtesy of James Crocker*

OPPOSITE PAGE BOTTOM: The New York soldiers came to Spartanburg to train, and that meant a lot of marching up and down the county's dusty roads. Most of these troops are looking at Alfred T. Willis as he photographs them, but some seem to be eyeing the motorcycle on which they probably wish they could ride off.
—*Courtesy of the Herald-Journal Willis Collection, Spartanburg County (SC) Public Libraries*

These non-coms of the 27th Division brace to demonstrate what the army hoped to produce from its training facility at the camp. Note the difference in the coats of the second and third men from the right and the leggings that button up the leg from the top of the shoe.
—*Courtesy of the Still Pictures Branch, National Archives II, College Park. Md.*

Many soldiers arrived at Wadsworth with medals for service on the Mexican border (left) and after the war received a World War I victory medal (right).
—*Courtesy of James Crocker*

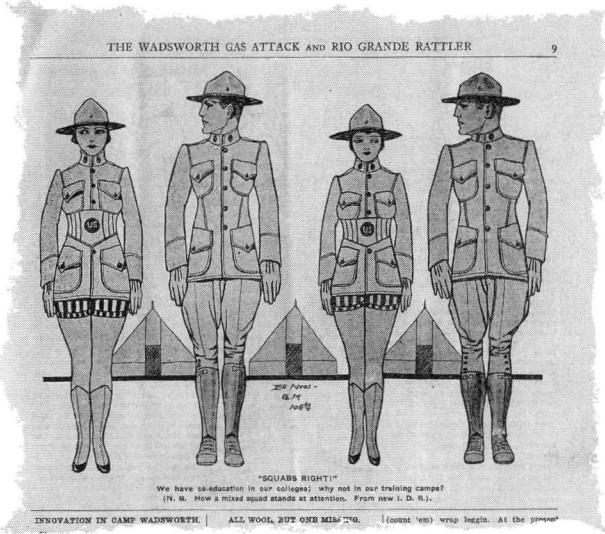

1918 Cartoon from the
Wadsworth Newspaper *Gas Attack*

"SQUABS RIGHT!"
We have co-education in our colleges; why not in our training camps?
(N. B. How a mixed squad stands at attention. From new I. D. R.).

INNOVATION IN CAMP WADSWORTH. | ALL WOOL, BUT ONE MISSING. | (count 'em) wrap leggin. At the present

Living at Camp Wadsworth in the summer heat must have
been a shock for New Yorkers; having to bear the hardships of
snow must have led to additional griping about the "sunny
South." —*Courtesy of the Spartanburg County (SC) Public Libraries*

BATTERY STREET

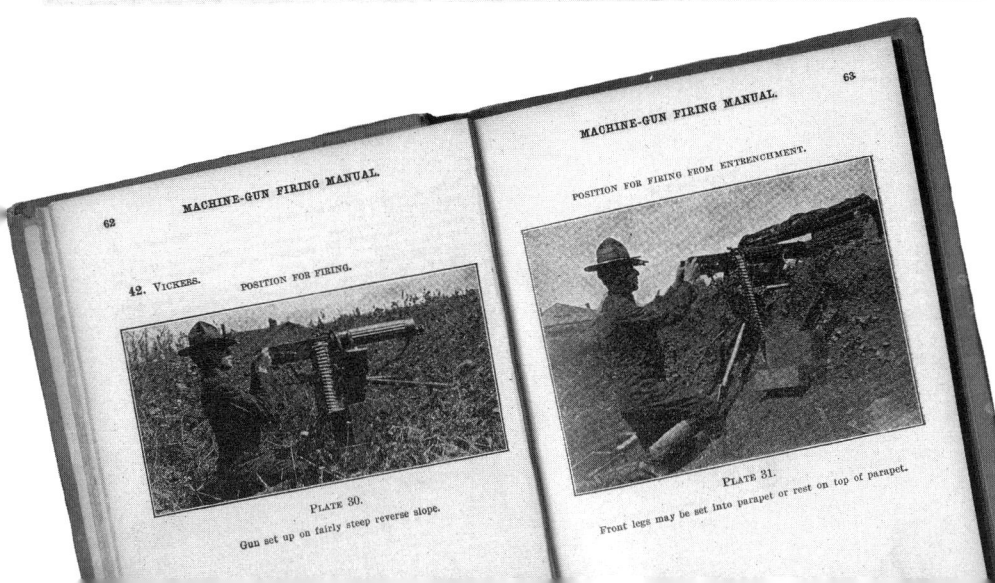

MACHINE-GUN FIRING MANUAL.   MACHINE-GUN FIRING MANUAL.

62   63

42. VICKERS.   POSITION FOR FIRING.   POSITION FOR FIRING FROM ENTRENCHMENT.

PLATE 30.   PLATE 31.
Gun set up on fairly steep reverse slope.   Front legs may be set into parapet or rest on top of parapet.

One of the Many Regulation
"How To" Manuals
—*Courtesy of James Crocker*

Boom and Subsistence • 199

It was inevitable that with an excess of males out at Camp Wadsworth, there would be some fraternization with the local Spartanburg girls, especially since the 27th Division was known as a Yankee "aristocratic" crowd; after all, one of its officers was a Vanderbilt. Sometimes the result was courtship and marriage, which was the case with Howard Andrew Gilmartin and Lois Dean, shown here at Camp Wadsworth with the appropriate chaperones. Lois was 18 at the time, and the South was the South, no matter how "aristocratic" the Yankees happened to be.
—*Courtesy of the Johnson family*

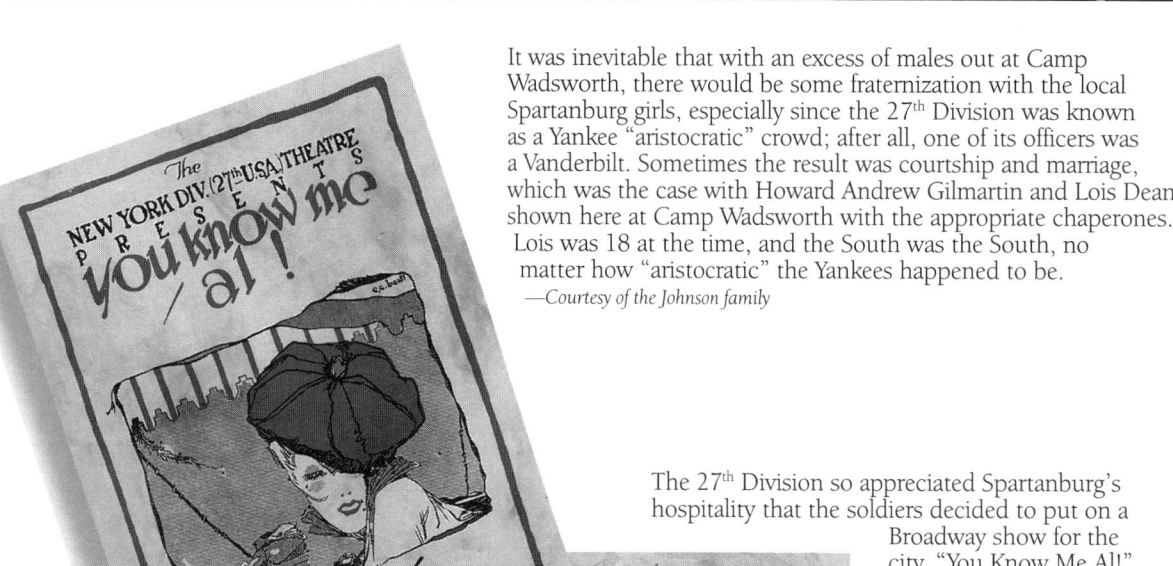

The New York Div. (27th) U.S.A. Theatre
P R E S E N T S
The You Know Me Al!

program

HOTEL CLEVELAND

The social center of Spartanburg and the one spot in the South that furnishes the New Yorker with a touch of his home town.

Drop in for supper after the theatre tonight and forget you ever left Broadway. You'll find our food, service and music excellent.

The 27th Division so appreciated Spartanburg's hospitality that the soldiers decided to put on a Broadway show for the city. "You Know Me Al!" with a cast of dozens was presented at the Harris Theater to large crowds of appreciative citizens. On the back of the program, the Hotel Cleveland, a relatively new facility then, offered the soldiers a bit of Broadway glamour of its own. —*Courtesy of the Spartanburg County Regional Museum*

Many soldiers sent these postcards home.
—*Courtesy of James Crocker*

At 2 a.m. on November 11, 1918, the news of the armistice ending World War I came to Spartanburg. Immediately, Major John G. Floyd called the railways and the fire department, and whistles began to blow all over the city. People thronged to the center of town, and the celebrations continued through the next day. Here celebrants crowd around General Morgan's statue where, earlier, the Kaiser had been burned in effigy. —*Courtesy of the Spartanburg County Regional Museum*

Despite a few boom years immediately following World War I, economic hard times came to the South and to Spartanburg County much earlier than to the rest of the nation. While much of the country was experiencing the economic boom and social iconoclasm characteristic of the "Roaring 20s," Spartanburg and other cotton counties were steadily sinking into economic depression. In spite of several attempts, tex-

Depression and War
Crisis
1920 - 1945

tile leadership in the Southeast would not cooperate in an effort to control production. Textiles were abundant, and prices dropped.

After 1923 the trend in the industry was toward fewer working days, shorter hours, and less pay. Agriculture also suffered as cotton prices moved steadily downward. Yet during the 1920s, the city of Spartanburg seemed prosperous as it feverishly promoted itself. The city undertook municipal projects that reflected optimism and confidence:

it organized and financed celebrations of the visits of national heroes, Charles Lindbergh and Amelia Earhardt; it rerouted the Southern Railway track off East Main Street; it constructed South Carolina's first municipal airport; it provided the state's first air mail service; and it built a new water works and a new skyscraper, the Montgomery Building.

Dogged determination, not optimism, marked the countryside. Farmers continued to use traditional farming methods, which eroded and exhausted the soil. Merchants, whose credit to the tenant farmer and sharecropper propped up the crop lien system of agriculture, risked losing money and, therefore, insisted that tenants plant cotton, which was non-perishable and for which there was always a market, however depressed. Economics and tradition prevented diversification of crops. Year after year cotton returned less and less on the investment of time and money. The agricultural future of the county was somewhat brightened in the early 1920s when several local farmers planted the first commercial peach trees. But it would be years before the fruit partially made up for falling cotton prices. Not until after World War II did peaches dominate the agriculture of the county. Finally, the introduction and increased popularity of synthetic fibers ended the growing of cotton in the county for 20 years. Recently, cotton planting has enjoyed a revival due to consumer demand for the fiber's unique qualities, but competition from Texas, California, and abroad has severely limited the scope of its rejuvenation.

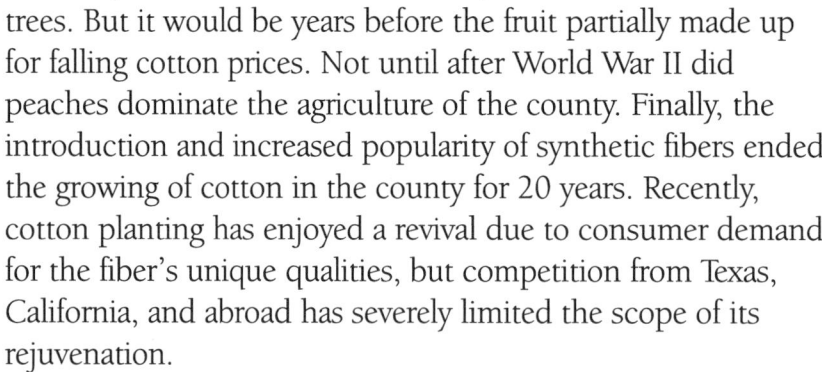

SPARTANBURG COUNTY PEACH LABELS

When the depression came to the rest of the nation in the early thirties, the condition of the county's beleaguered economy became dire. Many businesses closed. By the middle of 1933 all six banks in the city had failed, and poverty enveloped not only tenant farmers, sharecroppers, and mill workers, but also many other residents. During the thirties, all of the problems that had long plagued industry and agriculture were

magnified to calamity. The cotton mills that did not close shortened hours and lowered wages. The action worked in a fashion, for when combined with a resistance to "the dole," the number of county residents "on relief" never rose over 14 percent. There was no money with which to pay employees, and mills gave out tokens redeemable at the company store in the mill village. Hundreds of mill workers who, in the past, might have had reason to resent the company store, blessed it in the thirties.

MILL TOKENS FROM MAYFAIR, BEAUMONT & SPARTAN MILLS

Gloom fell over the land, and at times the animosities that had long existed between town and country, management and worker, land owner and tenant, exploded into bitterness and outright hostilities. Especially bitter was the strike of Spartanburg textile workers in 1934, a strike that included textile workers from Maine to Alabama, indeed, the largest strike in American history. The textile industry had voluntarily entered into an agreement under a federal program called the NRA in order to increase wages, profits, and employment, as well as reduce hours and protect labor's right to bargain. But the agreement did not turn out as workers had hoped. They struck mostly against the "stretch-out" (a practice in which mill management tried to get one worker to do what had traditionally been the work of two or three), the reclassifying of positions to reduce wages, and an uneven enforcement of the provisions of the NRA agreement. Spartanburg textile workers went from mill to mill in "flying squadrons" urging fellow workers to walk off the job and close the mill. Tension mounted until seven strikers were shot to death in Honea Path. Ten thousand people attended the collective funeral, but the strike collapsed. In violation of an agreement brokered by the federal government between strikers and mill management, the mills black-balled workers who had organized the strike, and they never worked in the mills again.

Throughout the Great Depression none suffered more than Spartanburg's farmers, many of whom had resigned themselves to hopelessness. Many believe that in hard times farmers can always get along because they can grow food. But by the 1930s

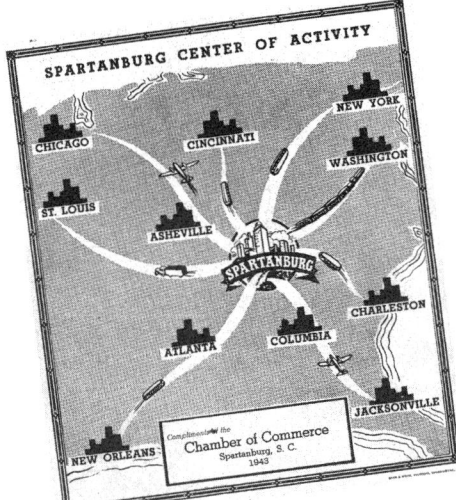

1943 BACK COVER
ADVERTISEMENT PROMOTING
SPARTANBURG AS A RAILROAD
HUB IN THE SOUTHEAST
—*Courtesy of James Crocker*

much of the county's land had been abused too long and was so depleted in essential nutrients as to be unreliable even for food crops. For decades people grew crops on hills in vertical rows. Even when some farmers sowed horizontally, they did not provide for proper runoff in heavy rain. The topsoil had long ago washed away, but fertilizers introduced in the 1870s had remedied that situation and given new life to an already troubled land. In the twentieth century, as farmers grew more and more cotton without trying to deal with erosion, the land simply continued to wash away. Most green, grassy, and pine-forested areas seen about the county today were wasted, washed-out dirt patches in the late 1920s. By the thirties, huge gullies marked the farms. Every road was bounded by deep crevices, and rivers and streams were gorged with sediment.

In 1933 the Soil Erosion Service of the United States Department of the Interior chose Spartanburg County for its pilot erosion prevention project. By 1935, when the service was renamed the Soil Conservation Service, the department's director, Dr. Thomas S. Buie, and his associates were experimenting with erosion prevention techniques on a large scale. With the introduction of terracing, the planting of trees, grasses, and kudzu, and the contouring of the land, the county's soil erosion and nutrient problems began to be managed, and the soil was gradually enriched and reclaimed for farming. No effort in the county's history has ever been so large and done so much to benefit its people. The Soil Conservation Service prevented Spartanburg County and many other similar counties from becoming wastelands. With initiatives such as rural electrification, soil conservation, and federal labor and industrial regulation, no region of the nation benefited as much from the New Deal as did the American South.

Landscape & Architecture

A 1924 panorama of downtown Spartanburg by Alfred Willis. Note the construction of the Montgomery Building on the far left.
—*Courtesy of Wofford College*

A photograph at dusk, looking down Magnolia Street (note the top of the Courthouse on the left) toward the Morgan Hotel.

A rare night image of Morgan Square from the east end looking down West Main Street. The last tall building on the right side of the street is the Cleveland Hotel.

In 1920 Spartanburg City Council voted to remove this fountain from Morgan Square and replace it with a drinking fountain. When John B. Cleveland gave the land known as Cleveland Park to the city in 1923, the concrete fountain was placed there. It now stands in a small greenspace at the intersection of North Church Street and Highway 9.

—*Photographs courtesy of the Herald-Journal Willis Collection, Spartanburg County (SC) Public Libraries*

Top: This is what Mills Avenue in Converse Heights looked like in the mid-1920s. The Converse College tower can be seen in the background center. Converse Heights, a farm area that had originally been part of the plantation of Major Govan Mills, was opened for development in 1906. In 1909 S. M. Bagwell planted shade trees on both sides and in the middle of Mills Avenue. —*Courtesy of Wofford College*

Bottom: Alfred Willis took this view of West Main Street looking toward Morgan Square in 1925. Notice the iron fences running along both sides of the street to prevent people from falling into what was at that time a fairly deep ravine. —*Courtesy of the Herald-Journal Willis Collection, Spartanburg County (SC) Public Libraries*

Saint John Street was not much more than an alley in the early 1920s. To the left of the photograph is the edge of the site of the Montgomery Building. The brick structure behind the workmen is the Southern Railway's freight depot, and just beyond it is the old Hastoc School founded in 1907. Into the 1920s the Hastoc School educated an exclusive clientele of boys under the direction of Professor Hugh T. Shockley. The upper floor had bedrooms for about 12 boarding students. A different building was used to educate girls. Although its location and appearance were unimposing, the academic standards of Hastoc were reputed to be very high.

—*Photograph by Alfred T. Willis, courtesy of the Herald-Journal Willis Collection, Spartanburg County (SC) Public Libraries*

The empty lot on the corner of Magnolia and Walnut was the future site of the Federal Building, and in the true entrepreneurial American spirit the emptiness was blocked from view by a string of billboards, rather artfully placed for a strictly commercial venture.
—*Courtesy of the Herald-Journal Willis Collection, Spartanburg County (SC) Public Libraries*

ABOVE: The residence of Captain John H. Montgomery stood at the corner of North Church and Elm (St. John) streets. Central United Methodist Church can be seen to its left.
—*Courtesy of Mrs. Victor Montgomery*

OPPOSITE PAGE: A wealthy New York businessman named Chapman built this building in 1912. In 1922 he sold it to Isaac Andrews and A. M. Law, who later sold his interest to Andrews. The Andrews Building was a classic example of the Chicago school of skyscraper architecture, and it was the county's finest early twentieth-century building. In 1922 the Central National Bank moved into the bottom floor, and banks occupied that space until the Andrews Building was destroyed in 1977. In the course of demolition, everything had been prepared for the building to be blown up when it simply collapsed, killing five men. —*Courtesy of the Charlie Mae Campbell family*

Top: Beginning construction of the Montgomery Building in 1923.
—*Courtesy of Mrs. Victor Montgomery*

Bottom: The original theater of the Montgomery Building as it looked in the 1920s. Notice the letter **M** over the stage. —*Courtesy of Lockwood Greene*

Opposite Page: The Montgomery Building was constructed on the site where John H. Montgomery had once built his home. At groundbreaking ceremonies in 1923, a large hole was dug with a steam shovel, and the house pushed into it. Over the remains of Captain John's house rose this wonderful structure with dark bay windows stacked one on top of the other, striped awnings, and iron marquee. The building had the look of prosperity, and the cars parked out front testify to the vibrant business life that went on inside. —*Courtesy of the Herald-Journal Willis Collection, Spartanburg County (SC) Public Libraries*

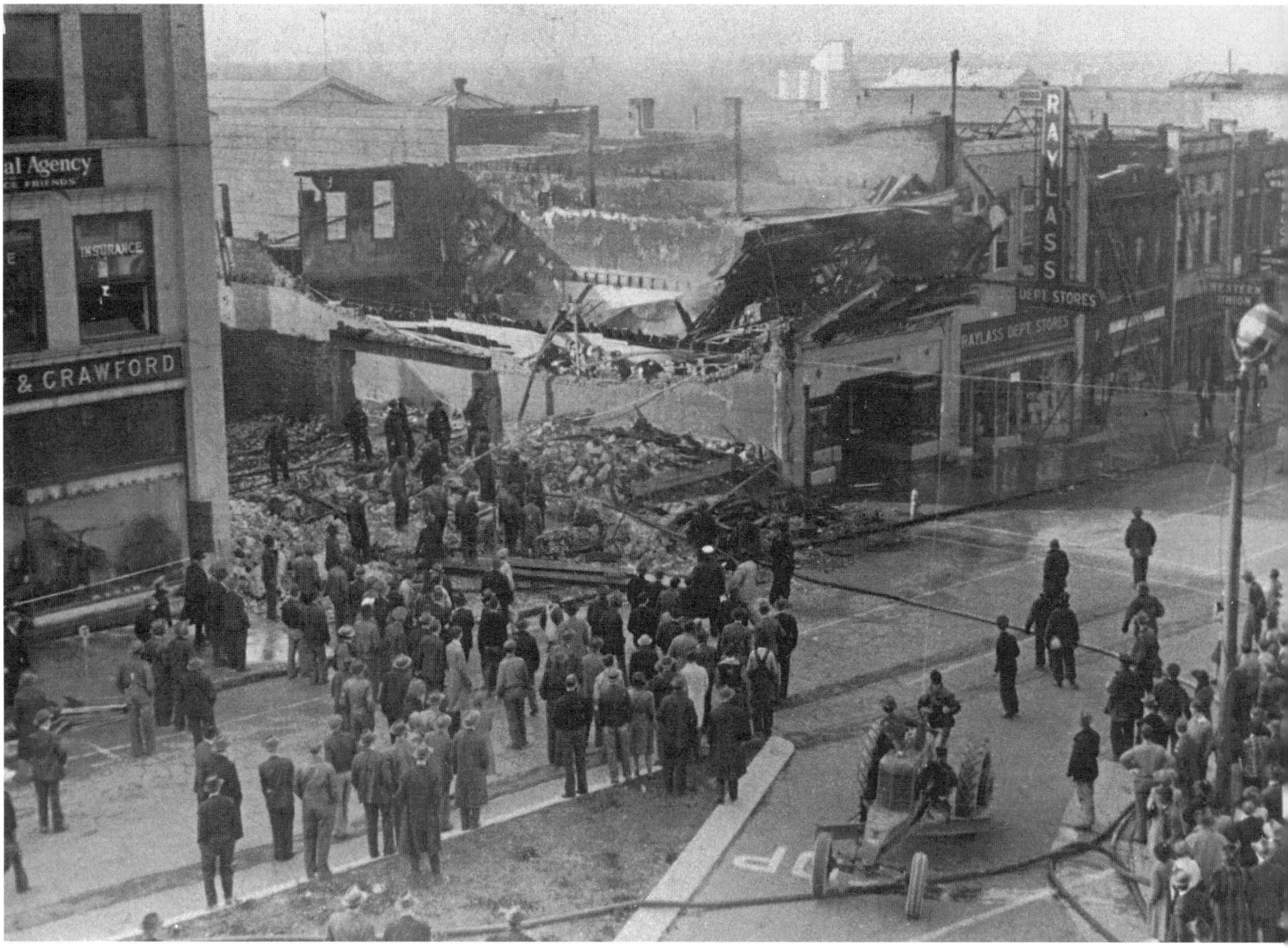
al Agency
INSURANCE
& CRAWFORD
RAYLASS
DEPT STORES
RAYLASS DEPT. STORES

SPARTANBURG
FIRE
AERIAL
No.1
DEPT.

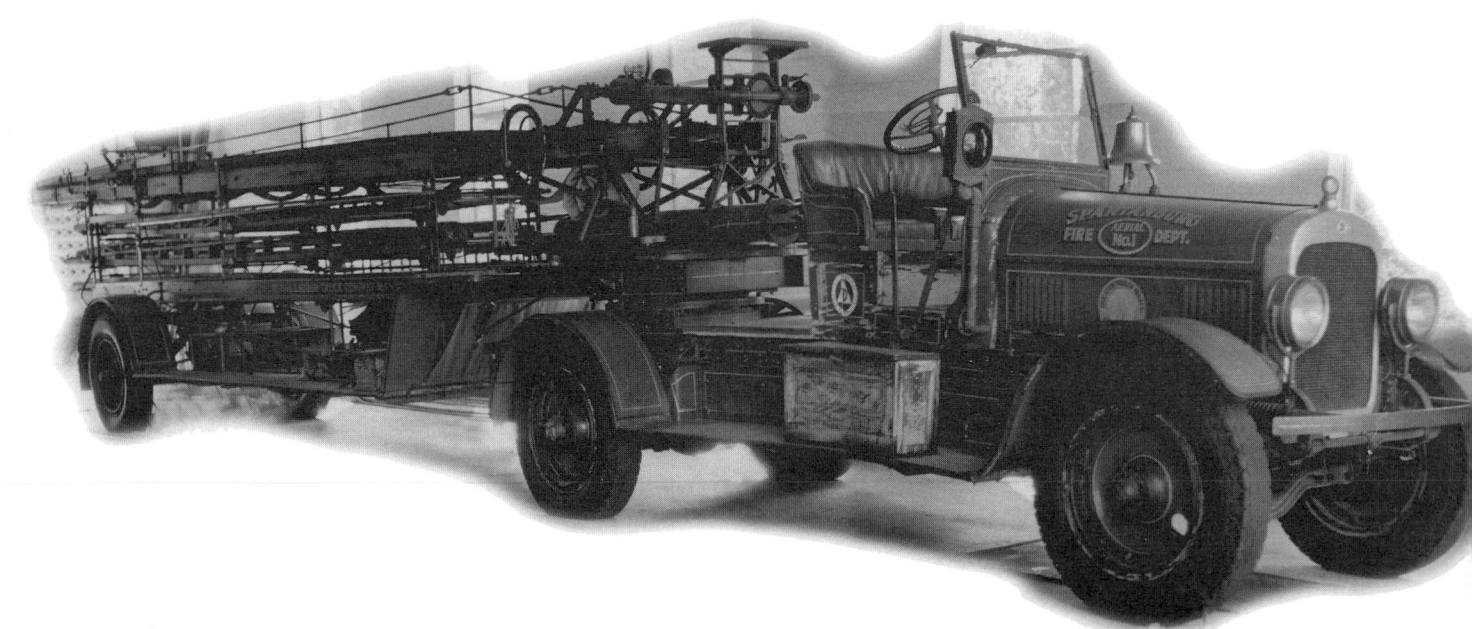

Opposite Page Top: Around mid-century there were three great fires that changed the look of the downtown area. This one took place at the Leader department store in the early 1940s. Two others occurred in the 1960s: the First Baptist Church and the old Elite, which had become a cafeteria. —*Courtesy of B & B Studio*

Opposite Page Bottom: A contemporary photograph of an actual 1926 fire truck kept at the fire department station on Union Street. —*Courtesy of the Spartanburg County Regional Museum*

Below: The original design of the First Baptist Church of Spartanburg on East Main Street. —*Courtesy of the Herald-Journal Willis Collection, Spartanburg County (SC) Public Libraries*

ABOVE: In the 1930s automobile traffic was becoming heavy in the city of Spartanburg. By contrast, in the country, many farm families (if they were lucky) traveled in wagons pulled by mules.

OPPOSITE PAGE TOP: By the late 1920s buses were competing with the streetcars. As seen here, buses were serving even the mill villages (in this case Saxon). This new form of public transportation, which did not need expensive rail tracks, could reach people wherever satisfactory roads existed. Thus reliable public transportation was extended beyond the capabilities of the electric rail system.

OPPOSITE PAGE MIDDLE: In the city the electric street car was still the transportation of choice for many.

OPPOSITE PAGE BOTTOM: Ford Model Ts and a lone tractor in the far end of the building were displayed in Ernest Burwell's showroom in the 1920s.

—*Photographs courtesy of the Herald-Journal Willis Collection, Spartanburg County (SC) Public Libraries*

ABOVE: By the early 1920s automobile and truck traffic made getting around downtown dangerous. To protect pedestrians from the trucks, cars, and trolleys converging at East Main and Liberty streets, the city installed this traffic control. Patrolman William C. Gash stands at his post; at the time he was the city's sole traffic officer.

OPPOSITE MIDDLE: Buses were beginning to compete with and replace streetcars by the mid-1920s when this photograph of the South Carolina Electric & Gas Company buses was taken.

OPPOSITE BOTTOM: A bicycle with a motor became surprisingly popular in the 1920s. Note the spelling of "Motocycles" on the window of the shop. Either the etymology of the word is obscure (it could mean a cycle that causes motion), or the painter could not spell.

—*Photographs courtesy of the Herald-Journal Willis Collection, Spartanburg County (SC) Public Libraries*

These jaunty bus drivers were photographed in the mid-1930s.
—*Courtesy of the Spartanburg County Regional Museum*

LEFT: Dr. and Mrs. C. E. Fleming built this fine home on the corner of East Main and South Dean Streets in 1884. The photograph probably dates from about the turn of the century when growing ivy had become faddish.
—*Courtesy of the Spartanburg County Regional Museum*

BELOW: In the 1920s the Rush Service Station was built into the front of the Fleming home; this strange adaptation was an indication of how the people in Spartanburg had taken to the automobile and how the commercialization of East Main Street had inevitably proceeded by that decade. Rush offered many services; as a member of AAA he offered "Free Road Service," as well as "Washing and Greasing" and an "Auto Laundry." —*Courtesy of George Mullinax*

ABOVE: Removing the tracks from across East Main Street in 1925 was a sign of progress to the city. Since the coming of automobiles, this railroad crossing had seriously impeded the flow of traffic. As the city became more sophisticated and train traffic increased, the fumes and noise from the engines grew more annoying. Southern Railway built a line around the center of town. The crossing guard directed traffic and lowered the railroad barriers across Main Street from the elevated small cabin to the left of the tracks.
—*Photograph by Alfred T. Willis, courtesy of Nicholas Harakas*

LEFT: By the middle 1930s the long track dispute in Spartanburg had been resolved. Buses took over public transportation, and only one trolley, the Clifton, remained in operation. In 1936 all trolleys, city and suburban, were discontinued. This photograph, made in 1935, shows three buses and the last remaining city trolley.
—*Courtesy of the W. S. Glenn Collection*

A new highway was built from Spartanburg to Camp Wadsworth in 1917. In the early 1920s the state decided to extend that road to Greenville. This photograph was taken of the work being done on S.C. 29 where I-85 now crosses it. Eventually the road would be widened into a four-lane highway, the first in South Carolina. —*Courtesy of Jane S. Cook*

One of the original mile markers for U.S. 29.
—*Courtesy of Mark Olencki*

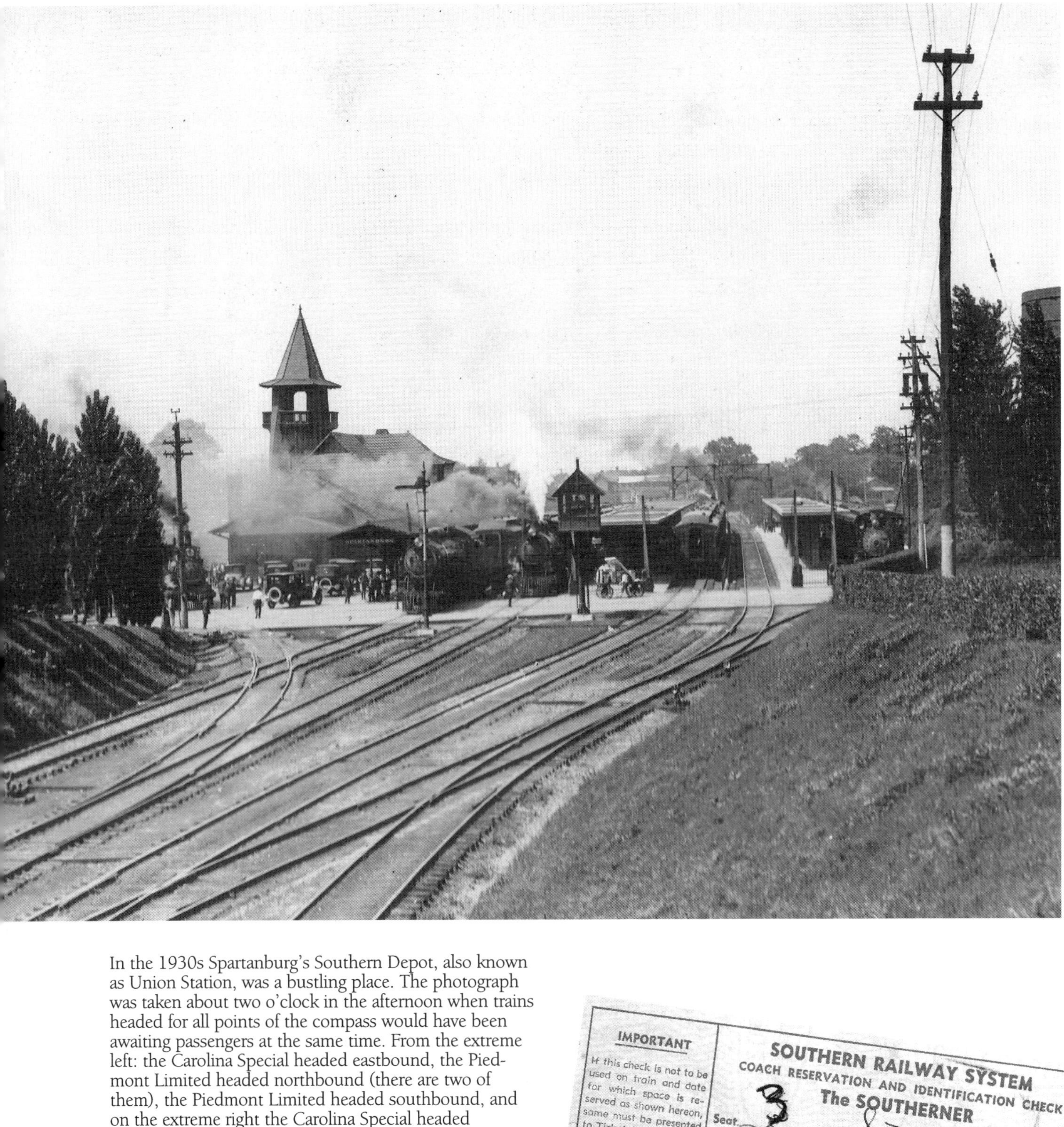

In the 1930s Spartanburg's Southern Depot, also known as Union Station, was a bustling place. The photograph was taken about two o'clock in the afternoon when trains headed for all points of the compass would have been awaiting passengers at the same time. From the extreme left: the Carolina Special headed eastbound, the Piedmont Limited headed northbound (there are two of them), the Piedmont Limited headed southbound, and on the extreme right the Carolina Special headed westbound. *—Courtesy of the Herald-Journal Willis Collection, Spartanburg County (SC) Public Libraries.*

IMPORTANT

If this check is not to be used on train and date for which space is reserved as shown hereon, same must be presented to Ticket Agent at least 24 hours prior to scheduled departure in order that reservation may be cancelled and reservation check exchanged for new date and reservation.

Form CRIC

SOUTHERN RAILWAY SYSTEM
COACH RESERVATION AND IDENTIFICATION CHECK
The SOUTHERNER

Seat 3 Car 83 Leave 6:14 P.M
FROM Phila. Pa. Date 3/31/43
TO Spartanburg-S.C. Ticket No. 68266

This check, good only in connection with rail ticket indicated above, should be shown when boarding train and presented to Conductor with ticket. Passenger should retain for identification and show to Conductor upon request.

GOOD ONLY ON DATE STAMPED ON BACK HEREOF

Not Good for Passage

Has No Cash or Refund Value

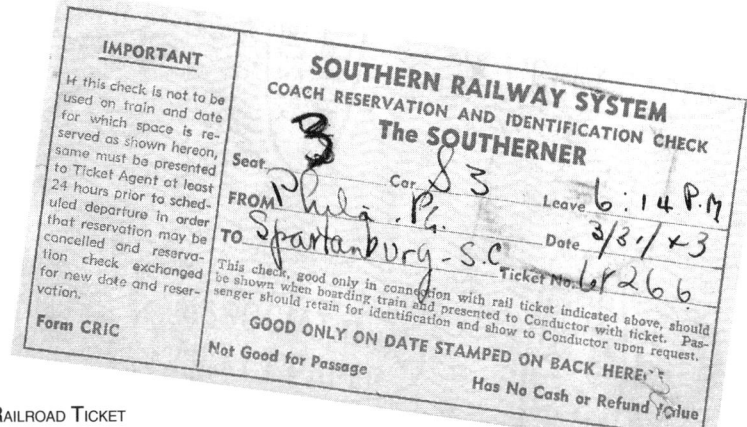

1943 Railroad Ticket
—Courtesy of the Spartanburg County Regional Museum

The Glenn Springs Hotel, 1930s.

A view of the main staircase above the
hotel lobby.
—*Photographs courtesy of the Herald-Journal Willis
Collection, Spartanburg County (SC) Public Libraries.*

Sitting rooms and lobby area of the hotel.

The Glenn Springs Hotel dining room.
—*Photographs courtesy of the Spartanburg County Regional Museum*

Sometime in the 1920s, a funeral procession of automobiles awaits its occupants before the Minter W. Bobo Funeral Company. Bobo's was located just south of the corner of Saint John and North Church streets. The double arches in the building next to it belong to the Harris Opera House. The Harris opened in 1907 and was used primarily for plays, musicals, and vaudeville. It claimed to be able to seat 2,000, but that figure seems exaggerated. In the years just before it was condemned, the Harris showed films. In this photograph the Harris billboard is advertising the LeRue Brothers, a vaudeville act.
—*Courtesy of the Spartanburg Herald-Journal*

Spartanburg opened the first commercial airport in South Carolina in September 1927. When Colonel Lindbergh came to the city one month later, the county's interest in aviation grew even brighter, but the greatest coup of all was the coming of air mail in 1928. On May 1, 1928, Eugene R. Brown flew Pitcairn Aviation's Mailwing, especially designed to carry mail, into the Spartanburg airport at 9:35 p.m. The plane could carry from 400 to 600 pounds of mail on the New York-to-Atlanta route. Spartanburg was one of only eight cities along the route that received the service.
—*Courtesy of the Herald-Journal Willis Collection, Spartanburg County (SC) Public Libraries*

Curtis military biplanes were on display at the Spartanburg Municipal Airport in the 1930s as part of a promotion for a flying school.
—*Courtesy of the Herald-Journal Willis Collection, Spartanburg County (SC) Public Libraries*

TOP: Congress established the Civilian Conservation Corps (CCC) in 1933 to provide jobs for the unemployed. The agency, run by the army, did most of its work in reforestation. Workers left their homes and lived in CCC barracks; for many village and city dwellers, this was their first rural experience. Since reforestation was part of the soil conservation effort in Spartanburg County (most of the pine forests evident today date from the 1930s), the government established a CCC camp at Switzer. This photograph of the camp dates from 1941.

BOTTOM: The Soil Conservation Service introduced Spartanburg County farmers to many alternative ways of preventing erosion. This 1941 photograph of Fernwood Orchard illustrates contour planting and strip cropping as well as the planting of various grains to hold the soil. In the background on the left is a kudzu meadow strip. Running along the top of the photograph is Highway 29, and the road running from top left to bottom right is Fernwood Drive. —*Photographs courtesy of Pat McKinney*

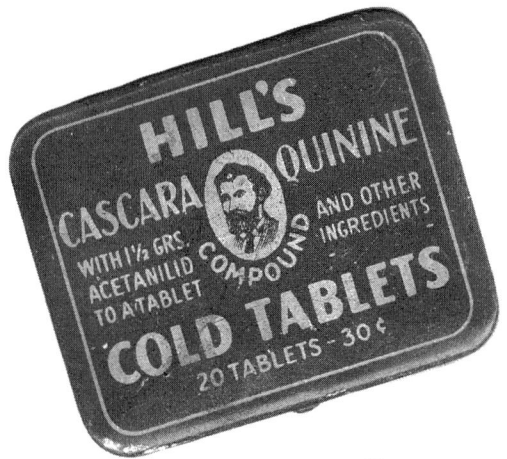

Although several private hospitals operated in the city, agitation for a tax-supported county hospital had existed since about 1910. After World War I the pressure for a public hospital increased, especially from the county medical association and the city council, which was giving $50 a month to each of to two private hospitals: Spartanburg and Good Samaritan. The new public hospital, Spartanburg General, was built at a cost of $250,000 and opened in 1921. Some Spartanburg residents complained that its location, out on North Church Street at the end of the trolley tracks, was too far out of town. —*Courtesy of Spartanburg Regional Healthcare System*

MEDICINE TINS, PILLS, & 1940S SYRINGE —*Courtesy of Dr. Charles Webb*

From the time of his arrival in Spartanburg, Dr. Hugh Ratchford Black had pushed hard for hospital facilities. He was instrumental in the establishment of the first city hospital and subsequently worked hard to persuade voters to pass the bond issue for General Hospital. Dr. Lewis P. Jones, in his biography of Dr. Black (*Hugh Ratchford Black: A Medical Pioneer*, privately printed, 1963), relates the tale that Dr. Black sent his son Paul with ballots and ballot boxes to precincts where no effort had been made to conduct the referendum. When General Hospital opened in 1921, Dr. Black performed its first operation on Paul. Several years later, the Drs. Black (Hugh R. had been joined in practice by two of his sons, Hugh S. and Sam) built a private hospital on the corner of East Main Street and Oakland Avenue. They named the facility for Dr. Hugh Black's wife, Mary Snoddy Black. In the 1960s the Mary Black Hospital moved to a new facility on Skylyn Drive.

—*Courtesy Marianna Black Habisreutinger*

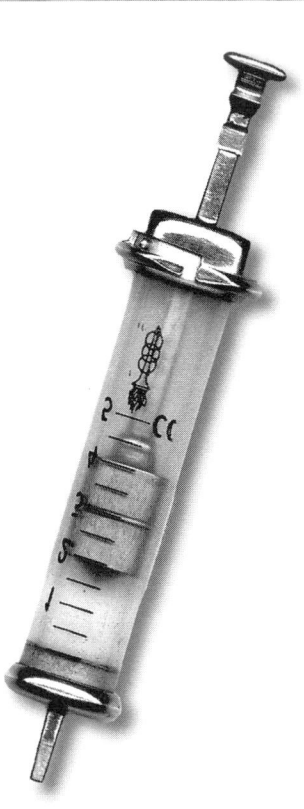

The East Main Street entrance and exterior clock tower of Wilson Hall at Converse College as they looked in the 1930s. —*Courtesy of Converse College and the Herald-Journal Willis Collection, Spartanburg County (SC) Public Libraries.*

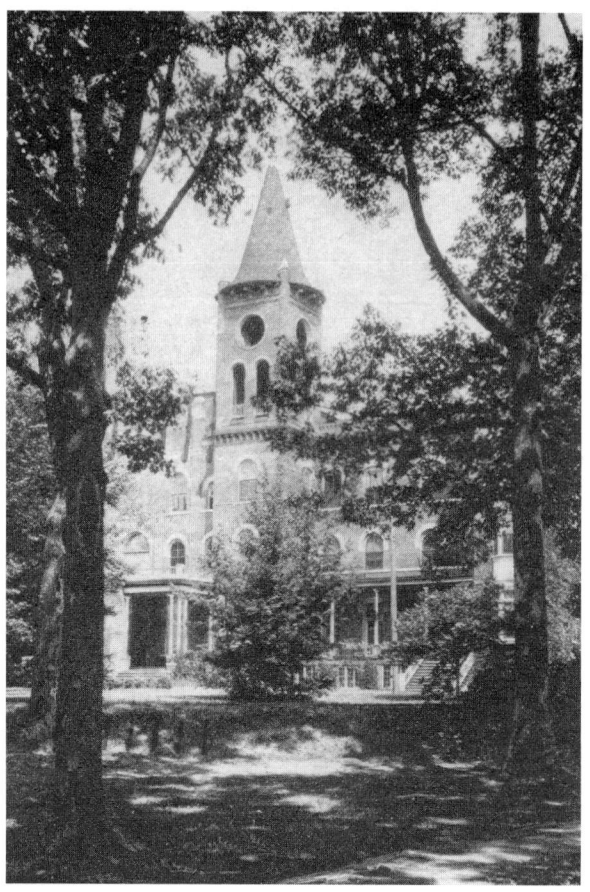

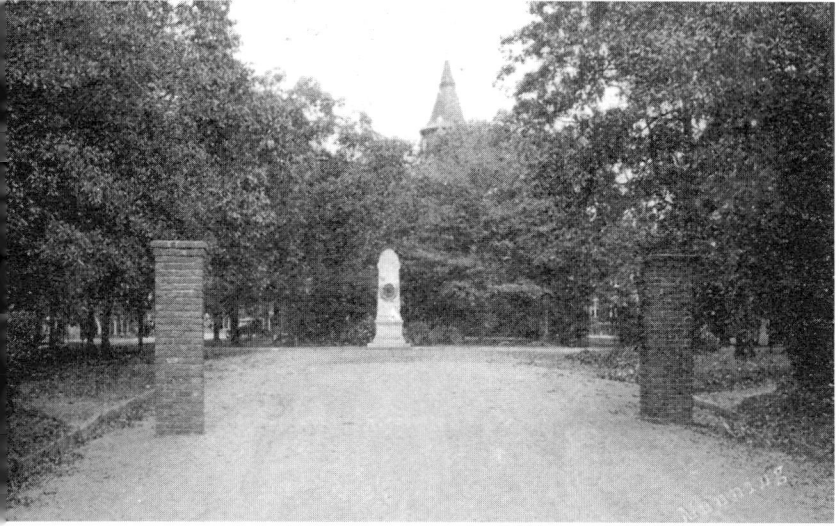

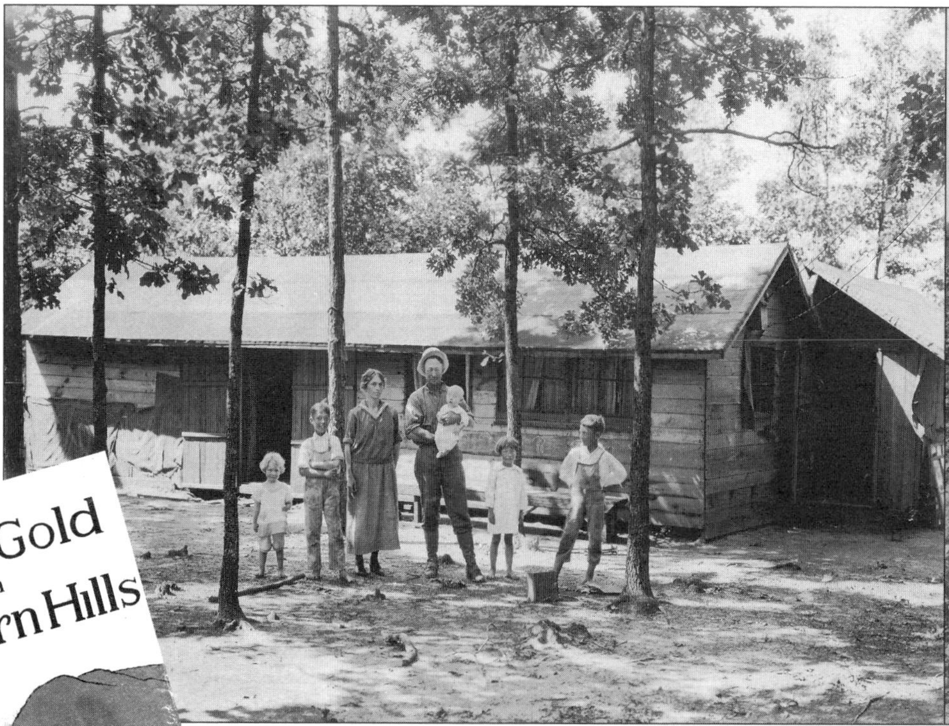

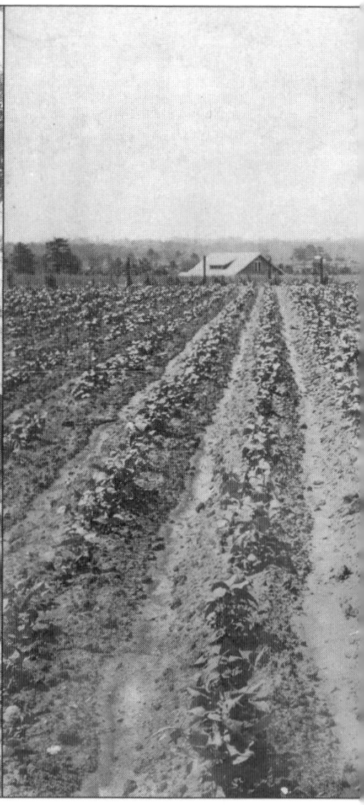

THE STORY OF THE FOUNDING OF TEXTILE INDUSTRIAL INSTITUTE

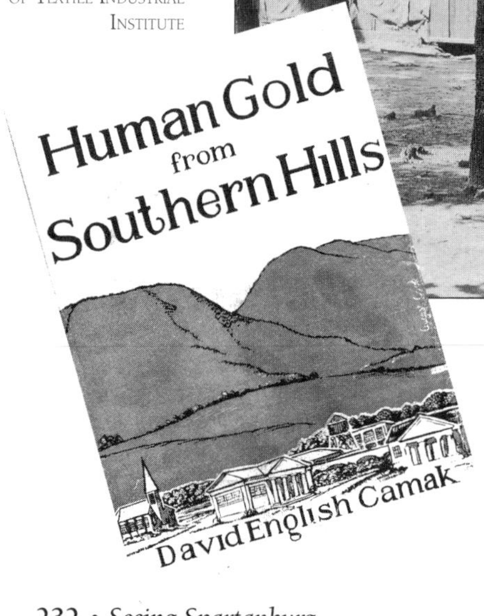

The Textile Industrial Institute, forerunner of present-day Spartanburg Methodist College, offered affordable education to a growing number of working class adults. TII experienced a boom in enrollment following World War I. Many married students came with their families, and tents and officers' barracks from Camp Wadsworth were pressed into service as temporary housing.

Wofford's ivy-clad Old Main building and Leonard Auditorium as they appeared in the 1930s. —*Photographs courtesy of Wofford College*

OPPOSITE PAGE BOTTOM: This student and his family lived in old barracks which were moved from Camp Wadsworth. The student eventually became a pastor in a cotton mill village.

CENTER: TII attracted many students from rural areas who found employment at the college's farm and dairy.

BOTTOM RIGHT: A former marine from New York and his family lived in tents until other housing became available.
—*Photographs courtesy of Spartanburg Methodist College*

By 1940 Morgan Square had a bandstand where concerts were held every Sunday afternoon. This photograph should be compared with Morgan Square of 1884 on pages 70-71. The Masonic Temple, built in 1928, stands on the far side of the Cleveland Hotel where the Opera House used to be. The Duncan Building, on the extreme right of this picture, stands where the old courthouse stood in 1884. The left side of the street has many buildings dating from the late nineteenth century that still stand. All the buildings on the left, west of the block with the building that has the word "Atlantic" painted on its front, have been torn down. The bare, fluorescent bulbs lighting the square, the presence of a filling station, and the nature of the vehicles are different, but the congestion is much the same. —*Courtesy of the Spartanburg Herald-Journal*

Community & Culture

ABOVE: A man proudly washes his Model T Ford. As Henry Ford had said: "You can have any color you want as long as it's black!"

OPPOSITE PAGE TOP: When they gathered for a group portrait in 1926, Spartanburg's finest had abandoned their "Bobbie" look and adopted a modern uniform, a style that was to endure. —*Photographs courtesy of the Spartanburg County Regional Museum*

OPPOSITE PAGE BOTTOM: The staff of the post office had grown considerably by the 1920s. —*Courtesy of the Herald-Journal Willis Collection, Spartanburg County (SC) Public Libraries*

The Campbell boys are dressed and ready for church (from left to right: Nathaniel, Cwright, and Clyde). —*Courtesy of the Charlie Mae Campbell family*

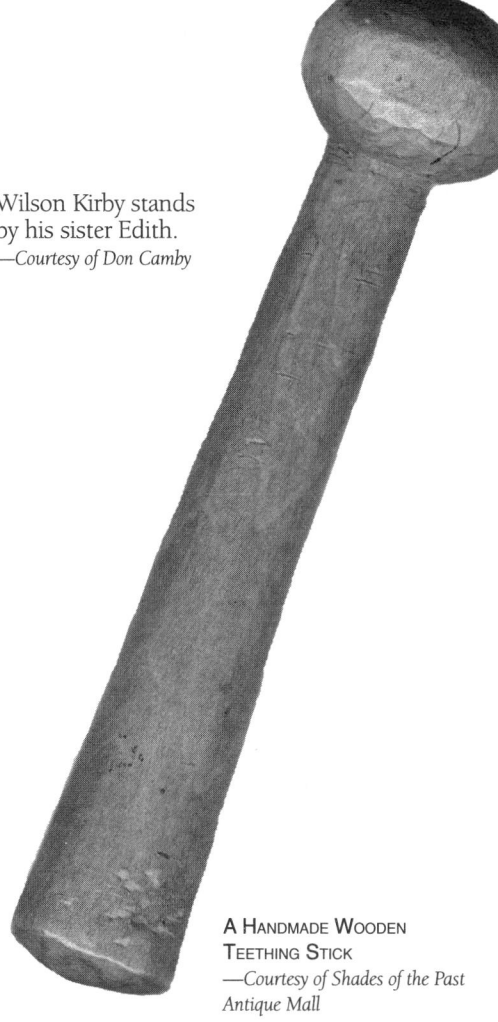

Wilson Kirby stands by his sister Edith.
—*Courtesy of Don Camby*

A HANDMADE WOODEN TEETHING STICK
—*Courtesy of Shades of the Past Antique Mall*

Jesse Franklin and Margaret Cleveland "take a ride."
—*Courtesy of Jesse Franklin Cleveland*

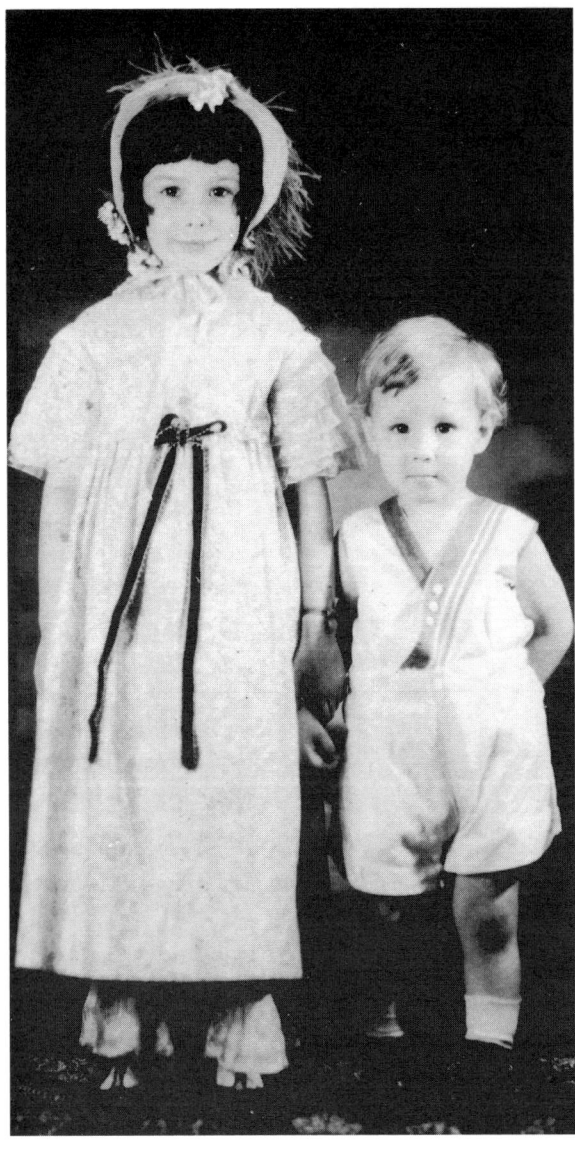

—Courtesy of the Johnson family

Harriet Roswell Ancrum at age three. *—Courtesy of the Johnson family*

Bob McKinney —*Courtesy of Jennie Rhinehart*

—*Courtesy of Elisabeth Bridgeman Jones*

ABOVE: A wedding party in the 1920s. The bride is Kate Montgomery, the groom is Fred Oates, the flower girl on the right is Peggy Gignilliat, and the father of the bride, second from the right in the second row, is Walter Montgomery. —*Courtesy of Kate M. Ward*

OPPOSITE PAGE: "Trottin' Sally," George Mullins, was a fixture of downtown Spartanburg in the 1920s. He would flit up and down Main Street playing his fiddle at the drop of a hat. If he sounds undignified, look at the photograph again. —*Photograph by Alfred T. Willis, courtesy of the Herald-Journal Willis Collection, Spartanburg County (SC) Public Libraries*

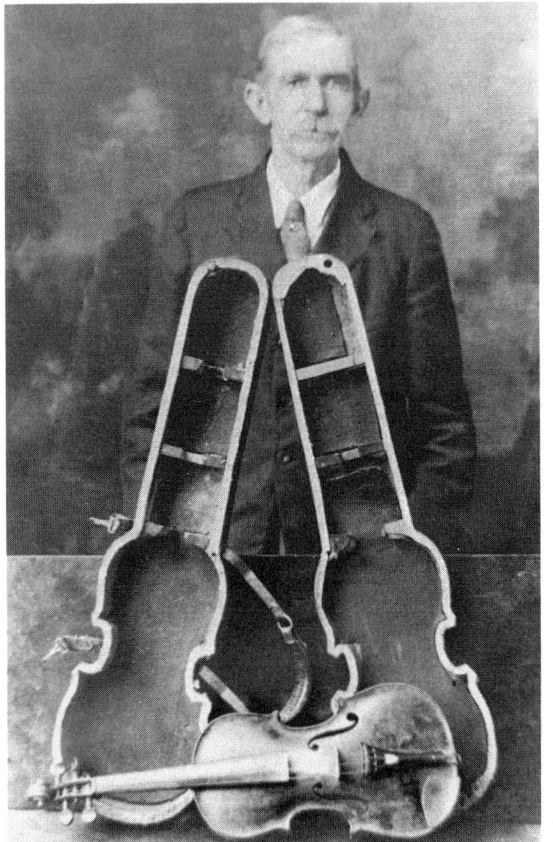

LEFT: John Weste Harris long kept a store and post office in the small community of Golightly just south of Fairforest Creek on present S.C. 56. An elderly black man came into the store one day carrying something wrapped in a worn cloth. The old man, who was called Uncle Dave, was hungry, so Harris gave him something to eat. Uncle Dave thanked Harris, took a violin from the cloth, and began to play old Southern airs. When finished, Uncle Dave handed the violin to Harris, saying that he was too old to play much longer and that Harris, being young and always having been good to him, ought to learn to play. Uncle Dave had played at Harris' wedding, and Harris always had a soft spot for him. Thus, Harris cherished that violin for the rest of his life—cherished it so much that he found the root of a walnut tree and carved a case for the violin out of that solid piece of hardwood. The violin fits the case so snugly that it is impossible to shake the violin about. John Weste Harris posed with his violin and case in the 1920s. Harris died in 1933, and the violin and case remain in the family. —*Courtesy of John Foster*

Depression and War • 243

ABOVE: Perhaps no entertainment was as ubiquitous among Southerners as Sunday school picnics. The setting for many stories, plays, and musical comedies, the mixture of scripture, good fun, and clandestine courting had long been part of the routine of Southern life. Here some members of Bethel Methodist Church set out on a church bus for an outing. —*Courtesy of the Spartanburg County Regional Museum*

OPPOSITE PAGE TOP: Billy Sunday never missed an opportunity to promote himself and his revivals. Here he poses with Spartanburg's Fire Department, cap and all (he also posed with the police department, among others). Notice the flamboyant signature that matched his animated demeanor. Sunday had resisted coming to the South because he opposed segregation, and finally consented only when local sponsors agreed to permit him to hold services for African Americans as well as whites. —*Courtesy of the Spartanburg County Regional Museum*

OPPOSITE PAGE BOTTOM: In the 1920s one of the greatest religious revivals in American history took place, and Billy Sunday was its most popular proponent. Sunday, a reformed alcoholic, preached abstinence from alcohol, patriotism to country, and faith in the Lord. When he came to Spartanburg in 1922, the local churches joined with him and provided booths with food and drink at the revivals. Sunday's sponsors built this "temple" for his six-week revival; the structure held seven thousand people and was located near the courthouse and only a short distance from Union Station to accommodate visitors from other towns in the Carolinas. As soon as Sunday left town, the building was torn down and the wood sold. —*Courtesy of the Herald-Journal Willis Collection, Spartanburg County (SC) Public Libraries*

ABOVE: The faculty of the Highland Elementary School had its picture taken in the 1930s. The first person on the left in the second row is Mary Homer Wright; the first person on the left in the third row is Charlie Mae Campbell, and next to her is Nancy Abercrombie. The man is the principal, W. A. Neill. Mary Wright was a pioneer in education for African Americans in Spartanburg; Charlie Mae Campbell became principal of the Mary Wright Elementary School, and Nancy Abercrombie long operated the Southside Cafe.
—*Courtesy of the Charlie Mae Campbell family*

OPPOSITE PAGE TOP: Education for African-American children progressed slowly after Reconstruction had gotten that community off to a good start. In 1909 Mary H. Wright had persuaded the city fathers to build Carrier Street School, seen here in 1928, for African-American students. Up to that time African Americans had had to walk to the Dean Street School, for a long time the only public school for black students. Mary Wright taught in Spartanburg's schools for 65 years before her death in 1945.

OPPOSITE PAGE CENTER: Highland Elementary School for African-American elementary school students in the 1930s.

OPPOSITE PAGE BOTTOM: Spartanburg pioneered the idea of junior high schools in South Carolina with the building on Howard Street of the Cleveland Junior High School, shown here in the 1930s. The Junior High School was named for Jesse Cleveland, whose home once stood on this land.
—*Photographs courtesy of the Herald-Journal Willis Collection, Spartanburg County (SC) Public Libraries*

From the 1920s until mid-century, there was not much in the way of athletics at Spartanburg High School that Hubert Roy Dobson did not coach. Here he stands in the late 1920s with his tumbling team, which includes two future army generals, William Westmoreland and Beverly Montgomery.

—*Photograph by Alfred T. Willis, courtesy of the Herald-Journal Willis Collection, Spartanburg County (SC) Public Libraries*

TOP: The city built its first public high school in 1897 on Converse Street. The building had only six classrooms and a small auditorium for its ten teachers and about 200 students. At the time most people considered education beyond the elementary grades a luxury. By the 1920s attitudes were changing, and it was obvious that Spartanburg needed a new high school. In 1921 a new high school on South Dean Street opened. The school board named the school for the superintendent of schools, Frank Evans. In 1924 and 1928 new wings were added to the building, which became a junior high school when the third high school was built in Fernwood. Presently, the Evans building houses social services departments and agencies. —*Courtesy of Wofford College*

BOTTOM: The Evans High School graduating class of 1930. —*Courtesy of the Spartanburg County Regional Museum*

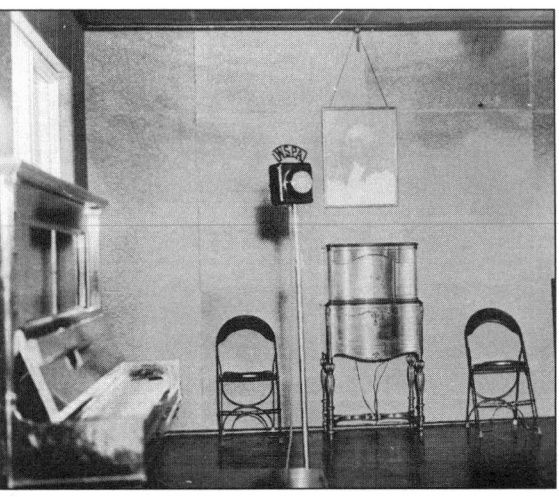

ABOVE: Reunions of Confederate soldiers were important events in the South. In 1928 Confederate veterans gathered in Spartanburg, and Alfred T. Willis was there to record the event.
—*Courtesy of the Herald-Journal Willis Collection, Spartanburg County (SC) Public Libraries*

OPPOSITE PAGE TOP: Politics was a form of recreation for Southerners, and the people of Spartanburg were no exception. Here, Ibra C. Blackwood, the first of four Spartanburg politicians who would be governors of South Carolina at various times from the 1930s to the 1960s, holds forth at what was then called a "stump meeting." Blackwood was governor of South Carolina in 1934 when the largest strike in American history broke out in the textile mills. Blackwood called out the National Guard to protect the mill owners and their rights; the Guard patrolled the streets of the mill villages, but Governor Blackwood had to hire "constables without compensation" to aid the Guardsmen as there were not enough of them to go around. In Honea Path, during a scuffle, the special deputies opened fire and killed seven of the striking workers. Ten thousand people attended the mass funeral. The strike eventually failed, and in spite of assurances from the mill owners, supported by the federal government, that there would be no retaliation, workers who had "agitated" the strike were blackballed from working in the mills. The union movement in the area has never recovered from this major setback.
—*Courtesy of the Herald-Journal Willis Collection, Spartanburg County (SC) Public Libraries*

OPPOSITE PAGE BOTTOM LEFT: Radio broke over the American scene in the 1920s. This transmitter was hand-constructed in 1930 and was WSPA's and the state's first. It began broadcasting from the top floor of the Montgomery Building.

OPPOSITE PAGE BOTTOM RIGHT: WSPA Radio's first studio, complete with a stand-up piano and a reproduction of Stuart's George Washington.
—*Photographs courtesy of Spartan Broadcasting Corporation*

ABOVE: Charles Lindbergh, in marked contrast to his hosts, looks solemnly uncomfortable at this testimonial dinner held at Converse College. His visit was a thrill for the county; it was probably something less for the shy hero. Some of the guests at the head table, from left to right: Senator Ellison D. "Cotton Ed" Smith, a Lindbergh aide; Mayor Ben Hill Brown; Lindbergh, Henry Arthur Ligon, Jr., Governor John Richards and Elizabeth Richards; and Dr. Robert Pell, president of Converse College. Seated in the front row from left to right: Cecelia Ligon; Pierre Fike, editor of the Spartanburg Journal; Rosco Beal; Dr. Henry Nelson Snyder, president of Wofford College; and Bessie Beal. *—Courtesy of Converse College*

OPPOSITE PAGE: When Charles A. Lindbergh landed a fragile monoplane, the Spirit of St. Louis, in Paris on May 21, 1927, he became a national hero. He had captured the imagination of the world by flying solo across the Atlantic just at a time when the sophistication and technology of radio and motion pictures could make the most of such an exploit. To his fellow Americans, this quiet and unassuming man epitomized the bravery and technical skill that was their pride. Lindbergh went on a national tour soon after returning to the United States, and he made Spartanburg one of his stops. On October 12, 1927, a parade and "civic dinner" were held in his honor. Thousands of people turned out for the parade, seen here on East Main Street. Lindbergh sits in the first car with his hands in his lap. He may have waved occasionally, but his overwhelming shyness, which was part of his charm, prevented anything but an occasional smile. The elevated box to the left of the picture was the perch from which the traffic officer controlled the light. *—Photograph by Alfred T. Willis, ourtesy of the Herald-Journal Willis Collection, Spartanburg County (SC) Public Libraries*

OPPOSITE PAGE INSET: The Spirit of St. Louis sits in front of the hangar at the Spartanburg downtown airport where Charles Lindbergh parked it during his visit to Spartanburg in 1927.
—Courtesy of the Herald-Journal Willis Collection, Spartanburg County (SC) Public Libraries

ABOVE: Mayor Ben Hill Brown greeted another of America's aviation heroes, Amelia Earhardt, when she touched down at Spartanburg's airport in 1931. Note the open cockpit and the resulting tousled hair of the young aviatrix. Her short hair, her obvious enthusiasm, and her youthful good looks endeared her to Americans nation wide. —*Courtesy of the Spartanburg County Regional Museum*

OPPOSITE PAGE TOP: The Spartanburg County Fair started in 1907 and immediately became one of the highlights of the year. Just as harness racing had been one of the special attractions of the Woodruff Fair, so it was with the fair in Spartanburg. This 1927 photograph shows a race in progress with the old wooden bleachers in the background. —*Courtesy of the Piedmont Interstate Fair Association*

ABOVE: By the late 1930s and early 1940s, when this photograph was taken, the county fair had replaced harness racing with automobile racing. —*Photograph by Alfred T. Willis, courtesy of the Piedmont Interstate Fair Association*

LEFT: In 1923 John B. Cleveland gave the city of Spartanburg land north of his home for a "playground for the children of the city." City Council built a public swimming pool in what was known as Cleveland Park. The photograph is dated 1927. The swimming pool no longer exists although the park continues to be used. —*Courtesy of Wofford College*

Trophy won by Tucapau textile
league baseball team. —*Courtesy of
the Spartanburg County Regional Museum*

The players on the American Legion baseball teams
from Spartanburg and Los Angeles stand together
before the start of the American Legion World Series in Duncan Park Stadium
in 1936. None of the players on the Spartanburg team was over 17 years of age.
They won five state championships in seven years and played in two Legion World
Series. The Spartanburg team won the Series in 1936 and came in second in 1938.
—*Courtesy of the Herald-Journal Willis Collection, Spartanburg County (SC) Public Libraries*

Baseball signed by textile league players.
—*Courtesy of the Spartanburg County Regional Museum*

Above & Opposite Page Top: One of the federally funded "New Deal" projects in the county was a new "Old Folks Home." The cluster of wooden buildings was the original county home for the elderly; the brick building with all the windows was its newly built replacement. Later this building was transformed into the county tuberculosis hospital.

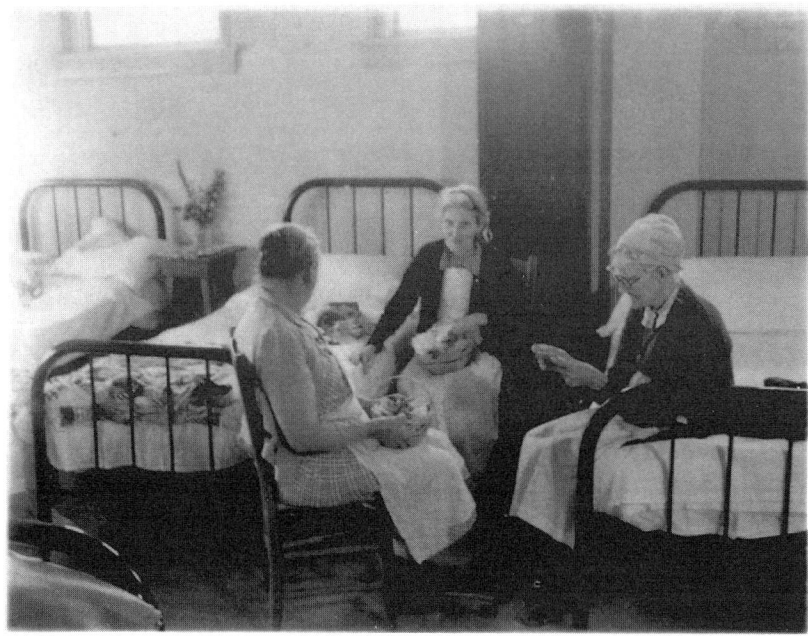

LEFT & OPPOSITE PAGE BOTTOM: The "old folks" enjoy the sunlight and other comforts made available to them through this federally funded project.
—*Photographs courtesy of the Still Pictures Branch, National Archives II, College Park, Md.*

LORD LOTHIAN'S TELEGRAM
—*Courtesy of Converse College*

UNION

NEWCOMB CARLTON
CHAIRMAN OF THE BOARD

R. B. WHITE
PRESIDENT

J. C. WILLEVER
FIRST VICE-PRESIDENT

DL = Day Letter
NT = Overnight Telegram
LC = Deferred Cable
NLT = Cable Night Letter
Ship Radiogram

(58)

The filing time shown in the date line on telegrams and day letters is STANDARD TIME at point of origin. Time of receipt is STANDARD TIME at point of destination

CF292 56=DUPLICATE CA WASHINGTON DC DEC 6 1940 655P

DABNEY GARRETT=

AM GRATEFUL TO HEAR OF YOUR ACTIVITIES FOR BRITISH WAR
RELIEF AND MUCH HOPE PERFORMANCE TONIGHT WILL BE
SUCCESSFUL BUNDLES FOR BRITAIN IS GIVING SPLENDID
ASSISTANCE TO THE DISTRESSED PEOPLE OF GREATBRITAIN
AND ON THEIR BEHALF I SEND MY WARM THANKS FOR THE
GENEROUS EFFORTS BEING MADE BY SOUTH CAROLINIANS ON
BEHALF OF THIS WORTHY CAUSE=

:LOTHIAN

THE COMPANY WILL APPRECIATE SUGGESTIONS FROM ITS PATRONS CONCERNING ITS SERVICE

BELOW: In 1940 Britain was under heavy attack by Hitler's military machine. Sympathy for the English was growing quickly in the United States, although the government seemed to many to be moving pitifully slowly in rendering aid. Officially, America was neutral, but by late 1940 it was abundantly clear where the nation's sympathies lay. There were many private efforts to help the British people, the major relief organization being Bundles for Britain. On December 6, 1940, the Spartanburg Lyric Opera Company presented a production of "The Gondoliers" for the benefit of Bundles for Britain. People from around the county, students from Converse, Wofford, and Spartanburg High School, plus the Union High School band all took part in the production. It was a triumph; the audience numbered about 1,500. They were treated to a telegram of thanks from the popular British ambassador to the United States, Lord Lothian. Ernst Bacon, who directed the production, read Lothian's telegram to the audience. In the next few weeks Lord Lothian, who had worked so hard and successfully to get help for his government from the Americans, died in Washington.
—*Courtesy of Converse College*

Three Spartanburg County GIs show typical American "cockiness" somewhere in Europe in 1944. From left to right: Orville Kirby, J. E. Hodge, and Joe Varner. —*Courtesy of Don Camby*

Prayer for Invasion

Almighty God... Our loved ones are now locked in death combat with the enemy who seeks to destroy Thy Word and our American Way of Life... Grant unto our dear ones of Thy Fatherly protection as they walk through the valley of the shadow of death... Bless, guide, and strengthen them... Be with them in all Thy dispensations... In prayerful obedience we humbly ask Thy Divine favor, Eternal God... Amen

Harry Smiley, who arranged for Rabbi Wrubel of Temple B'nai Israel in Spartanburg to prepare this prayer, made this display far in advance for the day when Allied forces would invade Europe. When news of the invasion, which had begun at 3:23 p.m. on June 6, 1944, was flashed, Smiley set his alarm for five o'clock the next morning and had the display ready at six. In the following weeks hundreds stopped, read the prayer, and wept. —*Courtesy of the Herald-Journal Willis Collection, Spartanburg County (SC) Public Libraries*

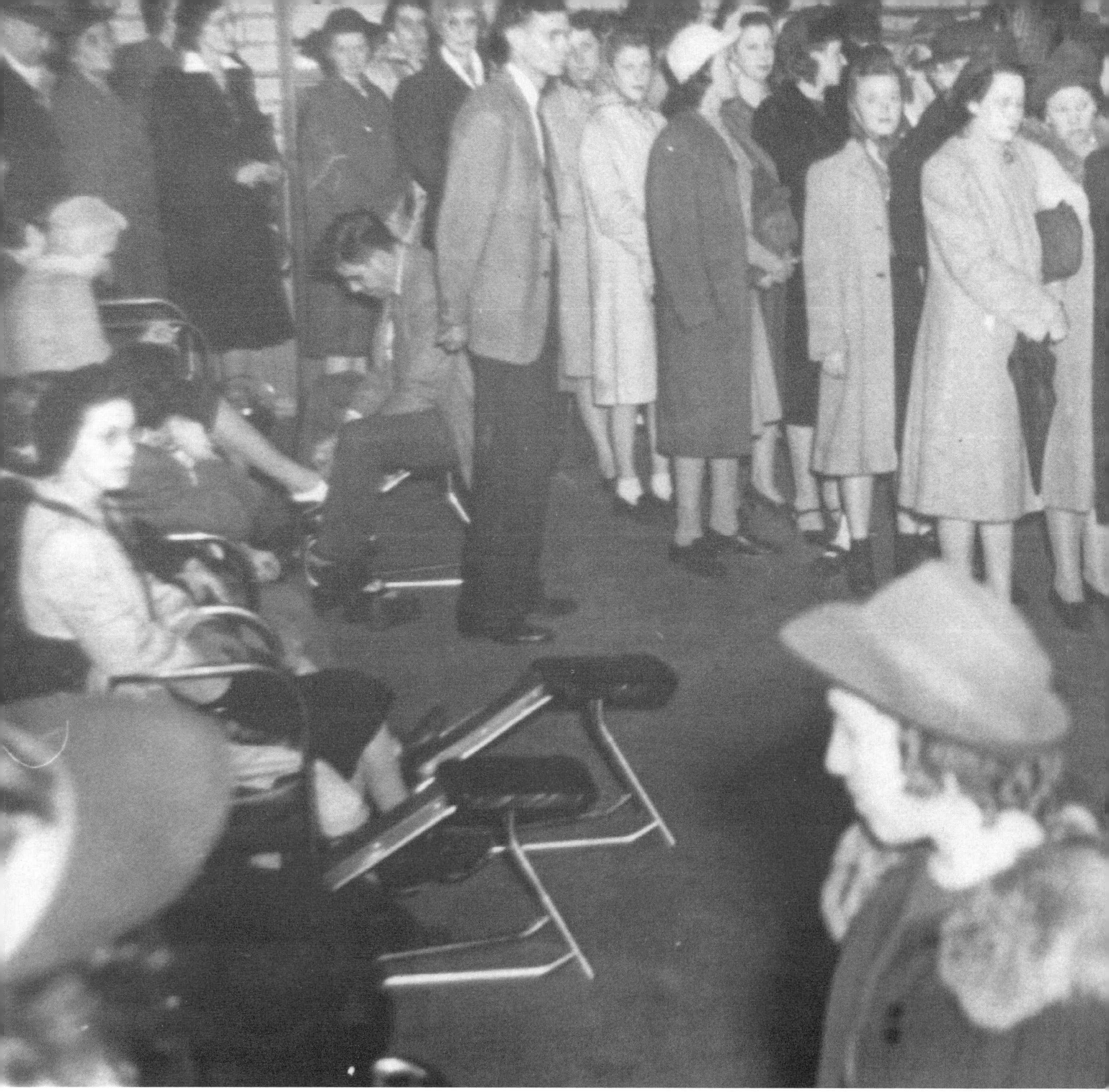

123503
DZ
UNITED STATES OF AMERICA
OFFICE OF PRICE ADMINISTRATION
WAR RATION BOOK TWO
IDENTIFICATION
123504
DZ
UNITED STATES OF AMERICA
OFFICE OF PRICE ADMINISTRATION
WAR RATION BOOK TWO
IDENTIFICATION
WARNING
OPA
RED POINT

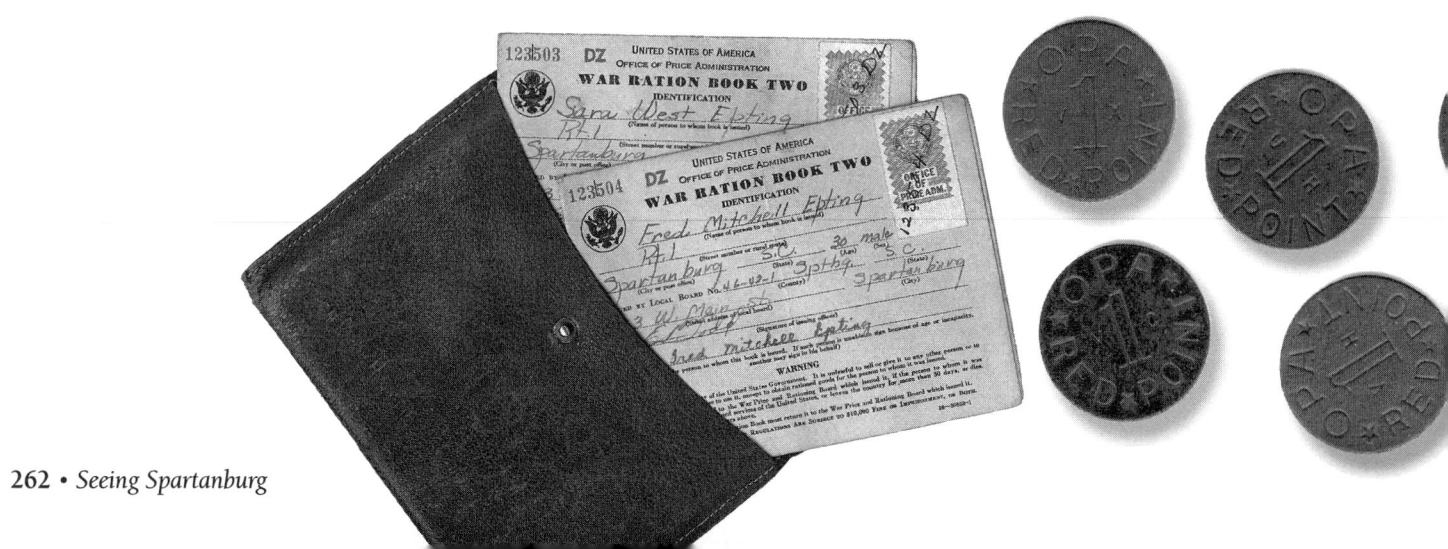

During World War II nylons were almost impossible to obtain. When Aug. W. Smith announced a sale on them in 1943 more than 600 women crowded the store. In 20 minutes the nylons were gone, but the store brought out 200 pair of silk hose it had set aside for the following week so the customers would not be too disappointed. —*Photograph by Kathryn Powell, courtesy of the Herald-Journal Willis Collection, Spartanburg County (SC) Public Libraries*

Americans conserved during World War II, and a large part of the effort was controlled by nationwide rationing. These are ration books and coins from that time. —*Courtesy of the South Pine Antique Mall*

On April 12, 1945, President Franklin D. Roosevelt died at his home in Warm Springs, Georgia. Roosevelt's death came as a shock to most Americans, who were unaware of the President's serious cardiovascular disease. Here the flag flies at half-mast over the Aug. W. Smith Company to honor the man who had led the nation since 1932. —*Courtesy of the Spartanburg County Regional Museum*

Work & Progress

PRICE CLOTHING

A wintery view of East Main Street outside Price's in the early 1920s.

Early collar wrapping and a machine that stamped initials into men's hats. —*Courtesy of Price's.*

J. E. Cauthen's General Store was the place to shop in Inman in the late 1920s. It was especially noted for its fine selection of handmade wooden toys. From left to right: clerk, Fletcher Golightly, Buddy Blackwell, H. W. Seawright, and J. E. Cauthen.
—*Courtesy of Nell Golightly*

ABOVE: The Montgomery Sandwich Shop was located diagonally across the street from the Montgomery Building on the corner of North Church and St. John streets. The popular deli was a favorite among businessmen and office people from the Montgomery Building. The man on the stool is unknown; standing in the middle behind the counter is Gus Patterson, and the man on the right is John Williams. The photograph dates from the early 1930s.
—*Courtesy of the Trakas family*

LEFT: H. T. Littlejohn Company was located on Wofford Street between North Church and Spring streets in 1926, when this photograph was taken. The company sold bulk feed and grain and other smaller items. Littlejohn stands on the left.

Top & Above: While Aug W. Smith's windows were usually interesting, James Buchanan always did something special for Christmas. Here is one of his designs on the marquee for a Christmas in the early 1930s. Buchanan made everything in his displays by hand with thimbles, needles, thread, and anything else he could get hold of. Buchanan was also a photographer—many of his photographs appear in the early pages of this book. Eventually, he became caretaker of Walnut Grove, the eighteenth-century residence of Charles Moore. —*Photographs courtesy of the Spartanburg County Regional Museum*

Opposite Page: The Elite (pronounced "a-leet") became the most popular eating place in the city from the 1920s through the 1950s. It was the epitome of the old-fashioned soda fountain. Soon the Elite drew a steady clientele who liked not only to eat but also to talk.

Opposite Page Insert: The first man on the left is George Harakas. The photograph was taken in 1914. Nicholas Trakas, the man with the moustache, had just decided to serve food and had installed a soda fountain. Trakas had a fruit stand on East Main Street for many years. —*Photographs by Alfred T. Willis, courtesy of Nicholas Harakas and the Herald-Journal Willis Collection, Spartanburg County (SC) Public Libraries*

Piedmont Laundry on the corner of Kennedy and South Liberty Streets lined up its delivery trucks and their drivers for this group photograph in the 1930s. Notice the short telephone number, a sign of simpler times.
—*Courtesy of the Herald-Journal Willis Collection, Spartanburg County (SC) Public Libraries*

In the 1920s and 30s, the Blue Bird Ice Cream Company provided Spartanburg with a frozen delight sold to stores and homes from these seven refrigerated trucks.
—*Courtesy of George Mullinax*

ADVERTISEMENT FROM CAMP CROFT PUBLICATION

Top: The Pierce Motor Company was on the southeast corner of Church and Broad Streets. Notice the streetcar tracks.

Bottom: The mechanics who worked for the Pierce Motor Company lined up for this formal photograph.

—*Photographs courtesy of the Herald-Journal Willis Collection, Spartanburg County (SC) Public Libraries*

Reflecting the continuing dependence of the county on cotton, R. V. Lanford stands amid his cotton in the Woodruff area in 1931. —*Courtesy of Ron Lanford*

Wagons loaded with cotton waiting to be
ginned and baled.
—*Courtesy of the Herald-Journal Willis Collection,
Spartanburg County (SC) Public Libraries*

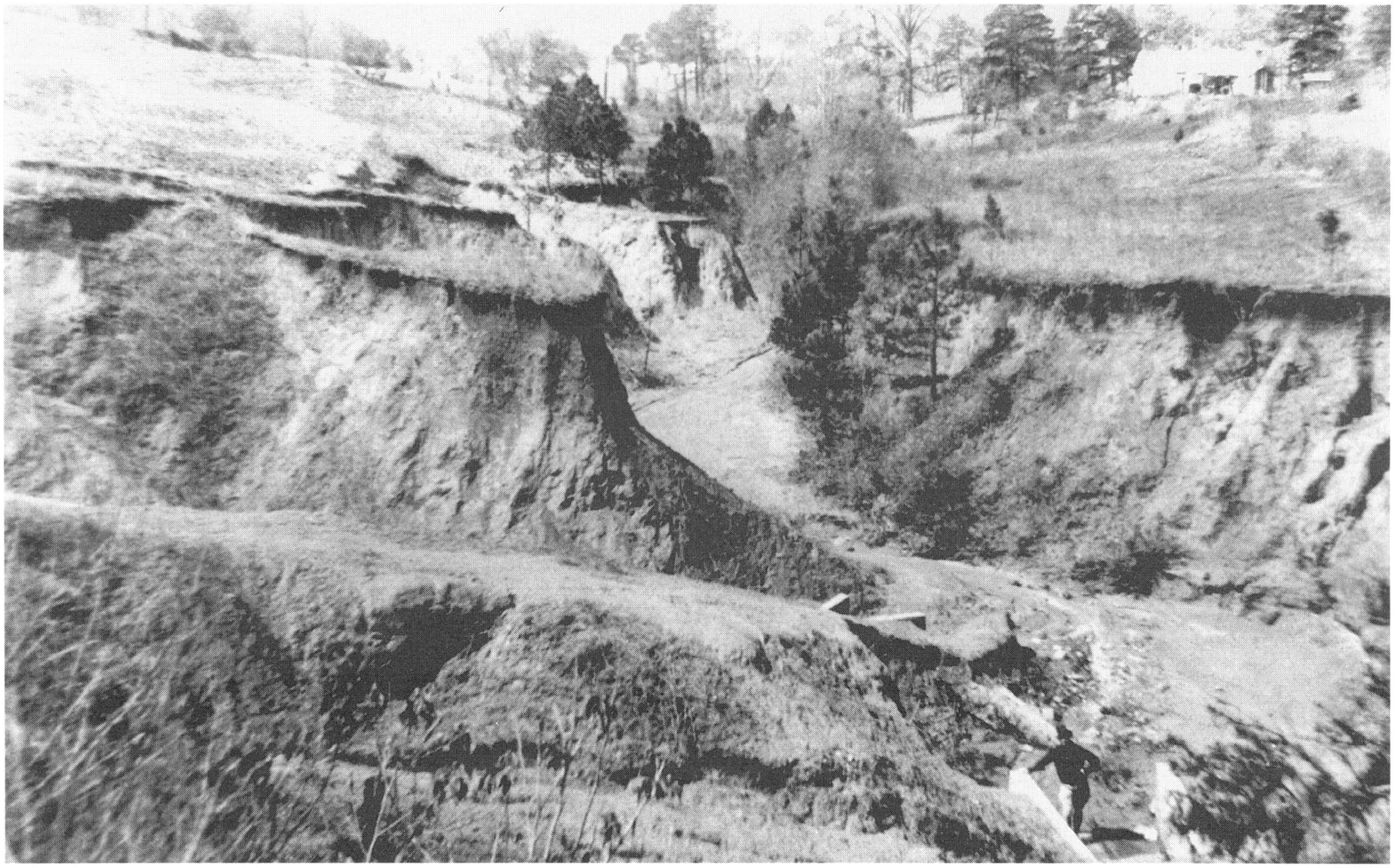

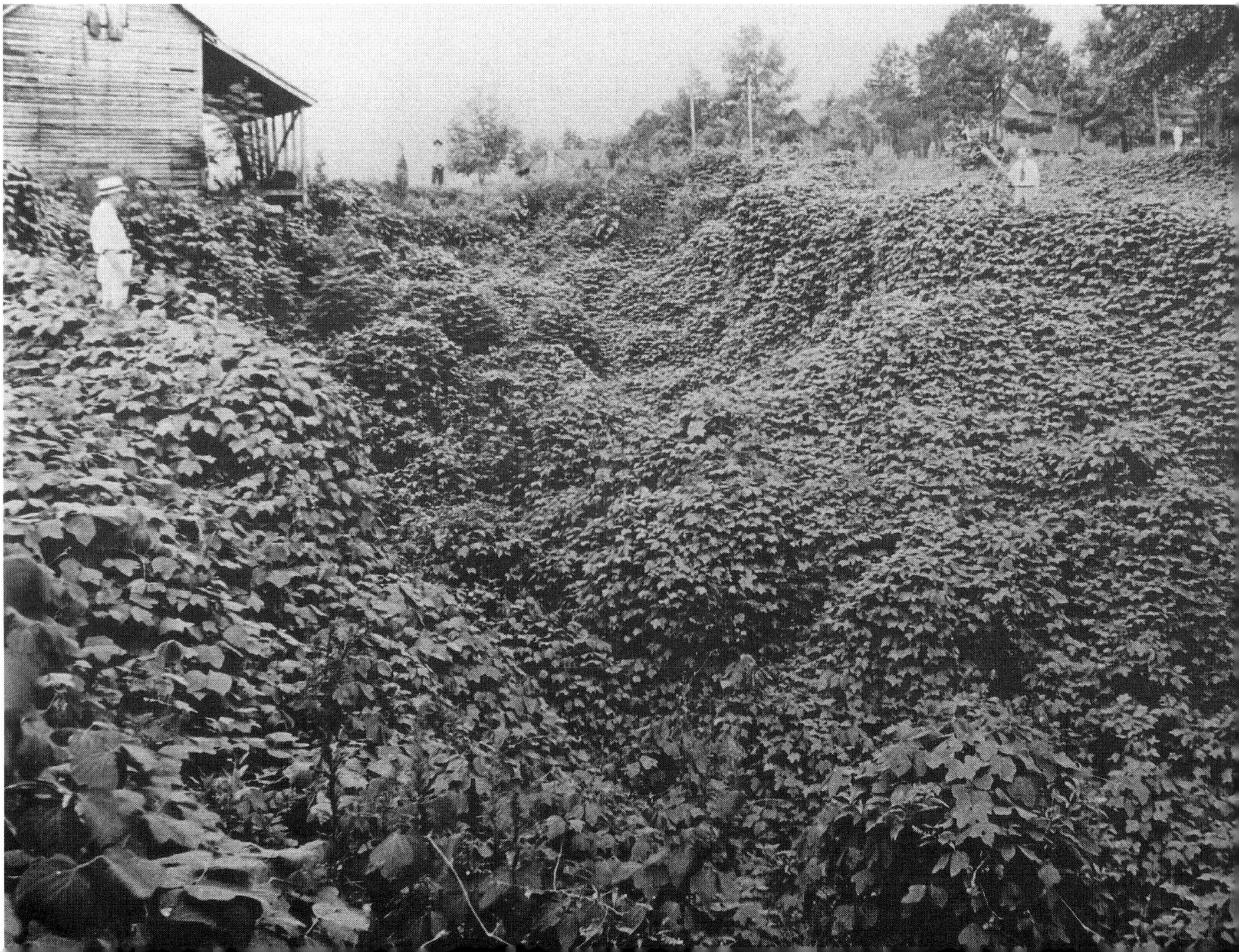

ABOVE: In response to the work of the Soil Conservation Service, J. T. Hudson worked to conserve the soil on his farm in Woodruff. The tractor is creating terraces, and the mule teams are dragging pans to level off the ridges. —*Courtesy of the South Carolina Museum Commission*

OPPOSITE PAGE TOP: Soil erosion had been a problem since colonial times, but the first national recognition of its economic and social effects did not take place until the late 1920s. By then erosion had become a national disaster, and Congress appropriated some funds to help protect the land. In 1933 Harold L. Ickes, Secretary of the Interior, authorized the creation of the Soil Erosion Service under the Works Progress Administration. One of the areas of the nation picked for demonstration and experimentation projects was the South Tyger River watershed. Directed by Thomas S. Buie, the Soil Erosion Service, which became the Soil Conservation Service in 1935, began its first project on the Berry Gully near Poplar Springs in Spartanburg County. The entire county was marked by years of neglect. Large gullies and smaller ruts long had made agriculture difficult and by the 1920s, almost impossible, and farmers were abandoning the washed-out land. The social as well as economic cost was enormous.

KUDZU
(*Pueraria lobata*)

OPPOSITE PAGE BOTTOM: One of the quickest and most effective methods of stopping erosion and rebuilding gullies was to plant kudzu. In 1933 a farmer near Woodruff planted 20 kudzu plants in this gully. Only six or eight lived. By 1935, when this photograph was taken, his gully was covered, and he boasted that it was filling up at the rate of two to four feet a year. Planting kudzu was rapidly adopted as an anti-erosion measure, and it appeared all over the county. Aggressive and difficult to kill, kudzu is despised by people who have built houses in areas where it has been planted.
—*Photographs courtesy of the South Caroliniana Library*

Top: In the fall of 1942 Spartanburg's cotton growers faced disaster. The cotton crop was a large one and was ready to be picked, but the war had so depleted manpower that the farmers could not possibly pick the crop by themselves. On October 8 all students in Spartanburg County were excused from classes to go out and pick cotton. Both Converse and Wofford students joined the pickers.

Opposite Page Bottom: Converse students board the bus to take them out to the cotton fields. A cotton-picking sack slung over her left shoulder, the young woman bends to roll her coveralls either up or down.

Above Insert: Wofford students are hard at work alongside Dr. Clarence Norton, Wofford's dean of students, and to his left, Charles P. Hammond of Hammond, Brown, Jennings' furniture store. Approximately 300 students picked 15,000 pounds of cotton in that one day.

—Photographs courtesy of Converse College; the Herald-Journal Willis Collection, Spartanburg County (SC) Public Libraries; Pat McKinney

Drayton Mill in the 1930s.
—*Courtesy of the Herald-Journal Willis Collection, Spartanburg County (SC) Public Libraries*

ABOVE: The cotton mills suffered depression conditions in the 1920s. Since Spartanburg County was dependent on the industry, it suffered also. Here workers check cloth at Pacolet Mills in 1925. *—Courtesy of Don Camby*

BELOW: The employees of Powell Mill in 1939. *—Courtesy of Mr. and Mrs. John Drennan*

The Beaumont Plant of Spartan Mills received the Army-Navy "E Award" five times during World War II. The plant, which dedicated its entire production to the war effort, was the only textile plant in South Carolina to receive this efficiency award. —*Courtesy of James Crocker*

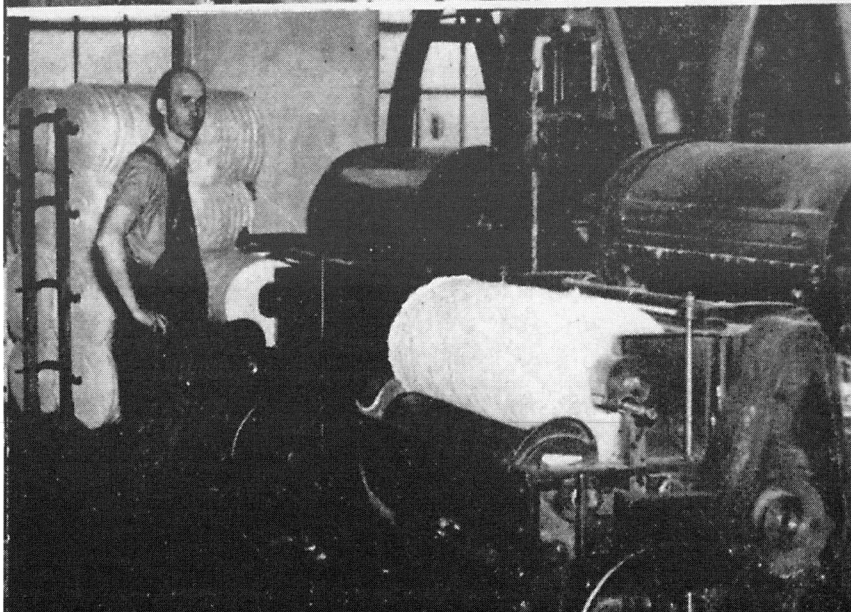

Cotton mill workers tend their machines during World War II. —*Courtesy of the Spartanburg County Regional Museum*

Textile mills provided not only housing but also social and religious activities. The textile mill authorities said that their intent was to provide their workers with a well-rounded life so the workers would miss nothing by not living in town. Others maintained that by providing employees with the important elements in a Southern worker's life, the mill could also influence the habits and ideas of its working force. The analogy was made to the company store where workers were expected to shop. Whatever the motivation, most of the mill villages had small churches as well as company stores. This is a Bible class at the Arcadia Baptist Church in 1927. Notice that some of the children have bare feet on a Sunday, evidence suggesting they were too poor to buy shoes. The cotton industry was depressed in the later 1920s, and workers were on shorter hours and less pay.

—*Courtesy of Elisabeth Bridgeman Jones*

Arkwright Mill children at play in the playground provided for them. —*Courtesy of Arkwright Mills*

This photograph, taken in the 1920s, reflects the unconscious nostalgia for rural life that seemed widespread among mill workers. —*Courtesy of Lockwood Greene*

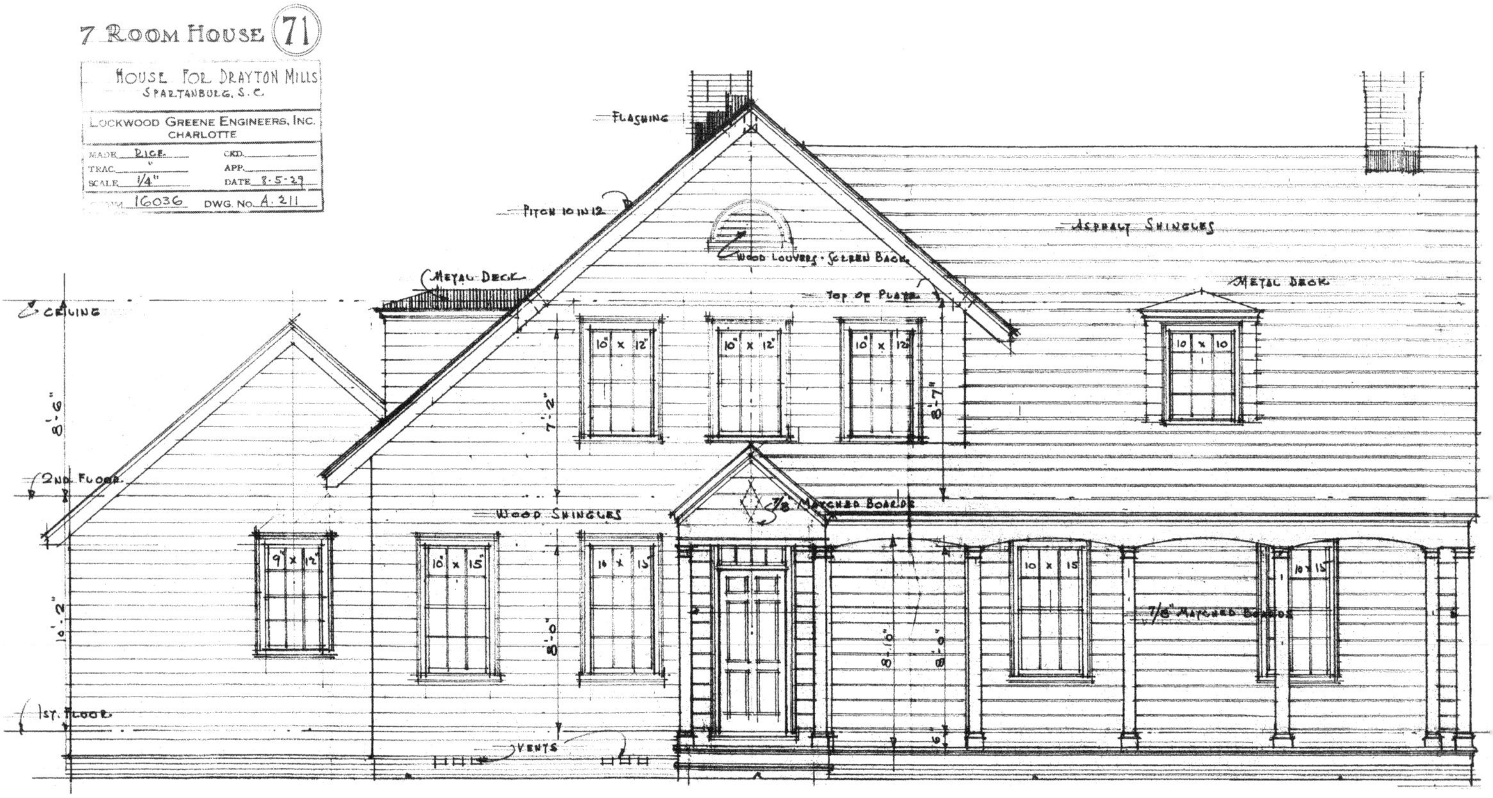

ARCHITECTUAL RENDERING OF DRAYTON MILL HOUSE
—*Courtesy of Lockwood Greene*

The Great Depression

I n remembering its past, Spartanburg should pay particular attention to the Great Depression and World War II. Perhaps no historical period save the Civil War has been as important in changing the fundamental conditions of life in the county. It was during the 1930s that writers, photographers, and sociologists from inside and outside the region exposed the fundamental conditions preventing progress: poverty rooted in sharecropping agriculture, a dependence on textiles (the least progressive industry in America in 1945), and legal segregation. On some of the following pages, images captured by two of America's most famous photographers illustrate the plight of rural inhabitants in Spartanburg County.

ABOVE: By 1930 the depression was causing panic. This scene was typical of thousands around the nation as people rushed to their banks to withdraw their deposits. On the extreme left of the photograph is part of the Central Bank, and on the extreme right is part of the Merchants and Farmers Bank. When newly inaugurated President Franklin Delano Roosevelt declared a bank holiday for March 6, 1933, the last of Spartanburg's six banks went under. Yet the city was not long without a bank, for the Citizens and Southern National Bank soon opened under sound "banking principles." —*Courtesy of the Herald-Journal Willis Collection, Spartanburg County (SC) Public Libraries*

LEFT: By 1930 the cotton mills in Spartanburg were in their death throes. There was no money with which to pay employees for even the few hours they were working, so the mills devised a system by which they could pay their workers in tokens. The tokens—common devices used at this time all over the country—were redeemable only at the company store. These particular tokens are from the Fingerville mill. —*Courtesy of Shelby Compton*

The Morgans leave their farm with all their worldly possessions, a common sight in the 1930s and '40s. Sharecroppers moved often (sometimes in the middle of the night) to escape a debt system in which they were trapped. In this case, however, the Morgan family is moving to a new home, which will provide them with their first electric lights, all due to the Rural Electrification Project of the New Deal. —*Courtesy of Pat McKinney*

D orothea Lange (1895-1965) was one of the most talented of the generation of photographers who chronicled America during the Great Depression. During the 1930s Dorothea Lange worked on and off (funding for photographers was uneven) for the photographic division of the Farm Security Administration. Most often they were given general instructions about what to do, then were left to photograph whatever caught their eye. Most of Dorothea Lange's work in the 1930s came from a collaboration with a professor named Paul S. Taylor from the University of California at Berkeley. Together, Lange and Taylor (they eventually married) produced some of the most important social documentary work of the decade. In 1937 they were asked to do a series on farm tenancy and make a swing through the South. Lange always did her homework before taking on an assignment ("my first concern is to obtain sufficient background for understanding of the problems"*), and she read extensively on the farm tenancy problem before taking her trip. She and Taylor began a countrywide automobile trip in California and ended by swinging up through the Carolinas to Virginia. These photographs of sharecroppers were taken during that trip, and they poignantly reflect conditions in Spartanburg County that were not, in any way, unique.

*Milton Meltzer, Dorothea Lange: A Photographer's Life (New York, 1978), p. 171.

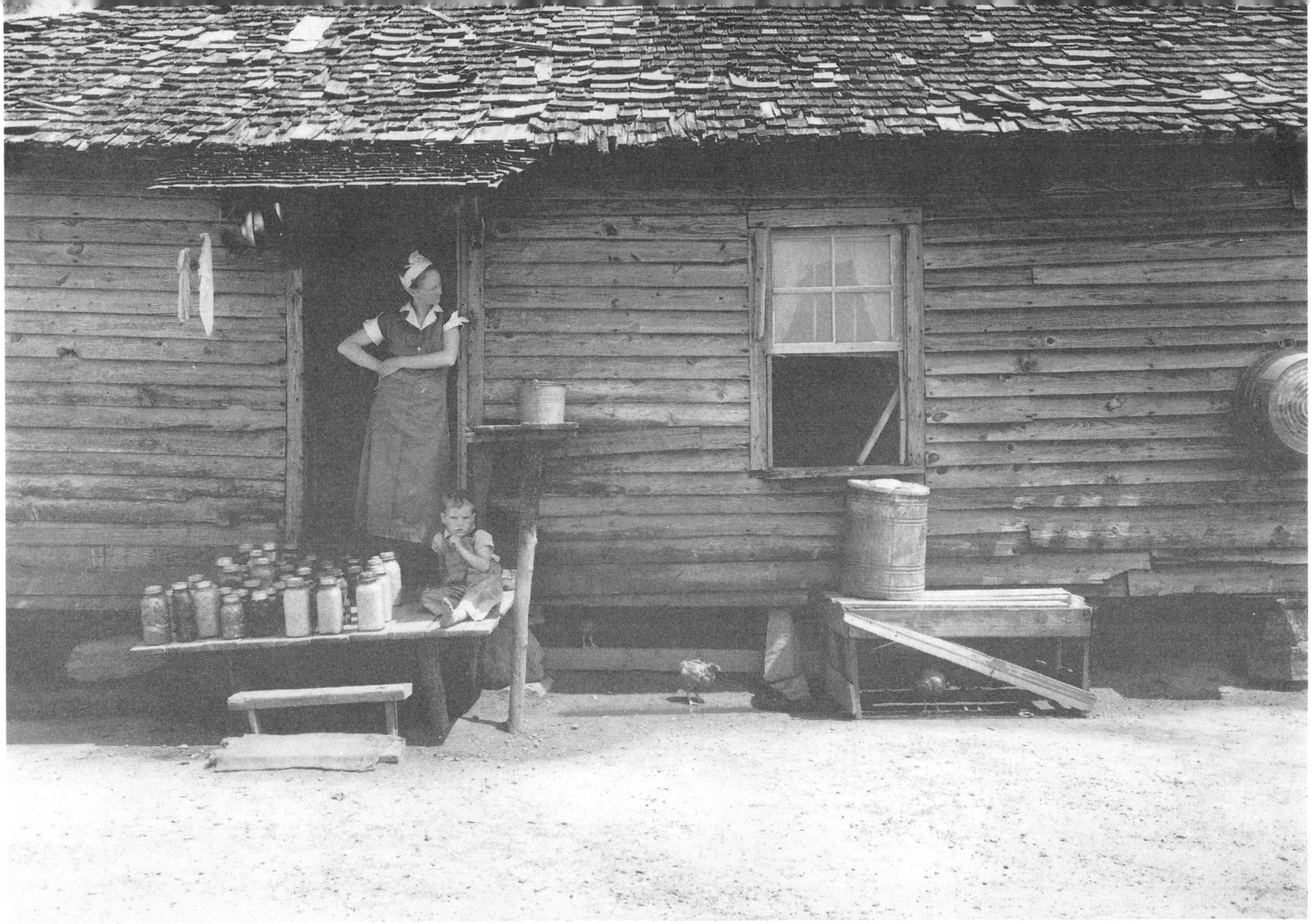

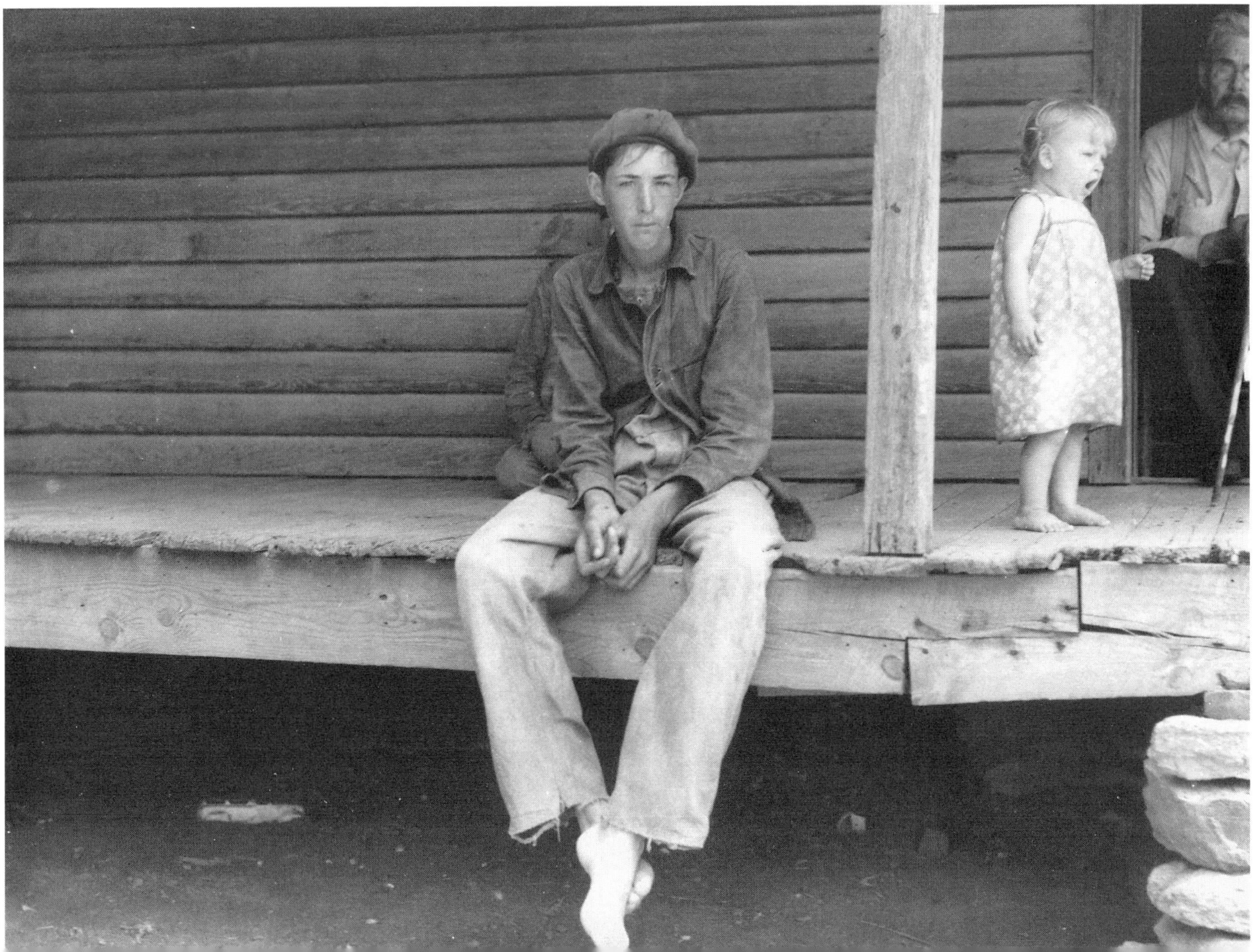

Although not quite as famous as Dorothea Lange, Jack Delano (1914-1997) was a principal photographer for the Farm Security Administration during the 1940s. In 1941 the Farm Security Administration sent him to Spartanburg to photograph the farmers who were being relocated from their farms in White Springs to Pacolet in order to make room for the building of Camp Croft. The following photographs are part of Delano's series recording that event; they are placed here because they show the conditions in which these people had been living during the 1930s. Of his work in Spartanburg Delano said: "Everywhere clusters of sad people huddled, seemingly stunned by the prospect of having to leave their homes and land, to be moved to they didn't know where, all in the name of national defense."* It seems strange to us now that people would be reluctant to leave this squalor, but they had been living on and farming this land all their lives, and they did not want to leave it in spite of their hardscrabble existence.

*Jack Delano, Photographic Memories (Smithsonian Institution Press, 1997), p. 69.

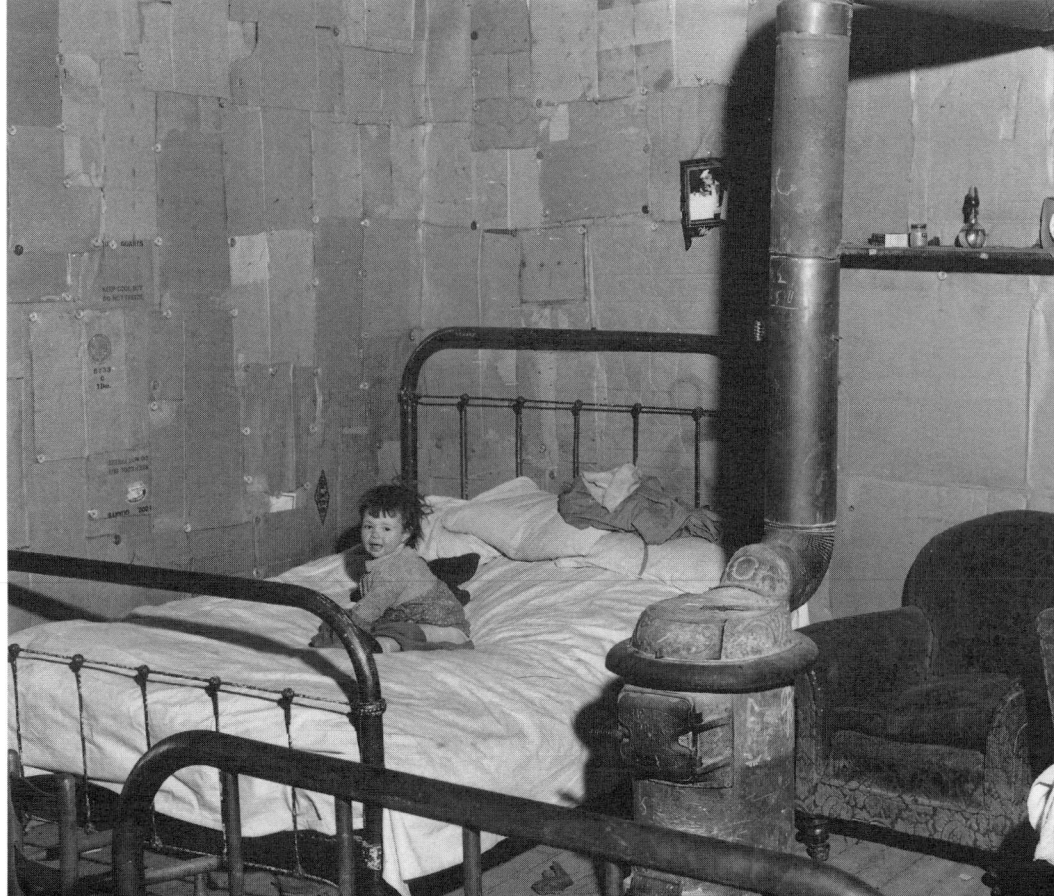

ABOVE: L. A. Anderson, one of the black small land owners who had to move out of the Camp Croft area. Although almost blind, he told the photographer that he was repairing an old house in preparation for moving in.

OPPOSITE PAGE TOP: Miss Mary Haines, who lived all her life on her small farm in the Camp Croft area. She told her photographer that she was planning to move but wanted to come back when "all the shootin' is over."

OPPOSITE PAGE BOTTOM: A combination bed and living room in the home of a "squatter" family in the Camp Croft area.

Above: Children of a "squatter" family preparing to move out of the Spartanburg army camp area.

Right: Mrs. L. A. Anderson, who lived in the Camp Croft area. She came to help a neighbor move.

Opposite Page: Mrs. Jennings resting after a day of moving into her pre-fabricated home.

—*Photographs by Jack Delano, courtesy of the Farm Security Administration, Library of Congress*

R. B. White, who owned a store and a farm in the Camp Croft area.
—*Photograph by Jack Delano, courtesy of the Farm Security Administration, Library of Congress*

When the United States War Department decided to build Camp Croft, it had to relocate hundreds of families from the area. The Farm Security Administration built the families new pre-fabricated houses in Pacolet. In spite of the poverty and poor housing conditions in which most of the families lived, many were reluctant to give up their homes or the land they had tilled as sharecroppers or tenant farmers. As part of its ongoing effort to record the history of the United States during its periods of crisis (the Great Depression and World War II), the Farm Security Administration sent one of its photographers, Jack Delano, to Spartanburg to photograph the resettlement; Delano took the following photographs in March and April 1941.

The Army Signal Corps made this aerial photograph of Camp Croft in the early 1940s. In 1940 the War Department bought a 22,000-acre tract between S.C. 56 and S.C. 176 southeast of the city of Spartanburg for the basic training of infantry troops. In February 1941 the United States Army activated Camp Croft, named for South Carolina-born Major General Edward Croft. Eighteen to twenty thousand men were trained at the facility every three months. At the end of the war, the War Department decided not to make the camp a permanent military base. The Spartanburg County Foundation bought it for more than $1 million in March 1945; the foundation had authority to dispose of the property in any way it wished, with the proceeds to benefit the county. Most of the land has been sold for industrial use. —*Courtesy of the Spartanburg Herald-Journal*

Belongings packed on a small trailer, this family told the photographer it was moving out of the military reservation area. —*Photograph by Jack Delano, courtesy of the Farm Security Administration, Library of Congress*

ABOVE: A tenant farmer's belongings being moved out of the Camp Croft area.

OPPOSITE PAGE TOP: An abandoned farm house in the Camp Croft area.

OPPOSITE PAGE CENTER: The family cow watches as a family moves into its new pre-fabricated house.

OPPOSITE PAGE BOTTOM: The Farm Security Administration rebuilt homes made from these pre-fab sections for families forced to move out of the military reservation area.
—*Photographs by Jack Delano, courtesy of the Farm Security Administration, Library of Congress*

Top: This boy was a member of a family who moved into one of the pre-fabricated houses. The photographer reported that the Pepsi-Cola can contained Pepsi syrup that had to be mixed with soda water to make the drink.

Bottom: A family having lunch at its new home. The young boy is William White, who now serves as the mayor of Cowpens. —*Photographs by Jack Delano, courtesy of Farm Security Administration, Library of Congress*

Camp Croft: War Years

The United States Army on dress parade at Camp Croft.
—*Courtesy of Bill Phillips*

Practicing at Duncan Park Lake.
—*Photograph by Army Signal Corps, courtesy of the National Archives Still Pictures Branch, National Archives II, College Park, Md.*

One of the grenades discovered at Camp Croft decades after the facility closed.
—*Courtesy of George Mullinax*

Pvt. Theodore Gates of Milwaukee, WI, and Pvt. Joseph B. Caputo of Newark, N.J., (right), exercise during calisthenics period at Camp Croft in 1942.

Camp Croft boasted the only mock boat in the Army. Christened "Col. B. J. Mills" after the commanding officer of the 8th Training Regiment, the boat was 32 feet high and 50 feet across the center line. The small invasion rowboat was 15 feet by five feet.

—Photographs by Army Signal Corps, courtesy of the National Archives Still Pictures Branch, National Archives II, College Park, Md.

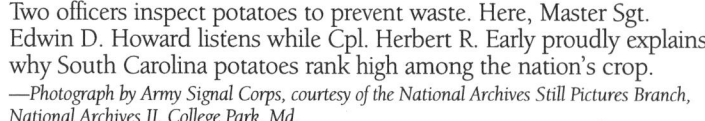

Two officers inspect potatoes to prevent waste. Here, Master Sgt. Edwin D. Howard listens while Cpl. Herbert R. Early proudly explains why South Carolina potatoes rank high among the nation's crop.
—*Photograph by Army Signal Corps, courtesy of the National Archives Still Pictures Branch, National Archives II, College Park, Md.*

MESS KIT
—*Courtesy of James Crocker*

Camp Croft women in combat camoflauge—even their nylons.

DECLASSIFIED MANUALS
—*Courtesy of James Crocker*

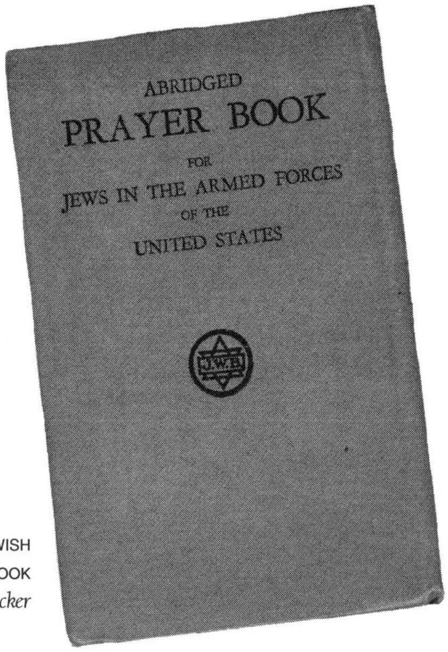

MILITARY-ISSUED JEWISH
PRAYER BOOK
—*Courtesy of James Crocker*

1943 CHAMBER OF
COMMERCE BOOKLET
—*Courtesy of James
Crocker*

The firing range at Camp Croft.
—*Photograph by Army Signal Corps, courtesy of the National Archives Still Pictures Branch, National Archives II, College Park, MD.*

Troops wait to enjoy a show at their theater on the post at Camp Croft. This building is now the home of the Spartanburg Little Theater.

—*Photograph by Army Signal Corps, courtesy of the National Archives Still Pictures Branch, National Archives II, College Park, Md.*

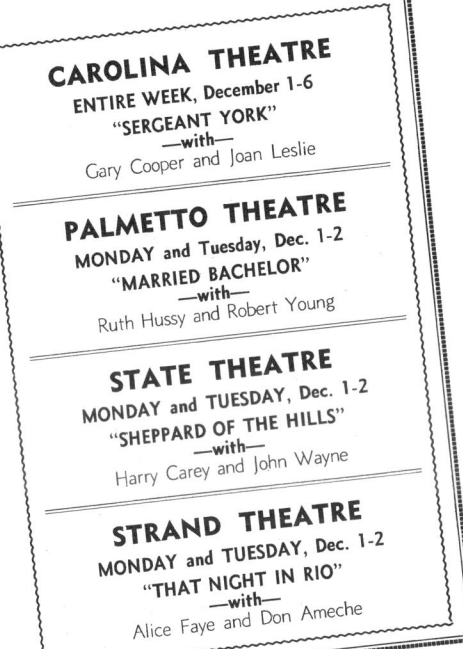

CAROLINA THEATRE
ENTIRE WEEK, December 1-6
"SERGEANT YORK"
—with—
Gary Cooper and Joan Leslie

PALMETTO THEATRE
MONDAY and Tuesday, Dec. 1-2
"MARRIED BACHELOR"
—with—
Ruth Hussy and Robert Young

STATE THEATRE
MONDAY and TUESDAY, Dec. 1-2
"SHEPPARD OF THE HILLS"
—with—
Harry Carey and John Wayne

STRAND THEATRE
MONDAY and TUESDAY, Dec. 1-2
"THAT NIGHT IN RIO"
—with—
Alice Faye and Don Ameche

OFFICIAL FOOTBALL PROGRAM

PRICE 10¢   PRICE 10¢

CAMP CROFT vs. WOFFORD COLLEGE
Saturday, Nov. 29, 1941 » » Duncan Park

Camp Croft football program (far right). This program contained the usual team statistics, ads for local movie theaters, and a reminder for upcoming games.

—*Courtesy of James Crocker*

"NEXT HOME GAME"
SATURDAY, DEC. 6, 1941
CAMP CROFT
VS.
Havana University
AT
DUNCAN PARK
KICK-OFF 2 P. M.

In this 1942 image, desk clerk Giller helps Miss Bunker sign in for a visit to Camp Croft. —*Photograph by Army Signal Corps, courtesy of the National Archives Still Pictures Branch, National Archives II, College Park, Md.*

Entertaining troops was an important part of the war effort; this candid snapshot shows one of the favorite "pin-up" girls of American troops, Betty Grable, as she prepares to entertain the troops in Spartanburg. The popular actress insisted that an enlisted man be her escort while she was visiting the camp and city, and the lucky man, Sgt. Thomas McDermott, is seen carrying out his duties. The sergeant reported that Grable had spoken to every man in the base hospital. To this day veterans fondly remember her gracious enthusiasm. —*Photograph by Army Signal Corps, courtesy of the National Archives Still Pictures Branch, National Archives II, College Park, MD.*

Like Camp Wadsworth during World War I, Camp Croft promoted fraternization between the soldiers and civilians, and many a wartime courtship resulted in a wedding.
—*Photograph by Army Signal Corps, courtesy of the National Archives Still Pictures Branch, National Archives II, College Park, MD.*

Busy soldiers could simply check boxes on these postcards to send messages home.
—*Courtesy of James Crocker*

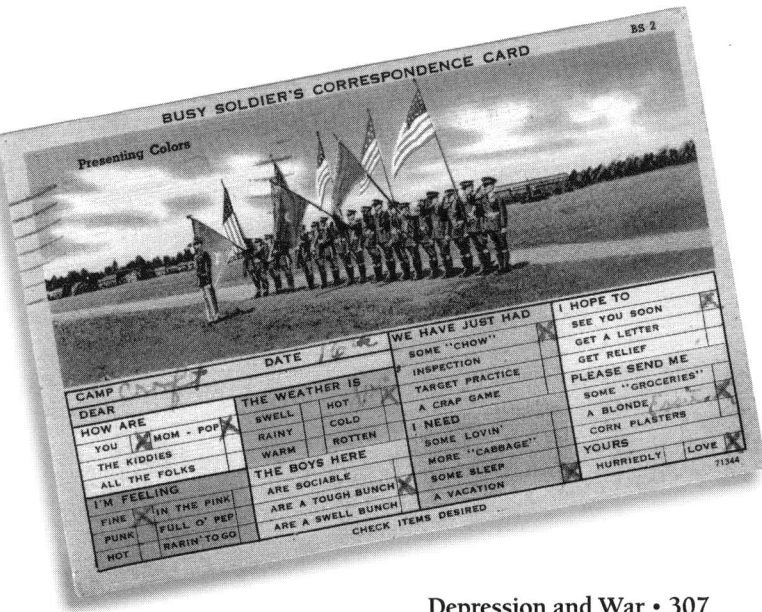

FREEDOM FIGHTERS

CAROLINA
STARTS MONDAY-NOVEMBER 28 FOR
"EASY LIVING" GREAT PRO-FOOTBALL

The Second World War marked a turning point in the history of the nation, the South, and Spartanburg County. After World War II Spartanburg County boomed. Its tradition of heavy investment in textiles, its selection as a site for experiments in soil conservation, its growing peach industry, and its aggressive leadership provided a sound basis for growth. Although Americans had not had to sacrifice as much as the people

Progress and Change

Recovery

1945 - 2000

of other countries during the war, they had rationed necessities, conserved, "made do," and done without. Luxury items had gone unsought and unsold. By 1945 the demand for consumer goods was almost insatiable. When American industry changed its output from war materials to consumer goods, the combination produced unprecedented prosperity. Indeed, from the late 1940s to the mid-seventies, Americans, including people living in Spartanburg County,

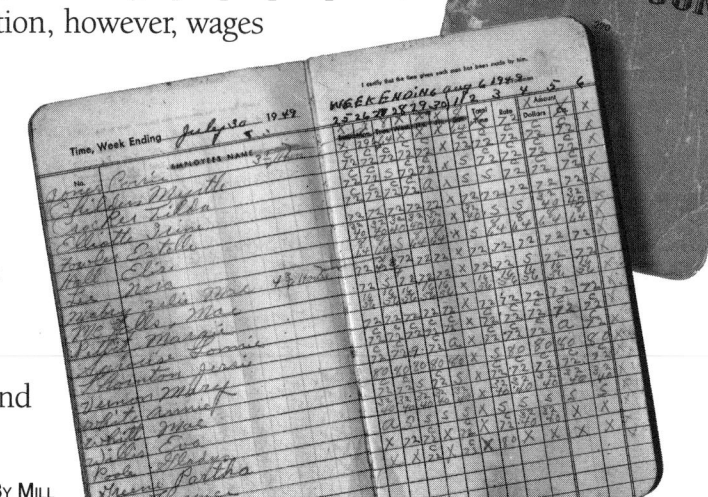

enjoyed the greatest period of prosperity in world history.

Prior to the war, the textile industry nationwide was backward by American industrial standards. During the half-century after the war, these same mills gained a leading place in the world's production of cloth by modernizing and investing in research and development. World War II had resuscitated the cotton mills, and postwar demands prolonged and deepened their recovery. As the county's primary industry expanded its vision as well as its product line, "cotton mills" became "textile mills." Eventually, world competition closed the weaker mills. The textile industry that remained survived by targeting niche markets and investing heavily in research, thus transforming what had been a backward industry into one of America's most innovative and far-sighted. The region's powerful Congressional delegation contributed directly to this transformation by promoting national policies that protected textiles from many forms of foreign competition. New industries recruited to the area provided work for people who would earlier have been in cotton mills. Although this diversification was sometimes painful, as textiles played a less exclusive but more robust role in the overall economy, Spartanburg County reaped long-term benefits. As the national standard of living rose, local wages followed that trend, and more people in Spartanburg than ever before enjoyed the benefits of prosperity.

By Southern standards Spartanburg's people prospered; relative to the rest of the nation, however, wages and benefits remained low. The State Development Board and the local Chamber of Commerce took advantage of this discrepancy, among other factors, to lure businesses from the North. Desperate for jobs and economic development, state and

LAMINATED SHUTTLE USED BY SPARTAN MILLS UNTIL 1990.
—*Courtesy of Spartan Mills*

TIME BOOKS COMMONLY USED BY MILL SUPERVISORS. —*Courtesy of the Spartanburg County Regional Museum*

local officials put together economic incentives too good for business to ignore. Immediate success was achieved in the textile industry. By the 1960s extraordinary efforts lured both domestic and foreign companies with the promise of a lack of organized labor, a history of low wages, an enhanced system of transportation (aided by the federal program to build interstate highways), and a congenial climate made even more so by air conditioning. By the 1990s Spartanburg County had a low unemployment rate but was still plagued by relatively low wages, a tax system that was too dependent on residential property, and a lack of effective long-range planning.

J. W. WOODWARD FUNERAL HOME FAN.
—*Courtesy of James Crocker*

In the postwar world, Spartanburg took advantage of its economic differences from other sections of the country, yet in many ways Spartanburg became much like the rest of the nation. The Great Depression had focused attention on many of the problems of the region: a debilitating form of agriculture built on sharecropping and tenant farming, an industrial base too dependent on one industry, and a system of legal segregation that resulted in an enormous waste of talent and economic resources. After 1945 legal segregation was finally destroyed by a combination of local African-American initiatives and pressure from outside the region. The federal courts and Congressional civil rights legislation provided the foundation and incentives for careful cooperation between local white and African-American leaders, which in turn led to progress by the county's African-American population. The integration of both textile mills and schools broke barriers to cooperation between the races which had seemed insurmountable a few years before. Also, by the end of the century, a combination of factors had significantly reduced the importance of agriculture in the county's economy. New Deal programs, migration north for steady and better wages, and the mechanical cotton picker destroyed the sharecropper and tenant farmer system of agriculture.

As the South lost some of its distinctiveness, technological innovations enhanced its similarities to the rest of the nation. Some people interpret these developments as showing how much the South has become like the rest of the nation, while others believe that the nation has become more like the South. Whichever you choose to stress, the change is evident. Linked with everyone by radio and television, people in Spartanburg saw the same advertisements, listened to much of the same music (although it remained a center of "Southern country" music), watched most of the same television shows (although cable provided the possibility for an extra heavy dose of stock car racing, demolition derbies, and wrestling) and shared generally in a national culture. In the 1950s the local television station, WSPA, aired Spartanburg's versions of national television shows: spinoffs of "Howdy-Doody," of "Kukla, Fran and Ollie," of "American Bandstand," and of quiz bowls. Yet, despite the tendency toward the homogenization of American culture, Spartanburg County kept much of its distinctive Southernness, defined by different people in different ways. Almost all who came here to live from other parts of the country testified to a slower pace, a less frantic demeanor, and a continuation of a "drawl," of Southern hospitality, and of "manners." If people don't know what all this means, then they are new to the area or immune to their surroundings; the first will pass, and the second is their loss.

In the last half of the twentieth century, living in the South meant sharing not only national prosperity but also its peculiar growing pains. Spartanburg now shared the problems associated with rapid growth and a consumer culture. It suffered from a decaying downtown, its businesses lured to malls that would themselves begin to destroy one another by the end of the century as bigger definitely became better. The city was surrounded by suburbs (now called "developments"), which increasingly were protected by walled entrances, sometimes manned by guards. The distance that had emerged between the mill villagers and the town dwellers from the 1880s through the 1930s was recreated by the movement of the middle class outside the city limits and by a stolid opposition to annexation. Where once the city had been the haven of the middle class surrounded by the workers living on the periphery of the city, now the geography had been reversed. While the socio-economic situation remained generally the same after desegregation, it was complicated by issues of race. Such a twist in social history was aptly described by Mark Twain: "History does not repeat itself, but it rhymes."

In the second half of the twentieth century, Spartanburg underwent fundamental change, much of which many would describe as progress. One of the most remarkable characteristics of these events and trends has been the absence of confrontation, social upheaval, or even violence. Although upheaval could have resulted from any one of these changes, the most obvious case is the civil rights revolution. Comparing Spartanburg with the rest of the region, the peaceful equanimity with which this change took place is noteworthy. This is not to deny the existence of frustration, anger, or anxiety, but that such feelings did not exhibit themselves in any more overt violence is astonishing. It may also be one of our finest legacies.

The photographs in this collection reflect a tenacious and ambitious people, a people sometimes beset with single-mindedness in agriculture, in business, and in race. The last half of the twentieth century has witnessed the disintegration of that single-mindedness, the creation of a sensitivity to the use of the land, the diversification of the types of industry, and the bringing about of increased opportunities for African Americans. Foreigners from abroad and from "the North" have moved into the area and benefited it with diversity and increased tolerance. Many would argue that a new foundation for a changing society has been created, a foundation that builds on the very best of Southern tradition and which makes possible constructive change. Perhaps that is progress.

The future of the area looks bright, but in looking to the future we should not neglect its past—not because the past will teach us any specific lessons but because it can give us perspective from which to judge and act. Since the early 1800s residents of Spartanburg County have bragged about its pleasant climate and its fertile soil. They have also despaired of their poverty, but they have stayed, persevered, and looked to the future. This is our legacy. We must see to it that the better part of their world, the world of these images, endures.

MALCOLM BALDRIGE NATIONAL QUALITY AWARD WON BY MILLIKEN AND COMPANY IN 1989.

Landscape & Architecture

Top: In the late 1930s Morgan Square had taken on a new look. The iron fountain with its trees and iron fence had been replaced by a rectangular bandstand surrounded with globe lights; the old street lamps had been replaced by vertical florescent bulbs; and the increasing traffic had forced the city to better regulate the flow of traffic by installing traffic islands.
—*Courtesy of the Herald-Journal Willis Collection, Spartanburg County (SC) Public Libraries*

Bottom: In the late 1940s a covered bus waiting station had been built between the bandstand and the statue of General Morgan. —*Courtesy of the Spartanburg County Regional Museum*

Top: In the 1950s the block of buildings at the top of Morgan Square was being demolished to enlarge the square so it would front North Church Street, and the bandstand and bus waiting area were gone. The problem of traffic control, which had plagued the area since the turn of the century, continued to make itself manifest in this conglomeration of arrows, parking spots, and converging streets, a problem that has never been satisfactorily solved. The cannons and cannon balls that had flanked the statue of Daniel Morgan were melted down for other uses during World War II.

Bottom: Morgan Square in the1960s had Daniel Morgan at its east end. The old Palmetto Building had been covered by the facade of Belk-Hudson, and further attempts had been made to handle the traffic congestion in the square. In the lower right is Pete's lunch, which had by then taken over from the Elite as the local hangout for newspaper people, local historians, lawyers and politicians. If you wanted to know what was going on in the city, you went to Pete's for breakfast.

—*Photographs courtesy of the Spartanburg County Regional Museum*

Right: In 1960, in order to ease traffic congestion in downtown Spartanburg, city officials decided to move the statue of General Daniel Morgan from its location in the middle of Morgan Square opposite Magnolia Street to its present location on the east end of the square. To continue to face the general in his traditional direction—northeast—would be to have him look directly into the building on the east side of North Church Street, so it was decided to turn him around and have him face out over the square in a southwest direction. It seemed bad enough to many old-time Spartanburg residents to move the general at all, but to have him face southward, as if he expected enemies to come from that direction, was even more unsettling. One resident summed up the feelings of many: "The general would not approve!" Nevertheless, the change was made in September 1960. This photograph shows Morgan being lowered from his pedestal in the middle of the square. The tall building to the left of the pedestal is the Andrews Building, now destroyed.
—*Courtesy of B & B Studio*

Opposite Page Top: North Church Street from the intersection with Main Street in the 1960s. Belk-Hudson has yet to cover the Palmetto Building with a tin facade, Price's men's store occupies the back of the lower floor, and Smith's Drugs has a store in the next block. The Montgomery Building still has the iron marquee extending over the sidewalk, but its dark-colored stacks of bay windows have been painted white.

Opposite Page Center: The north side of East Main Street looking west to the intersection with Church Street. This 1965 photograph shows Belk-Hudson with its facade and Woolworth's, which was directly across the street from Kress and Montgomery Ward, making for a treasure of department stores in the same block. The turn-of-the-century building in the center of the photograph looks isolated in the midst of all the sheet metal, glass and ubiquitous signs of the time.

Opposite Page Bottom: Montgomery Ward and S. H. Kress & Co. were some of the major national department stores that marked downtown shopping in the 1960s. The Elite Restaurant had become the W & W Cafeteria, perhaps indicating the beginning of the movement to fast food and faster living that were to mark the coming decades and change the physical character of the city. The people on the left of the photograph look as if they are charging across the street, probably intent on "making the light"–another indication of a changing lifestyle that would grow increasingly hectic.
—*Photographs courtesy of the Herald-Journal Willis Collection, Spartanburg County (SC) Public Libraries*

ABOVE: An aerial view of downtown Spartanburg. Notice the single water tower in the downtown landscape.
—*Courtesy of the Spartanburg County Regional Museum*

OPPOSITE PAGE TOP: Robert Willis was standing in the middle of South Church Street just below Milster Street (identified by the white stone marker on the left just below the gas price sign of 29.9 cents a gallon) looking north toward Hampton Avenue and the center of town when he took this photograph in the 1960s. The street on the right with the stop sign is Young Street. The wooded area to the right of the photograph has since been cleared as part of urban renewal and is now the site of Carver Junior High School and the Spartanburg Swim Center.

OPPOSITE PAGE CENTER: In the 1960s and '70s the open-air vendors' stalls of the Farmers' Market on Kennedy Street provided fresh vegetables, fruits, and flowers from around the county to city dwellers. By the end of the century, the spaces had been turned into enclosed shops.

OPPOSITE PAGE BOTTOM: The intersection of South Converse and Henry Streets. Note the ruts for the Southern railroad tracks, which were removed in the 1920s. The track used to proceed to just beyond Liberty Street (which parallels Converse) where they curved to the right and crossed Main Street.
—*Photographs courtesy of the Herald-Journal Willis Collection, Spartanburg County (SC) Public Libraries*

1970s view of the Main Street Mall. —*Courtesy of B & B Studio*

The clock tower was the centerpiece of the downtown shopping mall. The tower held the clock and bell that had been part of the old Opera House. It has since been moved to the western end of Morgan Square.
—*Courtesy of the Spartanburg County Regional Museum*

In the 1960s suburban American shopping centers drew shoppers away from the traditional downtown stores. As business in the center of town declined, city officials and downtown merchants banded together "to save downtown." City officials believed salvation would come by way of creating open-air malls in the city center with convenient off-street parking and an inviting atmosphere in which to spend a few hours. The city of Spartanburg suffered from the same problems as other towns and sought her solutions in the same way. The Main Street Mall, dedicated in 1974, stretched from Converse Street to Church Street. The street was reopened in the 1980s. —*Courtesy of Spartan Communications Corporation*

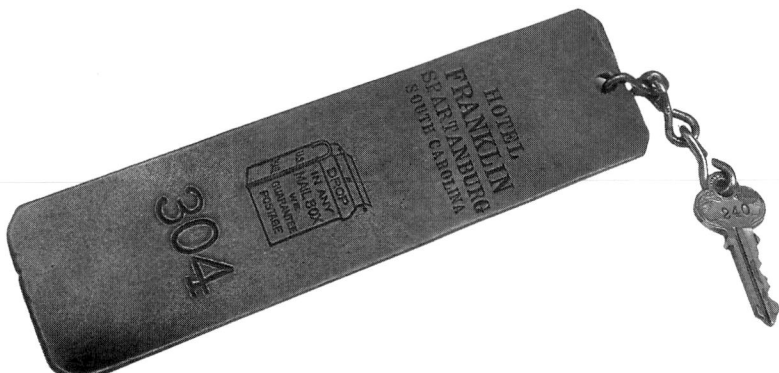

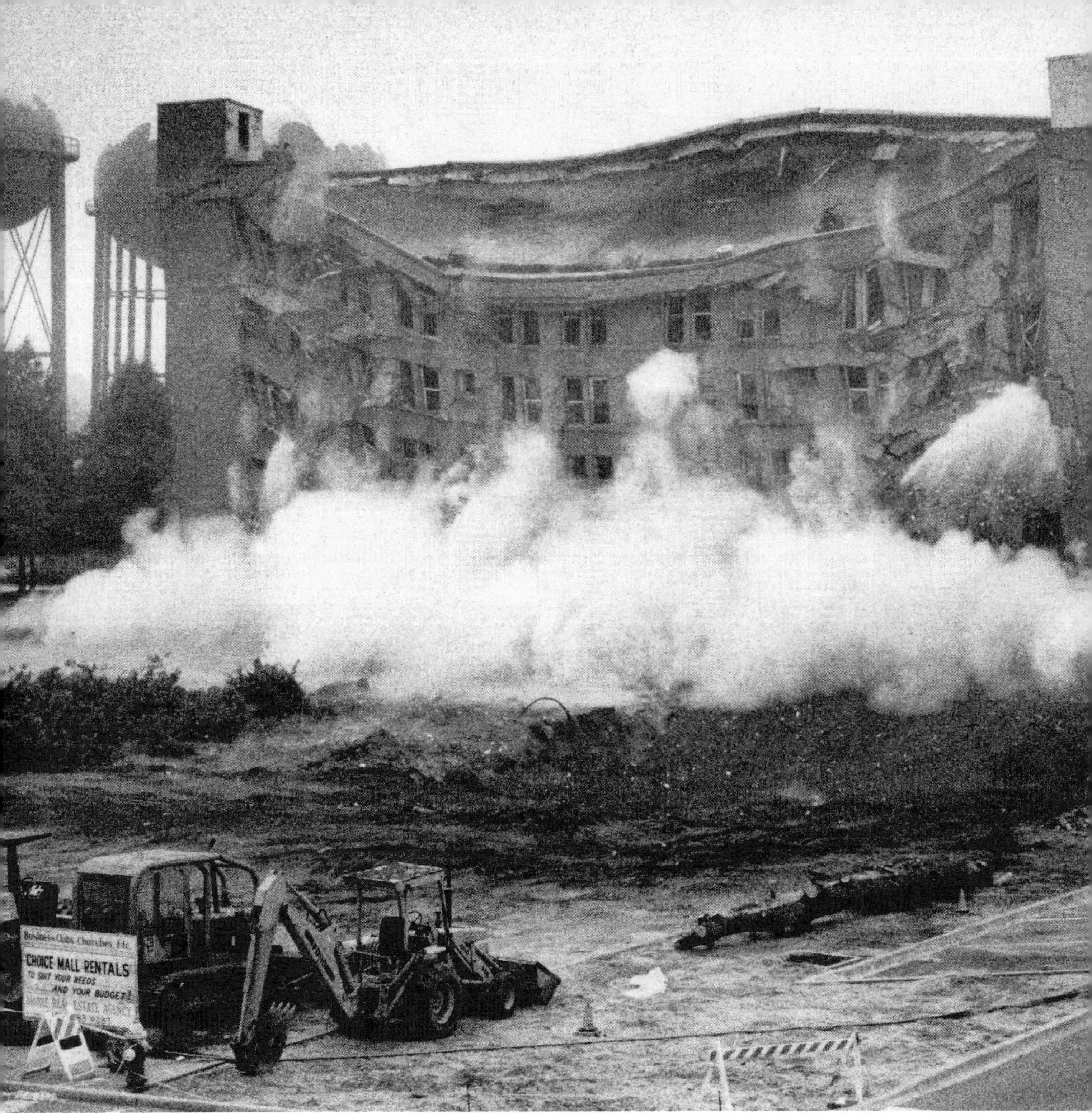
CHOICE MALL RENTALS
TO SUIT YOUR NEEDS
AND YOUR BUDGET!

HOTEL
FRANKLIN
SPARTANBURG
SOUTH CAROLINA
304
DROP IN ANY MAIL BOX WE GUARANTEE POSTAGE
240

HOTEL FRANKLIN KEY
—Courtesy of the Spartanburg County Regional Museum

The Hotel Franklin was in its heyday in the 1940s. Betty Grable stayed there when she visited Camp Croft during World War II. Located on East Main Street in the heart of the downtown shopping area, the Franklin served meals to its clientele as well as to shoppers. In the image at left, the structure had been enlarged, and its grand facade with the columns and the large cornice gave it an almost whimsical look, especially when its essentially mundane general structure was exposed by the parking lot. The building was imploded to make way for the Spartan Foods tower in the 1980s, and its stained glass windows now hang in the Broadwalk office building (above image).

—*Photographs courtesy of the Herald-Journal; the Herald-Journal Willis Collection, Spartanburg County (SC) Public Libraries; and Mark Olencki*

Gas Bottom was an area that stretched from Pine Street along Daniel Morgan Avenue up to the vicinity of Church Street. It got its name from the gas works plant located on Pine Street next to the railroad overpass across from Daniel Morgan Avenue and from the low lying land on a creek that ran through it. In antebellum days land that was next to streams was referred to as "bottom land." The houses in Gas Bottom were small and  dilapidated; many had outdoor toilets and no electricity. They were called "shotgun houses," so named because you could fire a shotgun from the front door right through the house. Typical of housing built by whites for African Americans all over the South, shotgun houses were quickly and easily built. By the 1970s Gas Bottom had become among the worst "slums" in the city. On the upper right of the bottom photograph, you can see the steeple of Central United Methodist Church, the Montgomery Building, and the top of the Andrews Building. This Gas Bottom area was cleared for urban renewal, and much of it is part of the proposed "Renaissance Park" —a plan for a hotel, golf course, outdoor theater, shops, and other amenities aimed at attracting conventions. The photograph of the gas works spewing black smoke was taken in the 1920s. —*Photographs courtesy of the Herald-Journal Willis Collection, Spartanburg County (SC) Public Libraries*

OPPOSITE PAGE & LEFT: The County Courthouse, which dated from the 1890s, was demolished in the 1960s to make room for a new building. In the photograph on the opposite page, note the signs just above the rubble that say "COLORED WOMEN," "WHITE WOMEN," and "WHITE MEN," reminders of a time when all public and private facilities were strictly segregated.
—*Photographs courtesy of the Spartanburg County Regional Museum*

The new County Courthouse was built in the "International Style" of flat planes, as if the walls were a thin skin drawn tightly against a rigid frame. The style is broken up, however, with the recessed glass wall and the elongated wing, both with prominent framing. The style was reflective of one of the twentieth century's most influential architects, the Swiss architect Le Corbusier.
—*Courtesy of Spartan Communications Corporation*

Beginning in the late 1930s, the federal government was determined to provide better housing for America's poor. Various types of housing projects were one result. These projects were meant to provide affordable and comfortable living quarters to help spawn feelings of community among people who had been, until then, unable to afford decent housing. Several of these multi-family projects were built in Spartanburg, and this one, Tobe Hartwell, was among the largest. As it turned out, the hopes for these communities went awry, and recently some–among them Tobe Hartwell—have been torn down. The inset photo shows the new Tobe Hartwell community under construction in 1999. This neighborhood will have single-family dwellings. *—Photographs courtesy of the Spartanburg County Regional Museum, Mark Olencki*

The residential Schuyler Building was another structure that contributed to Spartanburg's changing skyline. This concrete design was also reminiscent of Le Corbusier, although much more vertical in its emphasis. Concrete and steel were the rage in the 1950s and '60s, and Spartanburg's new buildings reflected the trends of the day.
—*Photograph courtesy of the Spartanburg County Regional Museum*

The YMCA built a new building with the city's first indoor swimming pool in the 1920s on East Main Street between Dean and Converse Streets. It has since been demolished. —*Courtesy of George Mullinax*

Built on the corner of North Liberty and Dunbar streets and opened in 1940, the Greyhound Bus Depot heralded a new age in public transportation with the advent of air-conditioned buses. Buses, along with automobiles, helped bring about the demise of train travel. Indeed, the bus station appropriated part of the name—"Union Station"—of the old train depot.
—*Photograph courtesy of the Herald-Journal Willis Collection, Spartanburg County (SC) Public Libraries*

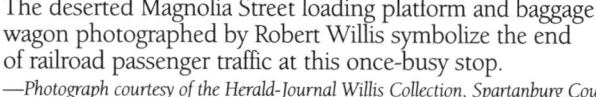

The deserted Magnolia Street loading platform and baggage wagon photographed by Robert Willis symbolize the end of railroad passenger traffic at this once-busy stop.

—*Photograph courtesy of the Herald-Journal Willis Collection, Spartanburg County (SC) Public Libraries*

Railroads continued to play an important role in transportation after the 1940s, but the number of passenger trains declined, while the number of freight trains increased. Here is one of the last photographs of a much reduced railroad station in Spartanburg with one of the new diesel engines pulling the Southern Crescent on the left and a freight train on the right. —*Courtesy of George Mullinax*

In 1977, the Magnolia Street Station shows the freight shunting activity of a working hub of the Southern Railway. This part of the station has since been demolished. —*Courtesy of Mark Olencki*

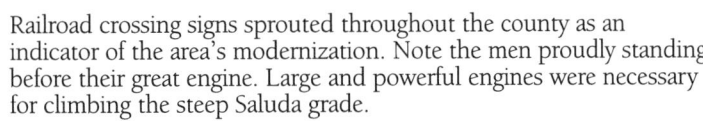

Railroad crossing signs sprouted throughout the county as an indicator of the area's modernization. Note the men proudly standing before their great engine. Large and powerful engines were necessary for climbing the steep Saluda grade.
—*Courtesy of the Spartanburg County Regional Museum*

The last of the types of travel that doomed the railroad was air travel. The interest in aviation only increased after World War II. Spartanburg's downtown airport catered to commercial air passengers. Note the sign for Eastern Airlines on the hangar on the right. —*Courtesy of the Spartanburg County Regional Museum*

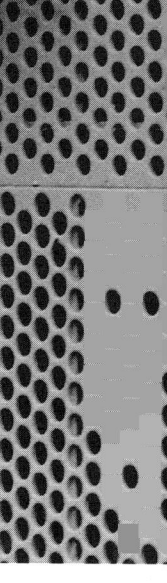

A typical "clover-leaf," part of the federal government's plan (under the administration of President Dwight D. Eisenhower) to crisscross the nation with interstate highways. The interstate highway system resulted from the realization that nothing was going to stop America's love affair with the private passenger car and that trucks were going to become American business's favorite mode for transporting goods. The Spartanburg area is served by I-85, which runs north-south, and I-26, which runs east-west. This photo was taken during construction of the intersection of these massive roadways.

—*Courtesy of Spartan Communications Corporation*

LEFT: The Spartanburg Downtown Airport was not large enough to carry the volume of traffic nor the size of commercial aircraft that Spartanburg's leaders saw in the city's future. Planning for the new facility began in the late 1950s, and the Greenville-Spartanburg Airport opened for its first commercial flights in 1962.

BELOW: Roger Milliken (second from the left), the head of the airport commission, sits aboard a Caterpillar tractor to break ground for the new airport. In the modern age, and for projects as large as the airport, one could not break ground with a common shovel! —*Photographs courtesy of Spartan Communications Corporation*

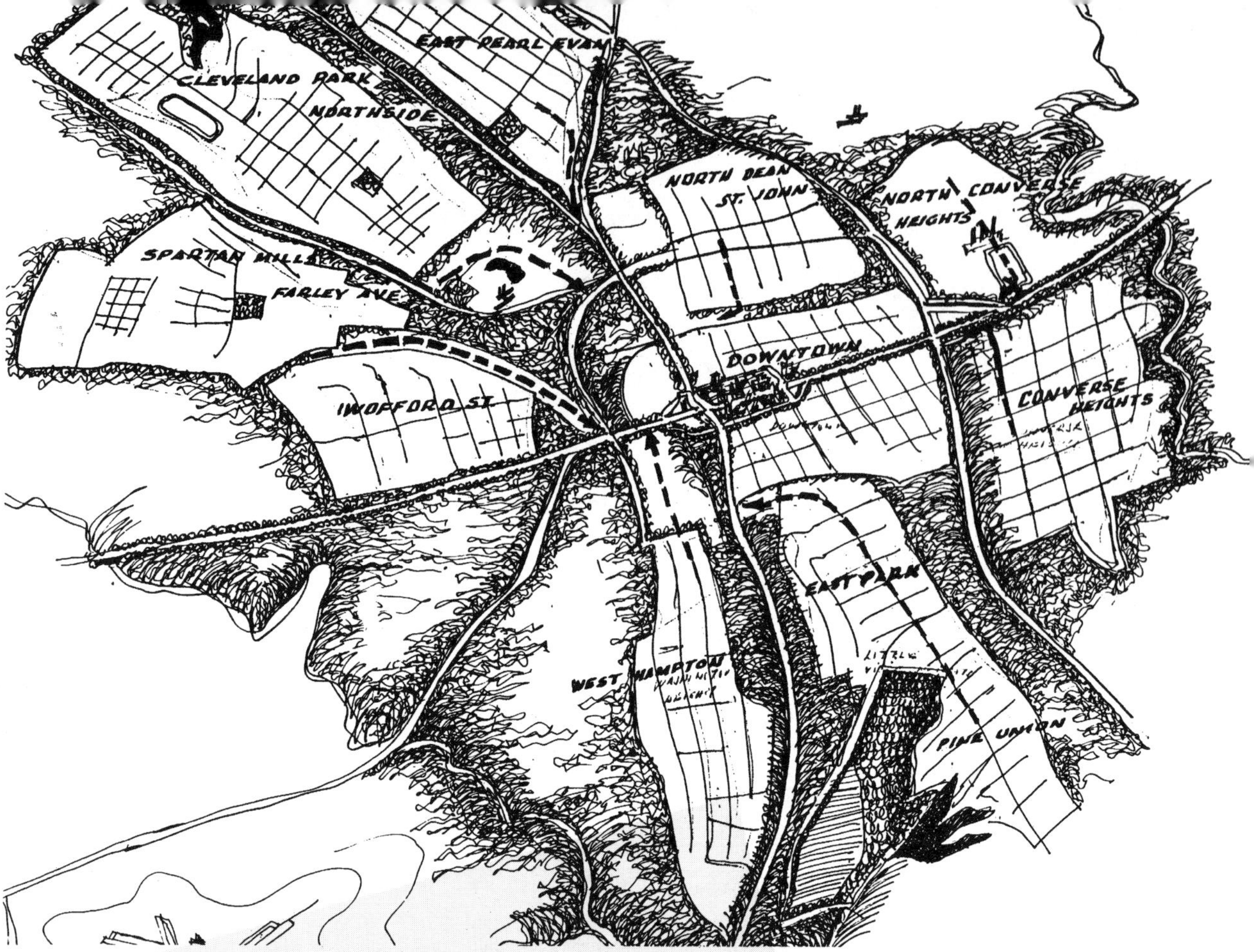
CLEVELAND PARK
NORTHSIDE
NORTH DEAN
ST. JOHN
NORTH CONVERSE
HEIGHTS
SPARTAN MILLS
FARLEY AVE.
DOWNTOWN
WOFFORD ST.
CONVERSE
HEIGHTS
EAST PARK
WEST HAMPTON
PINE UNION

Spartanburg Neighborhoods

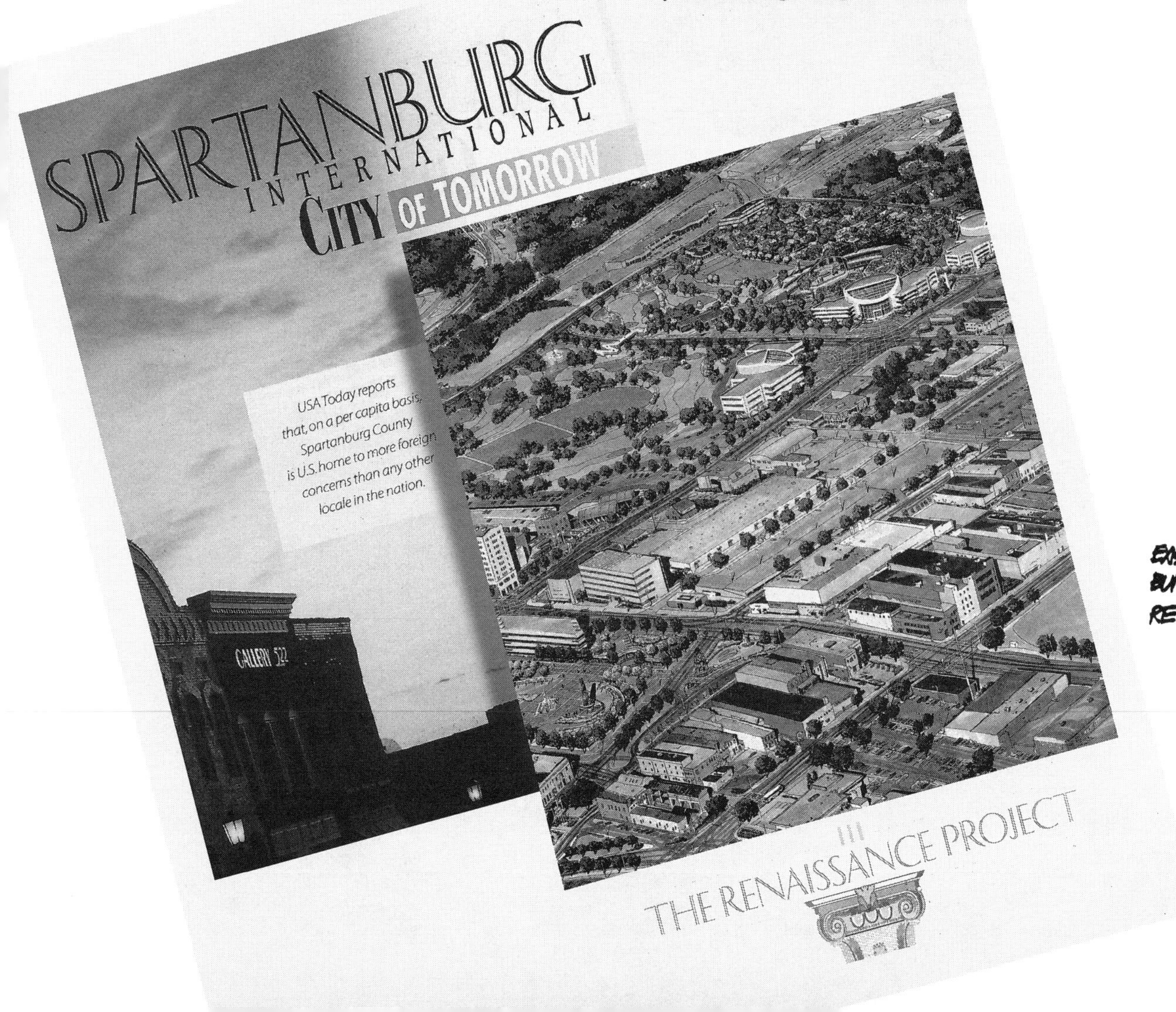
SPARTANBURG
INTERNATIONAL
CITY OF TOMORROW
USA Today reports that, on a per capita basis, Spartanburg County is U.S. home to more foreign concerns than any other locale in the nation.
GALLERY 522
THE RENAISSANCE PROJECT

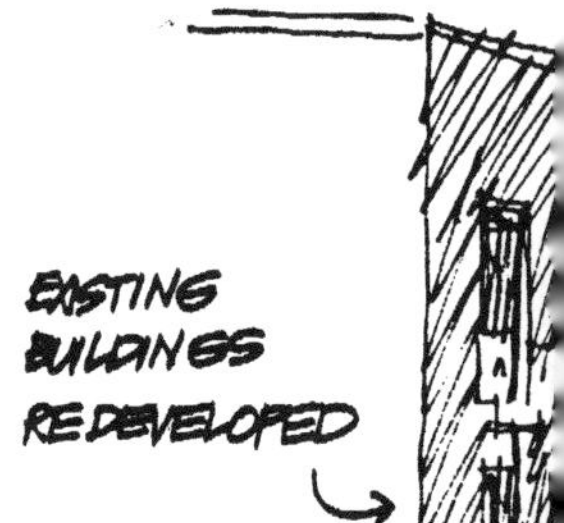
EXISTING
BUILDINGS
REDEVELOPED

The decades of the 1970s and '80s were a time for downtown planning in Spartanburg. A series of plans laid out possible redevelopment projects for the central city. In the early 1980s a group from the American Institute for Architects came to Spartanburg and sketched out ideas for Spartanburg neighborhoods and Morgan Square in the R/UDAT 100 plan. The most recent plan, the Renaissance Park, called for a hotel, amphitheater, and golf course. Construction began in 1999.

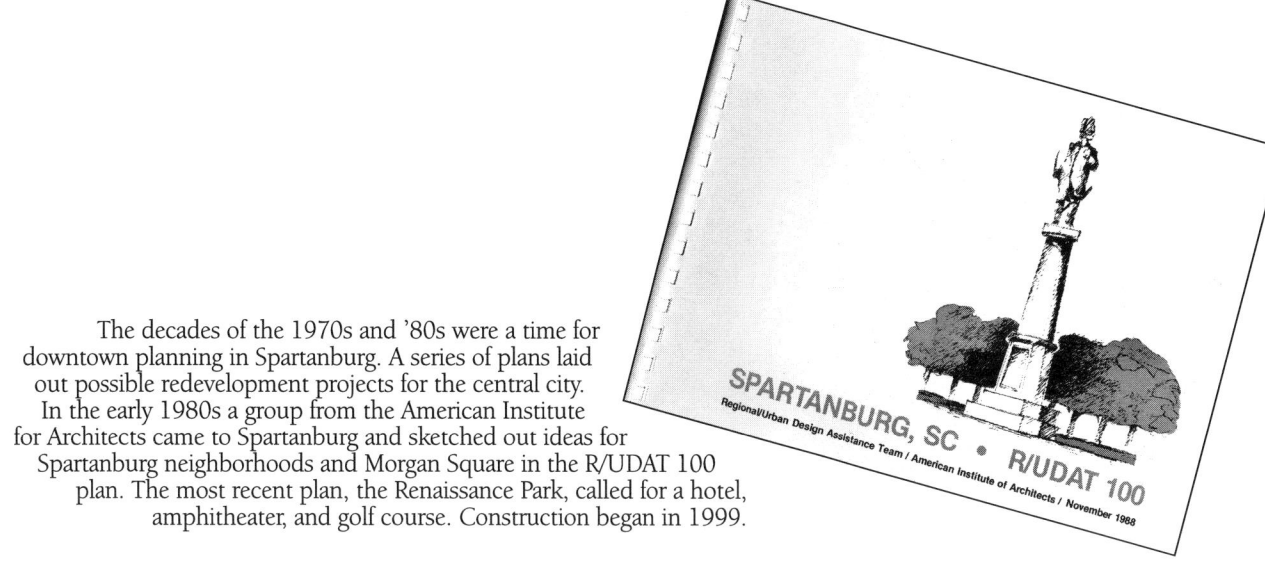

SPARTANBURG, SC • R/UDAT 100
Regional/Urban Design Assistance Team / American Institute of Architects / November 1988

New Morgan Square Development

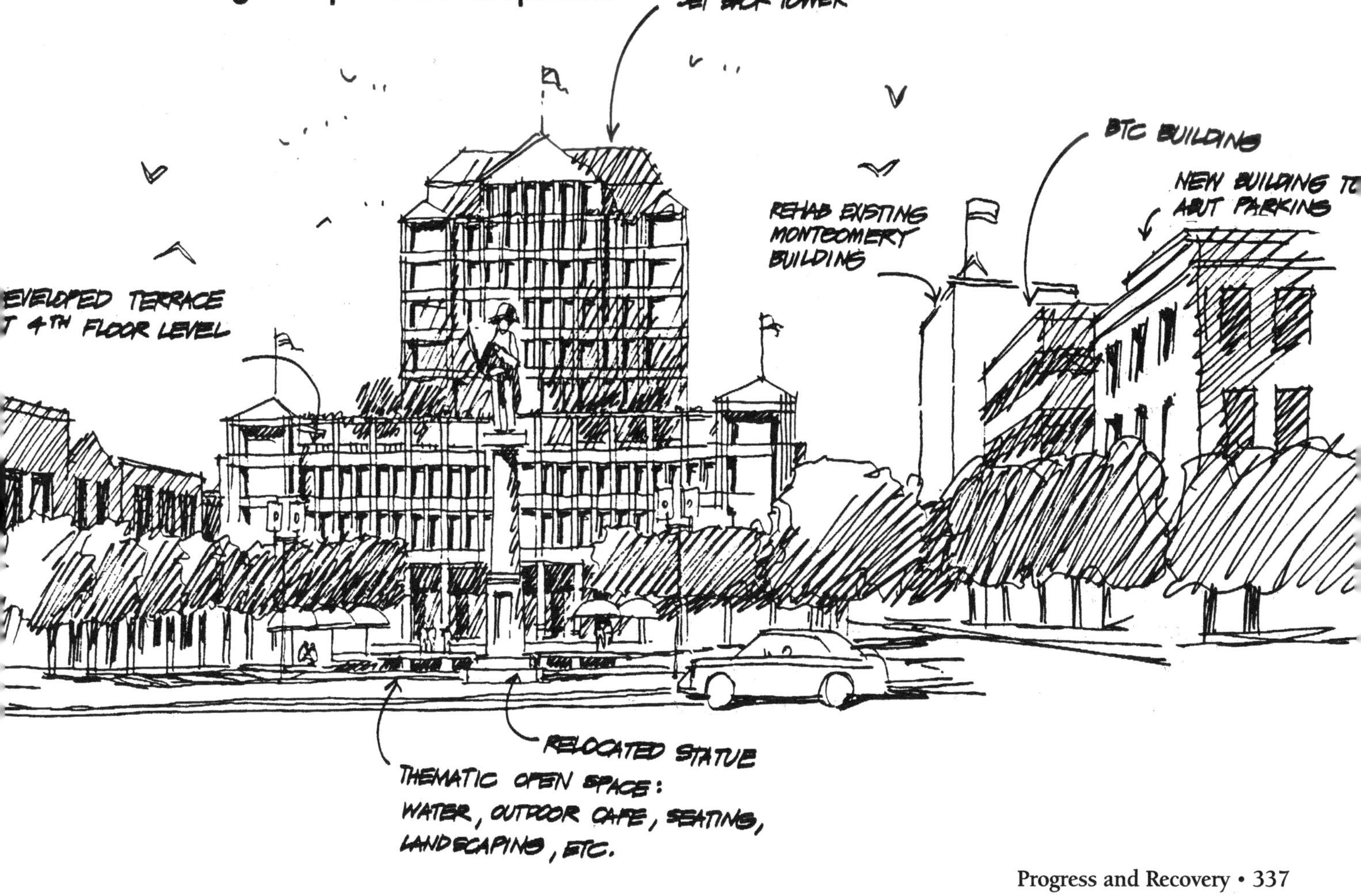

SET BACK TOWER

BTC BUILDING

NEW BUILDING TO ABUT PARKING

REHAB EXISTING MONTGOMERY BUILDINGS

DEVELOPED TERRACE AT 4TH FLOOR LEVEL

RELOCATED STATUE

THEMATIC OPEN SPACE: WATER, OUTDOOR CAFE, SEATING, LANDSCAPING, ETC.

Construction of the Spartan Foods (now Advantica) tower began in 1991.
Here, Chairman Jerry Richardson stands with fellow officers, Jody
Traywick, left, and Bill Phillips, right. Richardson and Charlie Bradshaw
began the company in 1962 with one Hardee's restaurant on Kennedy
Street. By 1993, the company had 130,000 employees worldwide.
—*Courtesy of Mark Olencki*

Right: Spartanburg Technical College opened with 150 students in 1963 during a statewide push to provide better job training for South Carolina citizens. This aerial image was taken in the 1970s. Today the campus has expanded several times and now serves more than 2,500 students. Insert: An architectual rendering of a Health Sciences facility, which will be the school's newest addition.
—*Courtesy of B & B Studio, Spartanburg Technical College*

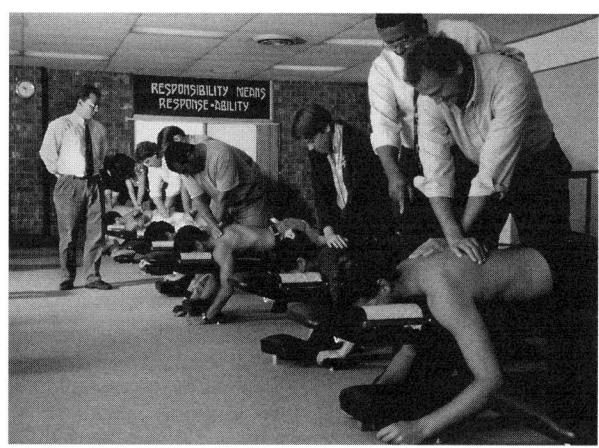

Sherman College was founded on Spartanburg's north side in 1973 to train doctors of chiropractic. Its student body is made up of approximately 400 students representing 42 states and 11 countries. —*Courtesy of Sherman College of Straight Chiropractic*

The University of South Carolina at Spartanburg was founded in 1967 when Spartanburg General Hospital announced that it was phasing out its nursing diploma program. The first class of 177 students included many who came to study nursing. Today USCS serves more than 3,500 students in a wide range of disciplines. —*Courtesy of Mark Olencki*

UNIVERSITY OF SOUTH CAROLINA
AT SPARTANBURG

A $14 million library opened on South Church Street in 1997. Its contemporary design included a brick wall slicing through the building, reminiscent of old textile mill construction. When the library opened, two water tanks were removed to make room for more parking spaces. One had stood since 1935, the other since 1986. —*Photographs courtesy of Mark Olencki*

Community & Culture

Construction began on the Spartanburg Memorial Auditorium in 1948 along North Church Street. Note the Wofford College buildings in the background. A major renovation of this building began in 1999. —*Courtesy B & B Studios*

Cleveland Park, which faces the Asheville Highway, had a grand swimming pool in 1946.
—*Courtesy of the Herald-Journal Willis Collection, Spartanburg County (SC) Public Libraries*

In 1946 the Piedmont Interstate Fair Association was organized to replace and enlarge the old county fair. The organization combined the efforts of six counties (Laurens, Polk, Rutherford, Cherokee, Union, and Spartanburg) to better showcase their industrial and agricultural potential. The fair built a concrete grandstand in 1956 to replace the old wooden structure, and harness racing was replaced by stock car racing—the highlight of the week's activities. —*Courtesy of the Piedmont Interstate Fair Association*

The Spartanburg Gun Club in the 1940s. —*Courtesy of the Spartanburg County Regional Museum*

Construction of a dam on the South Pacolet River (opposite page right) and Spartanburg's first reservoir began in the mid-1920s. Pictured below during construction in 1925 are R. B. Simms (left), who served as superintendent of the Water Works for 43 years, and Mr. Hackett (right), resident engineer.

Several water commissioners and water officials attended the grand opening of Lake Bowen, Spartanburg's second reservoir, in 1961. Among them were R. B. Simms, far left, and W. C. Bowen (without a hat), who was superintendent of the R. B. Simms Filtration Plant. —*Photographs courtesy of the Spartanburg Water System*

Rainbow Lake swimming area in the 1950s. Rainbow Lake was part of the Spartanburg Water System. Rather than integrating in the 1960s and '70s, local officials closed such swimming areas.
—*Courtesy of the Herald-Journal Willis Collection, Spartanburg County (SC) Public Libraries*

In the late 1940s, the Elite had changed into a full-fledged restaurant with live entertainment—in this case a blind piano player. The Elite also featured a "torch singer" named Rosa Thompson.
—*Courtesy of Nicholas Harakas*

James Buchanan worked for the Aug. W. Smith Company for many years. Buchanan designed the department store window displays and hand-painted and built elaborate decorations for various holidays. Spartanburg's people looked forward to what "Buck" Buchanan might have for them at any given time. Here he is seen preparing one of his scenes.
—*Courtesy of the Spartanburg County Regional Museum*

Blues artist Pink Anderson spent most of his life on South Forest Street in Spartanburg. He recorded numerous albums and influenced future generations of musicians, including the British rock group Pink Floyd and country artist Johnny Cash.
—*Courtesy of Mark Olencki*

Top: A post World War II scene outside the Montgomery Building's Carolina Theater.
—*Courtesy of B & B Studios*

Insert: The interior of the theater.

A popular national trend in the 1960s was the quiz show. In addition to the national quiz programs such as "The $64,000 Question," almost every local television station featured quiz bowls among local colleges and high schools. This 1960s photograph features the Spartanburg High School "Hi-Q" championship team and their popular coach, Tom Moore Craig, holding the trophy. From left to right: Bick Halligan, Venable Vermont, Kevin O'Neill, Chris Hoyle, Beth Hammond and David Lyles.
—*Courtesy of Spartan Communications Corporation*

Dance shows also were very popular. Of course, they all took their formats from the nationally broadcast "American Bandstand," which featured high school students. Many smaller stations also featured dancers from local colleges. An early 1960s Spartanburg dance show called "Dance Town" invited dancers from Wofford College and their dates. Third from the right among the dancing men is the author/professor Jim Kilgo of the University of Georgia.
—*Courtesy of Spartan Communications Corporation*

WORD radio regularly issued these lists of favorite tunes in the 1960s.
—*Courtesy of Sandy Camby*

If you lived in Spartanburg in the 1950s and '60s, you were likely to wake up to Cliff "Farmer" Gray, reporting the latest farm prices. His folksy, down home humor and his deep voice announcing the latest hog prices reminded everyone of where they lived and of what was truly important. Taken late in his career, this photograph shows Gray was far younger than his radio voice would have led one to believe. —*Courtesy of Spartan Communications Corporation*

Claudia Turner, center, was runner-up to Miss America in 1969. Here, she appeared on "The Nancy Welch Show" with her mother, left, and guest host Mary Willis, right. —*Courtesy of Susan Dunlap*

The manufacturers in the county had segregated baseball teams well past mid-century. This is the Draper African-American baseball team in 1954.

Thomas "Fox" Abrams, left, was the first African-American police officer commissioned by the city of Spartanburg in June 1950. He was hired by city Police Chief Ralph Prince. He also is the only police officer in Spartanburg history killed in the line of duty. He was shot in January 1962 when he answered a call at The Swing Club in an area near Henry Street. He is standing with Francis Dogan, another early African-American police officer, who died in March 1968.—*Photographs courtesy of the Spartanburg Community Development Office*

Dr. Ellen Watson, born in 1916, had a 41-year career as a guidance counselor and educator in Spartanburg city schools. She is credited with guiding many local youth through the difficult days of integration and helping scores of young African Americans go on to college. She served as president of the Spartanburg County Teachers Association and received awards from many national educational organizations for her work. She died in 1990. *—Courtesy of the Spartanburg Community Development Office*

Leaders of Silver Hill Methodist Church, the oldest African-American congregation in the county, stand among a meeting of ministers in the early 1950s. Mary Wright, a leader in the struggle for education for African Americans in Spartanburg, is the first person on the far right in the first row. *—Courtesy of Silver Hill Methodist Church*

Olin D. Johnston stands on the right with his daughter Elizabeth ("Liz") Patterson; her sister Sallie stands on the left with her uncle, David Jennings. They were all in Charleston to christen a new ship. Johnston served Spartanburg in the S.C. House of Representatives, as Governor, and finally, as a U.S. Senator. In the 1930s, Governor Johnston was instrumental in equitably settling labor disputes, especially involving textile workers. Throughout his political career, Johnston drew heavy support from textile workers, who considered him one of their own. As a governor, Johnston was a staunch supporter of the "New Deal." He died while serving in the U. S. Senate in 1965. His daughter, Liz Patterson, served on Spartanburg County Council, in the S.C. House of Representatives, and in the U.S. Congress. —*Photograph courtesy of the Herald-Journal Willis Collection, Spartanburg County (SC) Public Libraries*

OLIN JOHNSTON'S POCKET WATCH
—*Courtesy of Liz and Dwight Patterson*

Spartan Radiocasting Chairman Walter Brown and Spartanburg's Jimmy Byrnes attend the 1950 South Carolina state convention as delegates from Spartanburg County. At the time of this convention, Byrnes had served as a U.S. Congressman, a U.S. Senator, a U.S. Supreme Court Justice, and Secretary of State. Here, he had retired from federal service and was eager to get back into the political arena. He ran for Governor of South Carolina in 1950 and won resoundingly.
—*Courtesy of the Spartan Communications Corporation*

Perhaps no invention has so affected American households since mid-century as has television. WSPA-TV was South Carolina's first television station; this group gathered to view the station's first broadcast on April 29, 1956. In the first row, second from the left, is Sen. Strom Thurmond and next to him, Governor Jimmy Byrnes. —*Courtesy of Spartan Communications Corporation*

WSPA's "Dialogue" program focused on "problems between the two races." In that vein Dave Handy, third from the left, worked hard to promote racial understanding. By the 1960s television had become America's primary news source, and television networks as well as their local affiliates devoted much of their broadcast time to current events and news broadcasting. Here, Handy stands with his guests prior to hosting them on one of his interview shows. From left to right: Dewey Tullis, assistant director of the Spartanburg Model Cities Program; Dr. James Bruce, assistant professor of sociology at Wofford College; Handy; and E. J. Oliver, a Spartanburg druggist.

By the early 1970s desegregating public schools in the South had proven to be as divisive and contentious an issue as any this century. With the combined cooperation of leaders of both the African-American and white communities, desegregating Spartanburg's public school system was a tense but non-violent affair. The "Unitary School System," as the new desegregated system was then called, was explained to Spartanburg's population through every news outlet. Extensive preparation within the school systems and among the races included a series of programs aired on WSPA radio and television. Here Dave Handy, with his back to the camera, questions District 7 school officials about the Unitary School System. From left to right are: Dr. J. G. McCracken, superintendent; Charles Humphries Jr., assistant superintendent; Emerson B. Coleman, administrative assistant to the superintendent; Max M. Robbins, principal of Spartanburg High School; and Royce A. Justice, director of the Pre-Vocational Junior High School Program. —*Photographs courtesy of Spartan Communications Corporation*

Carver High School, which was the high school for African Americans in Spartanburg, is shown after its renovation in the 1950s. The "Unitary School System" of the early 1970s converted Carver into a junior high school.

When James Byrnes was elected governor in 1950, he pushed the state legislature to invest millions of dollars in building new schools for South Carolina's African-American community. Having been a Justice on the U.S. Supreme Court, Byrnes knew that many of the recent decisions of the courts had hinged on the violation of the "separate but equal" doctrine that had propped up the system of segregation in the South since the 1890s. Overall, schools for African Americans had always been vastly inferior to those for white students. Byrnes was convinced that if the South would provide equal facilities for African Americans, the Supreme Court would eventually rule in favor of "separate but equal." The state legislature appropriated millions of dollars to construct the schools, which proved a boon to the education of the state's and Spartanburg's African-American students, but the plan was unsuccessful. In 1954 when the U.S. Supreme Court overturned the "separate but equal" doctrine and ordered the integration of public schools, Byrnes and his fellow white South Carolinians were shocked and outraged. This photograph of the Mary H. Wright School was taken in the 1950s after it had been remodeled with the money Byrnes had squeezed out of the legislature.
—*Courtesy of the Herald-Journal Willis Collection, Spartanburg County (SC) Public Libraries*

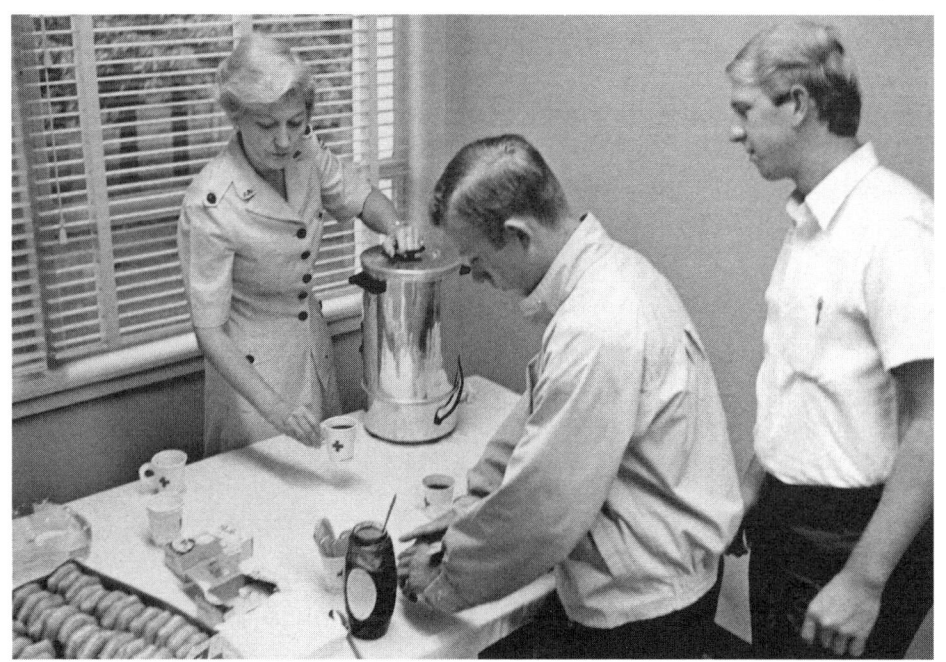

VIETNAM WAR MILITARY
IDENTIFICATION & DRAFT CARD
—*Courtesy of Don Camby*

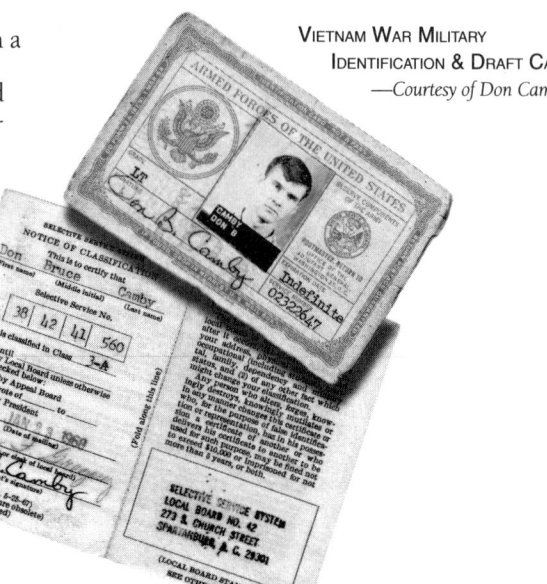

TOP LEFT: In the 1950s Admiral Richard Byrd visited Spartanburg. He participated in a show at the Camp Croft Armory in which Harriet Roswell Ancrum modelled a wedding dress made of cotton fabric manufactured by Reeves Brothers. Admiral Byrd had taken the fabric on his second expedition to the North Pole. WSPA Radio broadcast the show with its popular radio personality Jane Dalton, on the left, acting as mistress of ceremonies. —*Courtesy of the Johnson Family*

TOP RIGHT GROUP: The Korean War was America's first "limited" war, a concept difficult for many citizens to understand and support. However, many local men went to Korea to serve their country in all capacities.

BOTTOM LEFT: The tragedy of another "limited" conflict, the Vietnam War, struck all Americans, including citizens of Spartanburg, in the 1960s and '70s. Here Grace Cook of the local Red Cross serves doughnuts and coffee to draftees Allen Holcombe and Ricky Martin in 1966.
—*Courtesy of the Herald-Journal Willis Collection, Spartanburg County (SC) Public Libraries*

Work & Progress

When Ernest Burwell moved his Chevrolet dealership from his old location (top) to his new buildings (bottom) on the corner of North Church Street and Daniel Morgan Avenue, he planned a special event to celebrate.

People came by the dealership for weeks to see the new models and to sign up for the raffle of a new car. Thousands of people filled North Church Street on the day of the drawing, which was won by a professor at Wofford College, Virgil Ward Pettit, who had only recently received his Ph.D. and was driving an "old, beat up car," according to one of his colleagues. Burwell is shown here giving the keys to the lucky young professor. —*Photographs courtesy of the Spartanburg County Regional Museum*

Top: The employees of an East Main Street Esso station turn out for a group portrait. This station has been converted to American Fast Photo. —*Courtesy American Fast Photo*

Bottom: The work force at Southern Shops, located on the Asheville Highway, refurbished trains. —*Courtesy B & B Studios*

Peaches have been a major agricultural crop in Spartanburg County since the 1920s. These people are arranging the nicest peaches in shallow round trays that will be placed on top of the commercial peach basket to give it a finished and pretty look. This process is called "ringing." —*Courtesy of Marianna Black Habisreutinger*

There were 135,000 acres under cotton cultivation in Spartanburg County in 1920, and Spartanburg County led the state in cotton production. Erosion, over-fertilization, and the boll weevil gradually wiped out the crop, and by the 1950s, it ceased to be a major crop in the Piedmont. Here, Chad Cash operates a cotton picker as Cash Farms experimented with cotton production in 1996.
—*Courtesy of Mike Corbin*

ABOVE: Textiles continued to be the primary industry in the county after World War II. The industry was forced to modernize by foreign competition, and Spartanburg's mills became among the most progressive in the textile world. However, competition became more intense as time wore on, and many mills eventually closed, including Converse Mill seen here, the last of the Clifton Mills to do so. The modern U.S. Highway 29 bridge spanning the Pacolet River stands in stark contrast to the older buildings in the background, which represent a bygone era. The oldest mill, damaged by the flood of 1903, can be seen just above the highway bridge next to the river, and the newer mill, built on higher ground, dominates the scene to the left.
—Courtesy of the Spartanburg County Regional Museum

This 1960s aerial view of Pacolet Mill shows the mill village modernized but retaining its essential grid pattern. By the 1960s the textile mills had sold most of their houses to the workers who lived in them.
—Courtesy of the Herald-Journal Willis Collection, Spartanburg County (SC) Public Libraries

Top: Ever since 1884, when Seth Milliken negotiated to become the selling agent for the Pacolet Manufacturing Company, the Milliken name has been an important one in the county. This research facility opened in 1958 and is the largest privately-owned textile and chemical manufacturing firm in the world.
—*Courtesy of James Huff Photo/Graphic Services*

Bottom: Whitney Mill, left, and Beaumont Mill, right, were both closed by Spartan Mills in the 1990s. —*Courtesy of Mark Olencki*

The Cherry Hill Grill, located on East Main Street Extension, drew many patrons in the 1940s and '50s. Note the sign-of-the-times statement "We Serve White Trade Only" under the restaurant's name. —*Courtesy of George Mullinax*

The Piedmont Steak House operated on Magnolia Street from 1910 to 1997. Nick Lambroukos prominently displayed a chair that was used by Elvis Presley the night he performed in Spartanburg.
—*Courtesy of Mark Olencki*

CHILI-CHEESE A-PLENTY & SWEET TEA

Top: Wade's was a favorite on South Pine Street from the late 1940s until it moved to Pinewood in the 1980s.

Above: Louise Brown, the original yeast roll baker at Wade's, in the 1980s. —*Photographs courtesy of Wade's*

Above: The Sugar 'N Spice has been a popular drive-in on South Pine Street since 1961. From left to right: John Stathakis, James Meadows, Pete Copses, and Delores Mack.
—*Courtesy of Mark Olencki*

Destined to become a Spartanburg landmark, this is the Beacon Drive-In as it appeared in 1946. John White manned the cash register of the Beacon from its beginnings until he sold it in 1998. The Beacon has a wide menu of fried food in huge servings called "A Plenty" (featuring french fries and onion rings made from onions bought by the railroad carload) washed down by iced tea. The Beacon was once featured on Charles Kuralt's "On the Road" broadcast on the CBS Evening News.
—*Courtesy of George Mullinax*

BMW opened its first U.S. manufacturing plant in western Spartanburg County in 1994. This plant and its suppliers employed more than 3,000 people in the Upstate in 1999.
—*Courtesy of Steve Fincher*

The Carolina Panthers, owned by former Spartan Jerry Richardson, brought their summer training camp to Wofford College in 1995. The camp has become a major summer tourist attraction for the city.
—*Photographs courtesy of Les Duggins*

— Philip N. Racine

Born in Brunswick, Maine, Phil spent his elementary and junior high school years studying and praying in the private Roman Catholic School, St. John's, and his high school years (on the cusp of the age of Sex, Drugs, and Rock 'n Roll—he has shown no interest in *one* of these) in the public Brunswick High School where he was (insufferably) president of the student body.

An English major at Bowdoin College until he refused to spend a semester reading *The Faerie Queene*, he switched his major to history, became interested in the American Civil War, and edited the letters of a Maine soldier as a senior honors thesis. He then went on to Emory University where he earned masters and doctoral degrees in American history.

In 1986, he and his co-author, Richard B. Harwell, received the "Founder's Award" for distinguished research and writing on the Confederate period of U.S. history from the Confederate Memorial Literary Society of the Confederate Museum in Richmond, Virginia.

Presently, Racine is the William R. Kenan Jr. Professor of History at Wofford College, where he has taught since coming to Spartanburg in 1969. He is the author of several books and articles on Southern history, one of which, *Piedmont Farmer: The Journals of David Golightly Harris, 1855-1870*, is set in Spartanburg County.

Although he is originally from Maine (one cannot be any more "Yankee" than that), his life has been leavened by his wife, Frances, who is from the Deep South (Mississippi), and their two children, Russell and Ali, both Spartanburg natives. Racine hunts some, fishes more, but mostly does historical research.

The Hub City Writers Project is a non-profit organization whose mission is to foster a sense of community through the literary arts. We do this by publishing books from and about our community; encouraging, mentoring, and advancing the careers of local writers; and seeking to make Spartanburg a center for the literary arts.

Our metaphor of organization purposely looks backward to the nineteenth century when Spartanburg was known as the "hub city," a place where railroads converged and departed.

As we cross into the twenty-first century, Spartanburg is fast becoming a literary hub of South Carolina with an active and nationally celebrated core group of poets, fiction writers, and essayists. We celebrate these writers—and the ones yet born —as one of our community's greatest assets. William R. Ferris, former director of the Center for the Study of Southern Cultures, says of the emerging South, "Our culture is our greatest resource. We can shape an economic base . . . And it won't be an investment that will disappear."

Hub City Anthology • John Lane & Betsy Teter, editors
Hub City Music Makers • Peter Cooper
Hub City Christmas • John Lane & Betsy Teter, editors
New Southern Harmonies • Rosa Shand, Scott Gould, Deno Trakas, George Singleton
The Best of Radio Free Bubba • Meg Barnhouse, Pat Jobe, Kim Taylor, Gary Phillips
Family Trees • Mike Corbin
The Seasons of Harold Hatcher • Mike Hembree

— Colophon

Seeing Spartanburg was conceived during the summer of 1997 and reached full-term 26 months later. The production of this project *almost* overloaded our memory and storage systems (in the mental, physical, digital, and spiritual areas). Two additional hard drives totaling 18 gigs came to our rescue, along with another Power Macintosh® (a total of five computers were in constant use and never asleep). The usual array of zip®, jaz®, and CD-R drives are not to go unnoticed or unthanked. This, the eighth Hub City title, was released in a first printing of 5,000 soft-bound and a limited edition of 250 case-bound copies and a second printing of 2,000 soft-bound copies. The text typefaces are Berkeley Oldstyle from ITC/Bitstream, and the display face is Voluta Script from Adobe. The designer and editors began the book's maturation process on LONGMORN®, a "highly prized" 15-year-old single malt, continued with a 10-year-old "original cask strength" LAPHROAIG®, and finished with a constant supply of "cold-filtered" Miller® Genuine Draft.

*This index was compiled by the staff of the
Spartanburg County Public Libraries.*